Women and the Railway, 1850–1915

Edinburgh Critical Studies in Victorian Culture

Series Editor: Julian Wolfreys

Volumes available in the series:

Visit the Edinburgh Critical Studies in Victorian Culture web page at
www.euppublishing.com/series/ecve

Also Available:
Victoriographies – A Journal of Nineteenth-Century Writing, 1790–1914, edited by Julian Wolfreys
ISSN: 2044-2416
www.eupjournals.com/vic

Women and the Railway, 1850–1915

Anna Despotopoulou

EDINBURGH
University Press

Edinburgh University Press Ltd
The Tun – Holyrood Road
12(2f) Jackson's Entry
Edinburgh EH8 8PJ
www.euppublishing.com

Typeset in 10.5/13 Sabon by
Servis Filmsetting Ltd, Stockport, Cheshire,
and printed and bound in Great Britain by
CPI Group (UK) Ltd, Croydon CR0 4YY

A CIP record for this book is available from the
British Library

ISBN 978 0 7486 7694 1 (hardback)
ISBN 978 0 7486 7695 8 (webready PDF)
ISBN 978 0 7486 7696 5 (Epub)

Published with the support of the Edinburgh
University Scholarly Publishing Initiatives Fund.

Contents

Illustrations

Series Editor's Preface

'Victorian' is a term, at once indicative of a strongly determined concept and an often notoriously vague notion, emptied of all meaningful content by the many journalistic misconceptions that persist about the inhabitants and cultures of the British Isles and Victoria's Empire in the nineteenth century. As such, it has become a by-word for the assumption of various, often contradictory habits of thought, belief, behaviour and perceptions. Victorian studies and studies in nineteenth-century literature and culture have, from their institutional inception, questioned narrowness of presumption, pushed at the limits of the nominal definition, and have sought to question the very grounds on which the unreflective perception of the so-called Victorian has been built; and so they continue to do. Victorian and nineteenth-century studies of literature and culture maintain a breadth and diversity of interest, of focus and inquiry, in an interrogative and intellectually open-minded and challenging manner, which are equal to the exploration and inquisitiveness of its subjects. Many of the questions asked by scholars and researchers of the innumerable productions of nineteenth-century society actively put into suspension the clichés and stereotypes of 'Victorianism', whether the approach has been sustained by historical, scientific, philosophical, empirical, ideological or theoretical concerns; indeed, it would be incorrect to assume that each of these approaches to the idea of the Victorian has been, or has remained, in the main exclusive, sealed off from the interests and engagements of other approaches. A vital interdisciplinarity has been pursued and embraced, for the most part, even as there has been contest and debate amongst Victorianists, pursued with as much fervour as the affirmative exploration between different disciplines and differing epistemologies put to work in the service of reading the nineteenth century.

Edinburgh Critical Studies in Victorian Culture aims to take up both the debates and the inventive approaches and departures from

convention that studies in the nineteenth century have witnessed for
the last half-century at least. Aiming to maintain a 'Victorian' (in the
most positive sense of that motif) spirit of enquiry, the series's purpose
is to continue and augment the cross-fertilisation of interdisciplinary
approaches, and to offer, in addition, a number of timely and untimely
revisions of Victorian literature, culture, history and identity. At the
same time, the series will ask questions concerning what has been missed
or improperly received, misread, or not read at all, in order to present
a multi-faceted and heterogeneous kaleidoscope of representations.
Drawing on the most provocative, thoughtful and original research, the
series will seek to prod at the notion of the 'Victorian', and in so doing,
principally through theoretically and epistemologically sophisticated
close readings of the historicity of literature and culture in the nineteenth
century, to offer the reader provocative insights into a world that is
at once overly familiar, and irreducibly different, other and strange.
Working from original sources, primary documents and recent interdisciplinary theoretical models, Edinburgh Critical Studies in Victorian
Culture seeks not simply to push at the boundaries of research in the
nineteenth century, but also to inaugurate the persistent erasure and
provisional, strategic redrawing of those borders.

Julian Wolfreys

Acknowledgements

This book grew out of my participation in a research project entitled *Women in Spaces of Transit*, directed by Teresa Gómez Reus of the University of Alicante, and funded by the Spanish Ministry of Science and Innovation. I vividly remember meeting with the members of the project in Warwick and later in Cadiz in 2009 to discuss our individual contributions. It is in this context that the railway became my particular space of transit, and I would like to gratefully acknowledge Teresa Gómez Reus for including me in the project as well as the other members of our team for inspiring conversations and support: Janet Stobbs, Valerie Fehlbaum, and Aránzazu Usandizaga. Early versions of my readings of Mansfield's and Oliphant's short stories appeared in the article entitled '"Running on lines": Women and the Railway in Victorian and early Modernist Culture', included in the book that Teresa edited together with Terry Gifford, *Women in Transit through Literary Liminal Spaces* (Palgrave Macmillan, 2013); reproduced with permission of Palgrave Macmillan. The full published version of this article is available from: http://www.palgrave.com/products/title.aspx?pid=669457. Also, revised versions of parts of my article on Rhoda Broughton, 'Trains of Thought: the Challenges of Mobility in the Work of Rhoda Broughton', *Critical Survey* 23.1 (Berghahn Journals 2011): 90–106, special issue entitled 'Other Sensations', edited by Janice Allan, whom I thank, appear scattered in Chapters 1, 2, and 4.

Several ideas developed in this book were presented in embryonic form in various conferences in London (twice), Rome, Thessaloniki, Naples, and Venice. Thanks are owed to various colleagues who stimulated my thinking in new and refreshing ways during lively conversations: Tamar Heller, Tatiana Kontou, Greg Zacharias, Donatella Izzo, Anna De Biasio, Peter Walker, Sheila Teahan, Katerina Kitsi-Mitakou, Alicia Rix, Matthew Beaumont, Tina Choi, and Ilana Blumberg.

At the start of this process of writing, in the summer of 2012, I was very fortunate to spend time with my mentor Nicola Bradbury in Reading, and I would like to express my sincere thanks to her and to Lionel Kelly for stimulating conversations on literary railways, for their intellectual passion and generosity of spirit.

In the past years I have benefited from the academic and moral support of many colleagues at the University of Athens who have generously offered their time and expertise, helping to enlarge my thinking and my reading. I would like to thank Mina Karavanta for her reassuring and passionate presence and for enriching my theoretical perspective with enthusiasm and care. Many thanks are due to all the members of my Department of English Language and Literature for their encouragement and for granting me leave that enabled me to travel and conduct extensive research in libraries abroad. This research was also made possible by the generous University of Athens ELKE funding that was granted to me in 2012. I should also mention the help of my devoted students who, while studying for their graduate degrees in the UK, provided me with books and photocopies at a moment's notice: Thalia Trigoni, Charis Charalampous, Marouska Koulouri, and Danae Loukaki, many thanks to you.

At Edinburgh University Press, I am deeply grateful to Julian Wolfreys for his encouragement, his insightful comments, and for overseeing the manuscript with attention and care; the anonymous readers for thought-provoking remarks; Jackie Jones, Dhara Patel, and James Dale for their guidance throughout the production process and for securing funds which enabled me to acquire permissions for some of the images. I would also like to thank Nicola Wood for her expert copyediting and her careful attention to detail.

The four *Punch* images were generously offered by Mark Samuels Lasner and Curtis Small, Jr, of the University of Delaware Library, which I gratefully acknowledge for granting permission. 'Modes of Travelling in India', by Joseph Austin Benwell, was kindly and generously offered by a descendent of the artist, Dee Murray. The permission for the image reproduction of Rudolf Swoboda's painting was generously granted by the Royal Collection Trust, and of Augustus Egg's painting was given by the Birmingham Museums Trust. The *Funny Folks* image is reproduced by permission of the British Library. The George Gibbs illustration of 'Mrs Bathurst' has been scanned from my own copy of Kipling's book.

Finally I owe a special debt to my family – my parents for ongoing support and my mother especially for being such a careful and insightful reader of my work and for helping me with editing during the final stages of writing. My husband Kostas Vekrellis and my daughter Kalli have filled my life with inspiration, joy, adventure, and love. It is to them that I dedicate this book.

Introduction

You can't imagine how strange it seemed to be journeying on thus, without any visible cause of progress other than the magical machine, with its flying white breath and rhythmical, unvarying pace [. . .]
You cannot conceive what that sensation of cutting the air was; the motion is as smooth as possible, too. I could either have read or written; and as it was, I stood up, and with my bonnet off 'drank the air before me'. The wind, which was strong, or perhaps the force of our own thrusting against it, absolutely weighed my eyelids down [. . .] When I closed my eyes this sensation of flying was quite delightful, and strange beyond description; yet, strange as it was, I had a perfect sense of security, and not the slightest fear.

Frances Ann Kemble, *Records of a Girlhood* (1884), 281, 283

Fanny Kemble, the notable actress and writer, was one of the first women to experience the 'flying' sensation of the railway in August 1830, one month before the official opening of the Liverpool–Manchester line in September of the same year. By the side of the line's 'visionary' maker, 'the master of all these marvels', George Stephenson, with whom she professed to be 'most horribly in love' (280, 283), Kemble experienced the magic of locomotion. In the above-quoted letters she later collected in her autobiographical book, Kemble recorded the psychosomatic effects this trial journey had on her as well as the political climate and technological innovation that helped actualise the venture. Rhythmical motion, incalculable speed, identification with the mighty thrust of the engine and its 'cutting' power, and surrender to an invisible force which, nevertheless, inspires a sense of security, not dread or anxiety, are all felt by Kemble who, with bonnet off and no fear of exposure to the elements or to her fellow passengers, has a taste of a new social space which throughout the 'The Age of Transition' would become an important setting for the exploration of the subjectivity of women in literal and social transit.

This book examines Victorian and early modernist representations of women's experience of locomotion and the spaces of the railway at a period of heightened physical mobility and urbanisation. It looks at literary and non-fictional texts which concentrate on women in transit by train and explores the tension between women's boundless physical, emotional, and sexual aspirations – often depicted as closely related to the feelings of freedom and speed that train travel evoked – and Victorian gender ideology that imposed restrictions through discourses which constructed the spaces of the railway as topographies of patriarchy, fear, or manipulation. Women in trains were a 'hot' topic in the mid- and late Victorian period, as the hundreds of stories, news items, and cartoons in periodicals attest, and the texts in question construct them, on the one hand, as objects of admiration, and, on the other, as targets of humour, satire, and even hatred. Within a theoretical framework set by prominent feminist studies of women's appropriation of public space,[1] and acknowledging the little but certainly very suggestive work that has already been published on the subject of women and the railway,[2] I investigate the ideological tensions and changes regarding women's relation to spaces of transit that are negotiated in fiction but also in as yet unexamined printed materials found in the Victorian periodical press, texts which are in themselves transitory and ephemeral like the journeys they describe. The railway is examined as an ambiguously gendered space that highlights the artificiality of the private/public divide, giving prominence to woman's impulse to traverse boundaries, not only physically but also mentally and emotionally.

Women's presence in the streets of the big European metropoles or within the urban spaces of department stores and cafés has been widely discussed by scholars who have attempted to theorise female subjectivity within the public spaces of the city. The railway, however, relatively unexplored as a gendered space, seems to be a more complex setting of modern urban life as it defies definitions and baffles those who brave its challenges. In the words of Alan Trachtenberg, 'Nothing else in the nineteenth century seemed as vivid and dramatic a sign of modernity as the railroad' (xiii). Indeed influential critics such as Susan Stanford Friedman have been tempted to define modernity by using diction and imagery associated with the railway: 'The velocity, acceleration, and dynamism of shattering change across a wide spectrum of societal institutions are key components of modernity' (433). Yet women's relation to modernity has been long debated and often disputed, just as their occupancy of the spaces of modernity has been precarious and often misinterpreted. In order to address and study a different facet of women's response to modernity and their relation to transient space, I will concentrate on texts which represent them within settings of literal transit, the train and the railway station, as these were newly conceived Victorian spaces in which the rules of circulation for men and women had to be formulated anew, balancing social conventions concerning gender behaviour with the emerging demands of travel, industry, and work, served primarily by the railway. These spaces of transit are experienced subjectively by women and open up fresh possibilities for self-exploration and growth as they challenge women's sense of identity.

Women's reasons for travel by train and their choice of terrain traversed in the nineteenth century have not always been the same. Their trajectories within and beyond the city, within and beyond the nation, as urban passengers, commuters, travellers, tourists, expatriates, exiles, or even nomads play an important role in the making and remaking of their identity as modern subjects in an urban, industrial, and imperial setting. As many theorists and critics of women's travel writing have pointed out, for a long time travel was considered a male privilege, and the relevant discourse which emphasised the political and intellectual benefits of travel – scientific exploration, colonialisation, or just broadening the mind – concerned the white bourgeois Western man and thus, by comparison, served to confirm the moral and spatial association between women and home. Nevertheless, recent exploration of women's texts on travel has challenged the nineteenth-century division between public and private gendered spheres, rejecting the association of woman with spatial restriction, immobility, and passivity. More particularly, as Sidonie Smith has argued, 'The expanding mobility of certain women in the middle to late nineteenth century came as an effect of modernity – democratization, literacy, education, increasing wealth, urbanization and industrialization, and the colonial and imperial expansion that produced wealth and the investment in "progress"' (xi). The train 'that drove modernity' (Smith, xi) offered women the opportunity to participate in the wide, freely visitable world, a world that normally men were entitled to and which was often identified with the fluidity and flux of the modern pace of living. As a result the mobile worlds presented by women, at both national and international levels, potently describe both the pleasures of mobility and the dangers of displacement, the acceleration of urban life and the complexities of networks and routes, the randomness of encounters and the shifts in perception that rail travel effects. In fact, in women's texts on railway travel very often the map of the imagination displaces the transportation map, by taking precedence over the geographical, scientific, or sociological details of location. In particular, women's highlighting of dispersed and disparate objects, merged by the speed of the transportation medium, results from their new panoramic perception, which tends to privilege unstable representation over literal reporting of view, impressionism over realism.

I draw my arguments from a variety of cultural materials: novels, stories published in weekly and monthly journals, news items and commentaries, essays, illustrations, and paintings. In fact, the abundance and richness of short stories published in nineteenth-century journals, utilising the railway as setting for plots of romance, terror, domestic drama, humour, and the supernatural, testifies to the appeal that the railway had on the imagination of the Victorians who explored its ambiguities and the opportunities it offered for new terms of interaction. In these stories railway carriages and stations appear as settings at once public and private, open to crime and secure or comfortable like homes, spaces of fear or of comfort, of dizzying mobility or of boring immobility, of time lost or of time gained. Woman is ever present in these stories, identifying with but also fearful of the new drifting identity experienced through mobility. All texts which draw on the railway for their plots, imagery, or commentary, irrespective of the sex of their author, construct spaces of tension between woman's aspirations and society's impositions – spaces in which the conflicts of Victorian gender and domestic ideology are played out. In the narratives of train journeys, thus, two conflicting gendered worlds are juxtaposed: the objective with the subjective; technology with imagination; organisation with confusion; punctuality with irregularity; the rational with the irrational.

The importance of the railway not only as a means of technological development, economic growth, and imperial expansion but also as a cultural metaphor with 'educational, intellectual, emotional and psychological dimensions' (Freeman, *Railways*, 19), has been recorded in many books with historical, sociological, technological, or cultural focus. In his insightful and pioneering 1977 study, *The Railway Journey*, Wolfgang Schivelbusch first concentrated on the pervasive impact of the railway – the most dramatic technological change to affect everyday life in the nineteenth century – on socio-economic structures as well as on the modern industrialised consciousness, which experienced changes in perception and identity. Mechanised motion, panoramic vision, the annihilation of the space–time continuum, isolation, and the medical side-effects of train travel are just some of the issues introduced by Schivelbusch, whose book constitutes the starting point for most subsequent studies, my book included, of the cultural, social, and psychological impact of the railway. A second point of departure is Michael Freeman's comprehensive *Railways and the Victorian Imagination* (1999), which explores the ways in which socio-economic and geographic changes brought about by the railway interacted with the intellectual and cultural context to produce art and literature that reflected the fears and anxieties but also the thrill of and fascination with scientific technology, speed, and circulation via the revolutionary train. The train was, according to these studies, an important, perhaps the most crucial, means of urban growth and development – 'in terms of commodity circulation, the built environment of towns and cities, or of the city as a focus of conspicuous consumption' (Freeman, *Railways*, 29) – but also of suburbanisation, as population in the nineteenth century was constantly undergoing a process of displacement due to crucial socio-economic, demographic, and geographical parameters. The railway was ubiquitous, and the invasion, or despoiling, of rural towns and areas unavoidable, to the extent that railway companies had more power than gentlemen of social rank who were deprived of the authority to impede the purchase of their land which had been deemed a prescribed route.[3]

Moreover, as it becomes clear from both Schivelbusch's and Freeman's books, even though the railway, as a seemingly neutral technological space, appeared to initiate social progress and individual liberty, promising to introduce people to a more democratic era where passengers from all walks of life could partake of the technological advances which ameliorated the conditions of travel within a fast-moving, industrial society, in reality it naturalised even further social divisions by embedding the new practices within old hierarchical systems that took such social distinctions for granted. The railway then, rather than levelling out differences, became responsible for the further segregation of the classes (and the sexes) through their literal compartmentalisation in separate spaces (first it was separate trains and next it was separate – first-, second-, and third-class – carriages), which mirrored segregating policies in urban space. Therefore, the view that the railway was one in a series of institutional changes rooted in the processes of the democratisation of society is perhaps a truism that obscures rather than consolidates the issue of equal access to public space, and more poignantly the question of women's access to public space.

Bringing together the voices of many distinguished critics, Matthew Beaumont and Michael Freeman's edited collection, *The Railway and Modernity: Time, Space, and the Machine Ensemble* (2007), introduces or in some cases takes a fresh look at many problematics related to the railway as a seminal cultural experience. Chapters focusing on nineteenth- and twentieth-century literature and culture provide important insights into the ways the train affected space and social divisions, perception and consciousness, privacy and publicity, safety and danger. As the editors argue, 'The locomotive was after all the first industrial machine to which the middle classes had to adapt themselves in their everyday lives' ('Introduction', 21), but adaptation involved gradual transformation, and the 'machine space' (26), in which passengers found themselves increasingly cocooned in the long period covered in the aforementioned book, stood for both positive and negative social and personal advancements and transformations: train compartments are seen as utopic spaces of privacy and order as well as dystopic spaces of crime, segregation, and trauma. As Beaumont and Freeman argue, the compartment 'had an ambiguous ontological status, caught between private and public space, between interior and exterior, dream and reality' ('Introduction', 23).

Important studies, ranging from Janet Wolff's seminal 'The Invisible Flaneuse' (1985) and Deborah Epstein Nord's *Walking the Victorian Streets* (1995) to Deborah L. Parsons's *Streetwalking the Metropolis* (2000) and Teresa Gómez Reus and Aránzazu Usandizaga's edited volume *Inside Out* (2008), have elaborately described the challenges women faced as they ventured forth in the public spaces of Victorian cities, negotiating the impulse to wander in the metropolis and indulge in its spectacles with the objectifying and fixing gaze of society which deemed them exposed targets: at best objects of admiration and at worst disreputable or even fallen, but in both cases inviting harassment. The separate spheres ideology certainly dictated and checked the limits of women's desire and ambition, but as all these critics have suggested, with the rise of consumer culture and the increased participation of women in public spaces of work or entertainment, the boundaries between public and private had become blurry, and with them so had clear-cut distinctions between acceptable and unacceptable femininity, domestic passivity and transgressive agency.[4] Just as, in the words of Inga Bryden and Janet Floyd, domestic interior 'is never just private; it is a sign for public and cultural interaction' (12), the public spaces of modern transit, in their varied manifestations, were open to multiple and often contradictory signification, private and public, especially for women who within such unfamiliar territory had to reconceive their own femininity and identity in relation to these impalpably demarcated spaces. A recent book that includes many studies of the porosity of the boundaries between public and private is Teresa Gómez Reus and Terry Gifford's *Women in Transit through Literary Liminal Spaces* (2013). As the editors argue, 'liminality and transition are indeed marked by contingency and uncertainty. While being "in transit" inevitably entails the prospect of failure, liminality may also bring about the sudden emerging of agency' (6). If, as Rita Felski puts it, in line with social constructivist theory, 'Gender is continually in process, an identity that is performed and actualized over time within given social constraints' (21), women's interaction with ambiguous urban spaces was instrumental in the making and remaking of gender and in the fracturing of domestic and gender ideology which had posited an essentialist view of woman as by nature inclined towards the privacy of the home. By venturing into the public sphere, however, woman was not discarding one stereotype in order uncritically to adopt another; instead she helped to expose the instability of gender and spatial divides within the context of modern life of which she undoubtedly and most decidedly partook. And in doing so, woman pervades the culture of modernity 'as a powerful symbol of both the dangers and the promises of the modern age', according to Felski (3). For as Marshall Berman has pointed out, 'To be modern is to find ourselves in an environment that promises us adventure, power, joy, growth, transformation of ourselves and the world – and, at the same time, that threatens to destroy everything we have, everything we know, everything we are' (15).

Recently, in *Mobility and Modernity in Women's Novels, 1850s-1930s* (2009), Wendy Parkins has interrogated the ways in which woman's mobility aligns her with modern and modernising practices of the nineteenth and early twentieth centuries. With her comprehensive introduction which discusses the definitional and conceptual difficulties arising from the exploration of women's participation in modernity through mobility, as well as with her original look at authors ranging from George Eliot and Ouida to Elizabeth Bowen and May Sinclair, Parkins examines the trope of journeying far and near, identifying its stimulating but disorienting potential. Expanding on previous work done on women's passage through public space, Parkins also looks at mobility in non-urban spaces, considering the complex and often ambiguous identity and agency issues that arise when women adopt an urban as well as a cross-country trajectory. My study of women's mobility via the railway shares Parkins's scepticism of the unproblematic equation between mobility and agency, as mobility is not always empowering. Nevertheless, as Parkins argues, 'Despite the fact that the agency enacted is not unproblematic in itself [. . .] this does not diminish the strength of the association between women's mobility and agency in these novels but allows for the exploration of what an increased capacity for action might entail' (12). Diverging from Butlerian understandings of agency, Parkins, following Lois McNay, adopts a more productive view of agency, one that, in the context of gender ideology, allows for creative interventions which may initiate social change (12–13). In my examination of the commonplace experience of transportation, such a notion of agency is consistent with the theory of subtle resistance embedded in practices of everyday life described by Michel de Certeau, whose insight into the unheroic but definitely potent practices by which the subject resists assimilation into the institutional networks and discursive regimes of daily life informs my own ideas of the ways women's experience of the train destabilises social and gender hierarchies. The train, as will be shown, entrenched as it may be within the technologies of institutional stability and progress, exemplifies, nevertheless, one more conceptual space of ambiguity, where the unpredictable eruptions of heterogeneity disrupt what de Certeau names the 'grid of "discipline"' (xiv).[5] 'Mobility may be coerced or involuntary or simply the last resort,' Parkins admits, 'but even in novels where the heroine's mobility is not freely chosen [. . .] the woman's solitary journey takes on a heroic stature, often involves some claim to the right to act on her own behalf and challenges the actions of others consistent with modern understandings of autonomy' (12).

Urban and suburban mobility is also the topic of Ana Parejo Vadillo's *Women Poets and Urban Aestheticism: Passengers of Modernity* (2005), which discusses the effect of the London Underground, among other means of transit, on fin-de-siècle women poets who engaged with and even forged an urban aestheticism inspired by their use of transportation vehicles. Vadillo incisively asks, 'What did it mean [for a woman] to be a passenger at the *fin de siècle*?', observing that to the pre-existing scholarly investigation of 'a Victorian modernity based on walking, we must add the idea of an urban culture that incorporates public transport as a vehicle of modernity' (14). The mechanisation of life, consumerism, the transient gaze, as well as the new perception of space itself as a commodity item were all part of the passenger's experience within the city, and Vadillo's book evocatively shows how women poets transmuted the new sensations of automation and flux into verse. Vadillo is preoccupied with the fluidity of public and private in the vehicles of transportation she examines, but not as much as Amy Richter, whose examination of women and the railway in nineteenth-century America, in the book *Home on the Rails: Women, the Railroad, and the Rise of Public Domesticity* (2005), is based on the premise that

> In the confined spaces of the railroad, women and men renegotiated the boundary between private and public. They shaped public life to their will, reimagining it as a realm of moral and physical comfort, transplanting the values and expectations of the private/feminine home onto the public/manly world on rails. (8)

As a historian, Richter is particularly attuned to the historical, material, and factual details that showcase and determine the connection between women and the public space of the railway, examining not only popular narratives but also diaries, letters, advertisements, advice manuals, and timetables. At the same time she is interested in US racial segrega-tion policies, which were challenged in the railway, the site of contact between not only classes and sexes but also races. Thus, American cultural and ethnic diversity constituted additional parameters, compli-cating, on the one hand, the way gender and race were negotiated in the ambiguous space of the train and raising questions, on the other, about the ways in which the railroad accommodated anxieties about national identity and coherence. Richter's notion of 'public domesticity', which indicates the way the discourse of domesticity and of home – of lavish interiors and comfortable amenities but also domestic behaviour – per-vaded the experience and the stories of nineteenth-century American rail passengers, proves the shifting boundaries of public and private in such new settings of modernity as the train carriage but also the hotel, the department store, and many others. One reason that 'Victorian travelers carried domestic ideals with them onto trains' (64) appears to be, for Richter, the American need to infuse public life with the respect-ability that characterised their homes (72). Accordingly, lady travellers on trains were expected to embody the homely values they exerted in the domestic sphere, by showing self-restraint and modesty while at the same time adorning the luxurious surroundings. Nevertheless, as Richter shows, such a vision of an ethically and socially ordered public space was a fantasy often punctured by the realities of crime, aggres-sion, violence, discrimination, or even inappropriately expressed erotic desire which dissolved well established rules of decorum and interaction that had safeguarded the distance between men and women. Richter concludes that

> Even as the public life of rail travel became more domesticated, it remained a manly domain in contrast to the private sphere – regendered rather than ungendered by women's presence. Understanding this transformation and the place of women as actors and symbols within it explains how women entered into public but did not move about as men did. (160)

My own account of the challenges, frustrations, and pleasures of the railway for women owes a tremendous amount to the scholarly work discussed above, as my chapters will make evident. However, my book differs from Vadillo's study of fin-de-siècle women poets' approach to transport and Richter's history of American women's experience of the railroad, as it explores mainly fiction and non-fiction (some little known or read) – texts by and about women – that exclusively deal with the railway as a gendered space within a British, European, and Imperial context in the Victorian and early modernist period.[6] In this sense it sup-plements and expands on the work by Michael Freeman whose study of the impact of the railway on Victorian culture was formative, but with no consideration of the implications of gender. It could be argued that as a newly constructed space, the railway had no anterior ideological significance; therefore, unlike the city street, whose cultural, gender, and class politics developed through the centuries, and the omnibus, which, though similarly new, offered very brief experiences of mobility to women, the train offered women a more sustained involvement in the production of new space and in the ideological conflicts that helped formulate its meaning. However, even though the train may have been conceived as an integrated space, in which men and women carry out the shared, ordinary goal of transport, it was perceived, just as the street was, as a gendered, masculine space, in which women's presence was incongruous unless it conformed to the home-based virtues of patriarchal ideology. In *Moving Lives*, Sidonie Smith points out that while 'locomotion enhanced certain women's agency by offering a vehicle through which they could become less sessile, less ignorant, less dependent, and more autonomous', at the same time it 'reproduced normatively gendered patterns of work and leisure' (127). In fact, the comfortable domestic interiors of trains, with which railway manufacturers targeted women passengers, reproduced the setting of a woman's true place, the home, as described by John Ruskin in 'Of Queens' Gardens' (1865). Pertinent is the advice women received from Lillias Campbell Davidson, in *Hints to Lady Travellers at Home and Abroad* (1889), always to pack a pair of house-slippers when preparing for a long train journey (176). Though Davidson's recommendation has to do with women's comfort while travelling, it is also highly suggestive of mentalities which aimed at consolidating woman's association with the home. As many fictional texts in this book will show, when women took up the public function of active passenger, they were perceived as a threat to the attempt of patriarchal institutions to establish masculine socio-political signification in this new space of modernity.

In my approach to the railway as a social space, I draw on space theorists and geographers such as Henri Lefebvre, Michel de Certeau, Doreen Massey, and Tim Cresswell, who view space as socially constructed and constructing, as the product of an ongoing, dynamic process involving nature, politics, culture, and history. In his seminal *The Production of Space*, Lefebvre developed the idea of space not as a mere container, a frame, 'designed simply to receive whatever is poured into it', nor as 'apparently "neutral", "objective", fixed, transparent, innocent or indifferent', but rather as a 'social morphology' (93–4), forever becoming. Space for Lefebvre and his followers, however much the latter diverged from the former's initial premises, is engaged in a mutually formative relationship with social life, in the manner of a house or other static property which, rather than being 'the epitome of immovability' is, in actuality, 'an image of a complex of mobilities, a nexus of in and out conduits' (*Space*, 92–3). While being literally a space of 'in and out conduits', the railway is also, in a wider sense, constitutive of social meaning, just as social meaning continually shapes its spatial structures. In the spaces of the railway we see the tension that Lefebvre described between space conceived by engineers, planners, and 'technocratic subdividers' (representations of space) and space lived, that is, space which is produced and modified over time (representational space) by 'users' and artists who aspire to change and appropriate it through the imagination (33, 38–9). The railway, by which individuals fulfil the routines of their everyday life, is a site of social and spatial practices dictated, to a great extent, by socio-political interests which impose divisions and exclusions. However, at the same time, its political meaning is constantly reconfigured by unstable human interventions which make the train a site of challenge and contestation. But to what extent were women capable of disrupting political agendas which were implicated in the production of the space of the railway?

In order to address this question, this study, with its close readings of texts by female and male authors, is interested in the dialogue or, in some cases, the battle of the sexes concerning the way women's experience of the railway is represented. Men's texts, more often than not, served the crucial purpose of upholding the stability of gender ideology by constructing female rail passengers as either acceptably passive or unacceptably active, hence irksome or dangerous. As passive subjects female passengers served as spectacles on display for the entertainment of the male gaze, and as self-serving agents they were deemed criminals or prostitutes. In both cases in the figure of the female passenger we see merged a variety of attitudes or male fantasies about women which constituted them endangered or endangering. Chapter 1, with its focus on sensation fiction, demonstrates this tension between women's acceptable and unacceptable behaviour on the train. Other texts, by women especially, explored the emancipatory aspect of train travel, experimenting, in narrative terms, with woman's exploration of identity and sexuality as well as with the psychological anxieties and insecurities caused by travelling. The physical and psychological challenges of train travel for women are developed by a variety of authors, male and female. But while for the former (especially in short stories published in journals), more often than not, narrative functions as a discursive means of regulation and control, where men tacitly or even violently attempt to compromise and limit women's entitlement to such settings, for the latter it becomes a space for the subordination of technology and gender ideology to a subjective representation of the liminality experienced. It is such liminality, both of this in-between space of the railway itself and of the liminal spaces it literally crosses as it moves, that highlights potential slippages in gender structures and middle-class femininity in particular. In such circumstances train travel potentially becomes a metaphor for the bold transgression of woman who may appropriate and subvert the train's regulated mobility and speed, using them to her advantage. Women's personal itineraries, thus, often diverge from the ones rigidly delineated in Bradshaw's timetables, either literally or metaphorically, but in every case the train initiates a personal transformation, and the narrative of the railway becomes a strategy that helps them avoid objectification and fixing. 'Transgression,' Tim Cresswell argues, 'is often defined in geographical terms. Geography, then, can tell us a lot about transgression, and transgression, conversely provides valuable insights into the way places affect behavior and ideology' (*In Place*, 21). Of course, transgression is not uncomplicated and not always seen in a positive light; nor does it always lead to fulfilment or liberation, as can be seen in the studies of novels and short stories by Margaret Oliphant, Rhoda Broughton, Dora Russell, and Mona Caird.

As an emblem of the conquest of national and imperial space and of the staggering advances of science and technology, the train offered women passengers a taste of its omnipotence by inviting them to participate in the illusion of dominance over space and time. This feeling of power was also enhanced by the rail passengers' cultivation of the mobile, panoramic gaze – 'the tendency to see the discrete indiscriminately' according to Schivelbusch (61) – which facilitated the adapting of vision to the velocity and its control of the barrage of images flying past the carriage window. This illusion of mastery over the landscape did, to a certain extent, liberate and empower women's subjectivity, but by giving rise to desires, aspirations, or imaginative flights, it also confused women making them more conscious of their own limitations; for, as a space of technology and rational control, the train came to represent the totalising power of institutions and ideologies which applied rigid restrictions to women. Such limitations are applied as much in urban settings (see for example my studies of Henry James's London Underground) as in imperial settings, as can be seen in the tensions arising in the works of Mrs Humphry Ward and Flora Annie Steel, examined in Chapter 3. The railway's objective was to chart and divide space, but, in reality, and as has been shown by Richter, Parkins, and Vadillo, the carriage exemplified a crisis of boundaries that was particularly bewildering for women. The sense of indistinguishability between public and private, inner and outer (literally illustrated by the comfortable, domestic-like furnishings of the carriages) confused women, since, unlike the home, the carriage was not safe from contingencies like intrusions and accidents, and, unlike other public space, it could not foster invisibility. The imposed stasis and constant visual exposure to unidentified passengers in a compartment was more frightening to women than the circulation of city life which was quite comforting for the anonymity that it often protected through its openness.[7]

So the geography of the railway combines two clashing discourses: the spatial coherence and compartmentalisation of the subject aimed at by the rational technological minds who had designed and constructed it and, at the same time, the incoherence brought about by the fluidity of conceptual boundaries, as the train is first and foremost a site for the circulation of bodies who resist their compartmentalisation through anonymity and free mobility. While the carriage offers the illusion of enclosed and secured interiority within clearly demarcated material boundaries, it fails to prevent the psychological instability, disorientation, restlessness, and desocialising effects of a space without boundaries and, as a consequence, with no regulating rules of interaction. It is as such a liminal space, which defies rigid categorisation and ultimately resists disciplining tactics, that the railway becomes a site which may challenge ideological tools of power, and women often seem to thrive through this destabilisation and reconfiguration of boundaries. The fragmentation of consciousness experienced on the train, as we shall see in many women's narratives that move beyond the fear of violence and crime that such situations fostered, leads to self-development and even transformation. While not heroic, women's sense of liberation and even incoherence of consciousness is often figured as more valuable than the coherence experienced by men on the train, whose regular mobility ironically leads to passive demobilisation, as the ubiquitousness and inevitability of technology takes over physical and mental action. This distinction between mental activity and physical passivity, which becomes a gender difference, is examined throughout this book.

In his chapter entitled 'Railway Navigation and Incarceration', in *The Practice of Everyday Life*, de Certeau describes the railway carriage as 'A bubble of panoptic and classifying power, a module of imprisonment that makes possible the production of an order, a closed and autonomous insularity – that is what can traverse space and make itself independent of local roots' (111). As such the railway constitutes, in a microscopic way, a very potent grid-like institution, which aims at disciplining and classifying the subject through literal incarceration.[8] This 'perfect actualization of the rational utopia', as de Certeau calls it (111), functions on a par with the dominant politics that orchestrate everyday life, politics that aim at regularity and exclusions. At first glance, passengers seem to conform to these aims, accepting the divisions performed by means of the glass window or the iron rail, which separate while ensuring the fixity and silence of both inside and outside. 'But paradoxically,' de Certeau points out, 'it is the silence of these things put at a distance, behind the windowpane, which, from a great distance, makes our memories speak or draws out of the shadows the dreams of our secrets' (112). The railway thus 'combines dreams with technology'; 'the "speculative" returns, located in the very heart of the mechanical order. Contraries coincide for the duration of a journey' (113). If, therefore, according to de Certeau, the regularity of technology, which confirms and guarantees the regularity of rigid socio-political institutions such as the market economy, political regimes, and modern urban planning, may be contested by a myriad uncontrollable mental movements of passengers, then railway travelling may provide opportunities for resistance to ideology not in any revolutionary way but through one's everyday, quotidian, thoughts, fantasies, and activities. As Tim Cresswell puts it, 'The central tension in de Certeau's work is between a systemic grammar of space – an order that we inhabit and is not constructed by us – on the one hand and our ability to use this grammar in ways which are not predetermined' (*Place*, 39). It could be argued then that in its openness and with its fluid boundaries, despite its rigid and disciplined material structure, the train is the site of such contestational practices, an 'unstable stage', 'constantly struggled over and reimagined in practical ways', 'made and remade on a daily basis' (39). The train corresponds very well to this interpretation of place as an 'event' 'marked by openness and change rather than boundedness and permanence' (39).

As a site marked by transience, openness, and mobility, the railway – its carriages but also its stations – could also be conceived as a 'nonplace' in Marc Augé's sense: 'The traveller's space may [...] be the archetype of *non-place*', he argues (*Non-Places*, 86). Augé contends that in nineteenth-century travellers' accounts of space, one finds prophetic evocations of twentieth-century non-places, in which the traveller experiences 'an overburdening or emptying of individuality', and in contemplation of which 'only the movement of fleeting images enables the observer to hypothesize the existence of a past and glimpse the possibility of a future' (87). Such non-places, which are the products of what he terms 'supermodernity' (93), include the railway, the airport, the highway, and the supermarket, spaces in which individuals suffer a crisis of identity, due to the fact that they need to adopt a new way of thinking that lays emphasis on uprootedness and impermanence, which

affect the way they perceive personal and national histories and traditions: 'a person entering the space of non-place is relieved of his usual
determinants. He becomes no more than what he does or experiences in
the role of passenger, customer or driver' (103). In such an environment
passengers taste 'the passive joys of identity-loss, and the more active
pleasure of role-playing' (103). Train travel accelerated nineteenth-
century women's participation in modern life exactly because it made
them conscious of the need to learn to live for the present, in a perpetual present, embodying temporary and provisional roles. Women's
occupancy of the liminal and ephemeral spaces of the railway gradually
helped to unsettle their permanently anchored position within the home.
For Victorian women venturing forth from the home and risking an
infraction of gender ideology, such an experience was both exhilarating and terrifying. But in every case it required an encounter with and
confrontation of the self that is treated narratively through interior
monologue or other experimental stylistic effects.

Moreover, in his description of the preponderance of such non-places
in our contemporary times, Augé delineates the 'traffic conditions of
spaces in which individuals are supposed to interact only with texts,
whose proponents are not individuals but "moral entities" or institutions (airports, airlines, Ministry of Transport [. . .])' (*Non-Places*, 96).
It could be argued that in the nineteenth century we see the beginnings
of this fissure in communication traditions, as passengers struggle to reconcile their own customs of sociability with new institutional hierarchies
of interaction imposed by anonymous authorities. The depersonalisation of human relations is thus exacerbated in the spaces of the railway
in which, as Augé claims, 'people coexist or cohabit without living
together, where the status of [. . .] solitary passenger implies a contractual relation with society' (*Anthropology*, 110). As will be seen in the
chapters that follow, women and men struggled with the contractual
relations they entered into with the railway network, whose signs they
had to follow almost mechanically: the timetable, the ticket office, the
purchasing of tickets, the management of luggage, the choice of carriage,
and so on. But women especially faced the further challenge of juggling
two antithetical goals on the train: handling competently the contracts
of public life, the mechanics of travel, while at the same time preserving
and showcasing their private role as domestic angels. Together with
the new form of anonymous sociability this contractual relation with
the transportation network enabled women, for better or for worse,
to experience 'relationships as traffic', in Raymond Williams's words
(299).

As Williams ruefully points out, traffic is 'a form of consciousness and a form of social relations', an indication of the alienation experienced by daily travellers or commuters pursuing their 'ultimately separate ways but in a common mode' (296).[9] In his analysis of Dickens, Gissing, George Eliot, and Gaskell, among others, in *The Country and the City*, Williams describes the negative effects of what he calls 'scrambling and ambiguous mobility' on the male migrants of their stories (224), paying little or no attention to their female counterparts who similarly experience the mobility of urban or cross-country living. Yet, for woman forging new relations with the metropolis and its institutions, the railway – being perhaps the most formidable institution in and beyond the city – helped her cultivate an individuality which until the time of the railway was mostly unfolding within close quarters and in accordance with a socially prescribed role of femininity. Williams's poignant descriptions of railway circulation as 'the life's blood' and at the same time as 'the triumphant monster, Death' (163), thwarting human habits and purposes with its inexorable force, only partially fits the railway experience of women, for whom the train was a further means of reconfiguring the role of womanhood, of exploring subjectivity and the limits of desire. Moreover, the train was first and foremost a contact zone, and for women, ephemeral contact, which was diametrically different from the rooted relations fostered in the home, was a challenge both threatening – in cases where their ambition was cut short by assault – and productive, in the sense that it helped reconceive gender hierarchies and rules of interaction between the sexes. The women's narratives that will be examined from the age of sensation to early modernism negotiate and often resist the discipline and framing that railway mobility entailed in principle. Through plot and style women complicate or question the myths of connection, heterosexual romance, comfort, and fixed destinations that the railway conjured in the Victorian period.

Therefore, travelling through space by train becomes for women a socio-political and psychological adventure. Likewise, the production of the spaces of transit that the railway generated is complicated by the parameter of gender, by the everyday practices of women using them for ordinary or extraordinary purposes. The rail journey enabled women to experience ephemeral relations not only with co-passengers but also with places. The temporariness of places passed through, visited, or viewed from the window required of women the cultivation of a mobile gaze which characterised differently the tourist and the cosmopolitan. As will be seen in Chapter 3, the former applies her transitory glance on sites and landscapes briefly gazed at, swiftly consumed, and promptly exchanged for the next, while the latter adopts the borderless mentality activated by the precarious relations with place acquired by train travel, a mentality that enables her to experience as active, and not static, the ongoing, live trajectories of places through which she travels. As Doreen Massey evocatively describes, on a train, you are 'travelling not across space-as-a-surface [. . .] you are travelling *across trajectories*. The tree which blows now in the wind out there beyond the train window was once an acorn on another tree, will one day hence be gone' (119). Train travel often obscures the ongoing life of objects, people, and landscapes passed by, making one feel that they are 'trapped in the timeless instant' at which they were visually captured from the window (119); instead, Massey proposes, train travel should be imagined 'as a speeding across on-going stories' (119), through and across spaces already and continually inscribed with history and multiple becomings. Thus, space, according to Massey, 'presents us with the social' in the sense that it challenges the subject to become conscious of 'the contemporaneity of an ongoing multiplicity of others, human and non-human' (195) – a challenge brought into focus while one is journeying by train. In many stories that are examined in Chapters 3 and 4, women exhibit a dynamic model of mentation through an acknowledgement of this contemporaneity or simultaneity of trajectories. Women's subjective experience of the railway is described as particularly attuned to these complex temporal and spatial dimensions of locomotion, which have, in turn, a formative effect on the heroines themselves, and which find their expression in innovative narrative styles often resembling the modernist techniques of interior monologue and stream of consciousness. As a railway passenger, Massey argues, 'You are part of the constant process of the making and breaking of links which is an element in the constitution of you yourself', but also of the places travelled to and through, 'and thus of space itself' (118). For, as Massey contends, 'Since space is a product of social relations,' with a train journey one is helping 'to *alter* space, to participate in its continuing production' (118). Therefore, the image of the train navigating through places and lives makes women conscious of themselves, body and consciousness, in flux, alongside many parallel trajectories, and of space itself as alterable and altered by time as well as by their own superimposition upon it.

The book aims at presenting women's multilevel and multifaceted response to the railway within a period which spans approximately sixty years and during which the train remained the fastest vehicle of land transportation. Chapter 1, 'Geographies of Fear in the Age of Sensation', examines journalistic and fictional accounts of the dangers that railway travel incurred for women, considering the function of the discourse of fear that was used in both types of texts. Narratives of robbery, murder, sexual abuse, and even rape, on the one hand, served to acquaint the public, and women specifically, with the dangers of railway mobility, but, on the other, they helped perpetuate a stereotype of the woman who, finding herself in a space of transit, is rendered vulnerable by a presumed ineptitude, as far as the practicalities of travel were concerned, and by a disconcerting inability to defend her own person or her possessions. The railway as a new setting of uncertain signification, permeable borders, and tentative safety accommodated very elaborate sensation plots, which, however, did not always victimise women. The chapter looks at many short stories and novels by popular novelists such as Mary Elizabeth Braddon, Wilkie Collins, Rhoda Broughton, Ellen Wood, and Margaret Oliphant as well as by anonymous authors published in periodicals. As these texts show, the railway, in which all passengers's social and personal identity seems precarious due to anonymity, was also treated as a stage by women who found opportunity to manipulate their behaviour and appearance in order to pursue economic or even amorous aims. Ultimately, the train facilitated both the blurring of identity on which the sensation plot depended and the consequent subversion of gender conventions through female transgression that such fiction is famous for.

Chapter 2, 'Railway Speed', considers the metaphor of 'fastness' that was attributed to young women with unconventional behaviour, drawing connections between such manners fostered by the looser interaction that the railway encouraged, literal mobility, and sexual transgression. I examine railway short stories which expose young flirts or even more dangerous femmes fatales, whose provocative behaviour threatened the stability of domestic ideology by exposing the incompatibility between men's and women's intentions, manners, and morals. The outcome of these stories demonstrates that even though through its metaphors the Victorian period associated women with its most powerful emblem of speed and mobility, those women were, nevertheless, expected to follow prescribed, cast-in-iron paths. Uncontrollable 'fastness' in girls would inevitably lead them to crash. In the second part of Chapter 2, I look closely at three women authors' representation of female sexuality in relation to the railway, Rhoda Broughton's *Not Wisely but too Well*, Dora Russell's *Footprints in the Snow*, and Margaret Oliphant's 'A Story of a Wedding Tour', in which the train (and the idea of fast transit) becomes the conceptual means of exploring the heroines' potential for the bold transgression of social codes. In the third part of Chapter 2, I examine the presence of 'fast' women in Henry James's London Metropolitan Railway settings. Wandering in underground locations, the heroines of 'A London Life' and *The Wings of the Dove* negotiate sexual desire and social norms. It is argued that the underground scenes mark moments of undoing and rupture, moments during which codes of morality and manners fall apart or clash and are subverted. These settings, however, also point towards the dangers of displacement, of moving in the margins of binary gender rules (which is what happens in James's Underground), and at the disorientation that ensues.

Chapter 3, 'Breaching National Borders: Rail Travel in Europe and Empire' firstly addresses women's train travel in Europe through examples from Anthony Trollope and Henry James, arguing that the experience of the railway trained women in the tourist mentality, which many female characters exhibit as they roam through Europe on the grand tour. The tourist gaze, promoted primarily by the train, partly consisted in the mobile and transitory glance of sites and landscapes. Tourism by train also provided men and women with structured ways in which to interact, reconfiguring the terms and the intensity of emotional attachments, fostering a modern view of love based on transient feelings and fleeting impressions acquired by the mobile gaze. However, for James in *The Portrait of a Lady* the train may also become the figurative means of representing Isabel Archer's expansion of consciousness as she experiences the permeability of boundaries between self and world, thus acquiring an ethically cosmopolitan stance. In the second and third parts of Chapter 3, I turn my attention to women's ventures in spaces of empire, Canada and India, in fiction by Mary Humphry Ward and Flora Annie Steel, for whom the railway figures as a contact zone of colonial and gender encounters. It is my contention that the train narratives examined exhibit the incoherence of national identity within settings of empire, and that women in particular, who occupy a peculiar position as, at the same time, colonists and disenfranchised subjects of empire, expose the impossibility of monolithic, solidly impermeable identities within this context. The ideological tensions found in these narratives are strongly suggestive of the women's awareness of the aporias and impossibilities resulting from the railway's mission to discipline and homogenise the heterogeneous conceptual space of colonial culture and ethnicity.

Chapter 4, 'Railway Space and Time' goes back to the 1850s in order to study the ways women progressively dealt with the mechanisation of life and the concomitant alienation or estrangement from community that the railway brought about. In this period of increasing industrialisation and urbanisation, the railway contributed to the construction of a new social and spatial experience for which relocation seemed to be a prerequisite as well as an outcome. The issue of women's response to community loss and spatial displacement is examined in two novels which demonstrate development in women's mentality as well as clashing gender perspectives: Gaskell's *North and South* and Hardy's *Jude the Obscure*. It is argued that spatial displacement is increasingly connected to the nervousness and fragmentation experienced by railway women as we move towards the fin de siècle and modernism, during which women start developing new narrative techniques that reflect changes in the perception of time and space that the railway stimulated. The second part of Chapter 4 concentrates on railway time and women's late-nineteenth-century narratives which offer a more internalised experience of the railway, one that seems to defy the rigid standardisation of time, precision, and punctuality that train travel required. Rhoda Broughton, Margaret Oliphant, Mona Caird, Edith Wharton, and Katherine Mansfield experiment with the representation of fleeting vision and temporal experience, often prefiguring a stream of consciousness that combines coherent thought with incoherent free association. The heroines' mind wandering seems to defy the rigid compartmentalisation of experience that railway time enforces. Nevertheless, the train also remains a site of alienation and violence, as the modernist examples from Wharton and Mansfield demonstrate. With their restlessness, volatility, and increasingly impenetrable obscurity, the railway women of my narrative withstand their own assimilation within networks of institutional morality that the railway, as a battlefield of gender and class conflicts, paradoxically both challenged and strengthened.

Notes

1. See, for example, Karen Chase and Michael Levenson, *The Spectacle of Intimacy*, Monica Cohen, *Professional Domesticity*, Teresa Gómez Reus and Aránzazu Usandizaga (eds), *Inside Out*, Andrea Kaston Tange, *Architectural Identities*, Elizabeth Langland, *Nobody's Angels*, Wendy Parkins, *Mobility and Modernity in Women's Novels, 1850–1930s*, Deborah L. Parsons, *Streetwalking the Metropolis: Women, the City and Modernity*, and Deborah Epstein Nord, *Walking the Victorian Streets*.
2. Amy Richter's *Home on the Rails: Women, the Railroad, and the Rise of Public Domesticity* is the only full-length examination of women and the railway, but it focuses on America solely and from a historical perspective. Ana Parejo Vadillo's *Women Poets and Urban Aestheticism: Passengers of Modernity* partly discusses the effect of the London Underground on fin-de-siècle women's poetry. Wendy Parkins's *Mobility and Modernity in Women's Novels, 1850–1930s: Women Moving Dangerously* includes some discussions of the railway.
3. For a historical/technical account see Jack Simmons, *The Victorian Railway*; for details on the development of the railway in Britain, Christian Wolmar,

Fire and Steam, and in Europe and America, Wolmar, *Blood, Iron, and Gold*; on economic enterprise and regulation of the railway network in Victorian England, Mark Casson's *The World's First Railway System*; and for a critical tour of railway art, Kennedy and Treuherz's *The Railway: Art in the Age of Steam*.

4. See also the ground-breaking work of Lenore Davidoff and Catherine Hall, *Family Fortunes*, Elizabeth Langland, *Nobody's Angels*, and Monica Cohen, *Professional Domesticity*, all of which challenge the Victorian public/private binary, demonstrating its untenability.

5. See also Mark Poster's reading of de Certeau in *Cultural History and Postmodernity*, 125.

6. In Chapter 4 I briefly diverge from this rationale, by looking at a voyage within the United States by Edith Wharton, whose modernist treatment of the railway illustrates beautifully the themes of that section.

7. Wolfgang Schivelbusch has argued that the gradual introduction of the side corridor in train carriages after the mid-nineteenth century 'shone a light into the threatening darkness' of the previously isolated compartments 'by providing a connection to the general traffic' and by assuring the bourgeois traveller 'that his compartment and the possible events taking place in it were controled by the appropriate authority' (196). Circulation within the train eventually made travel safer and more comfortable for women.

8. Ian Carter has described the ways in which the railway applied discipline:

   Railway workers and passengers alike found themselves constrained by fierce discipline, blending features from older military organisation (uniformed staff, administrative procedures based on strict hierarchical delegation, senior staff as 'officers') with features drawn from newer capitalist industry (enforced rule-bound behaviour, intense divisions of labour, close surveillance, professional technical expertise, rigid time discipline). (10)

9. Williams describes the modern transportation network (which includes the railway but also the car) as indicative of modern alienation, and argues, in relation to *Dombey and Son* that

   In seeing the city, as he here sees the railways, as at once the exciting and the threatening consequence of a new mobility, as not only an alien and indifferent system but as the unknown, perhaps unknowable, sum of so many lives, jostling, colliding, disrupting, adjusting, recognizing, settling, moving again to new spaces, Dickens went to the centre, the dynamic centre, of this transforming social experience. (163–4)

Chapter 1

Geographies of Fear in the Age of Sensation

Ephemeral Chills and Thrills

I am the wife of Henry Deakerton Martin, of Cheltenham, and was travelling from [Gloucester] to Bristol, yesterday, by the express train. Defendant
entered the compartment of the carriage in which I was seated alone at
Gloucester. During the journey we talked, as people generally do in the train.
He had the impertinence to kiss me. He put his arm around my neck and
kissed me twice, and on my arrival at Bristol, I gave him in charge.
          Anon., 'A Gentleman Fined for Kissing a Lady in a Railway Carriage'
                                                  Reynold's Newspaper (1861)

He then proceeded to push his knee against her, and she withdrew her leg; and
in a short time he put his arm round her waist and kissed her. She was in the
compartment alone with this man, a strong, powerful man, and unprotected
[. . .] The defendant became more daring and kissed her lips, and placed himself
in front of her and endeavoured to raise her dress, and undoubtedly committed
an indecent assault. The lady screamed, but the train was going at the rate of
thirty or forty miles an hour, and her screams were not heard [. . .] She endeavoured to break the window with her elbow, but did not succeed, and she then
got the door open and got out. The defendant then put his arm round her and
endeavoured to pull her back into the carriage, but she got herself in a place of
safety so far as he was concerned, but in a place of great danger so far as her
life was concerned, but she determined to keep in that position even if death
overtook her rather than be further molested by this man.
          Anon., 'The Charge of Assaulting a Lady in a Railway Carriage'
                                                           Daily News (1875)

He pulled her from her seat and threw her upon the floor. The lady struggled
and resisted to the utmost of her power. Prisoner threatened to shoot her, to
administer chloroform, or to cut her throat if she resisted [. . .]
          Anon., 'Dastardly Assault on a Lady in a Railway Carriage'
                                                  Lloyd's Weekly Newspaper (1893)

A cultural account of women and the railway in the Victorian times
cannot but start with a review of the most popular narrative of the period,

that of women's vulnerability within the train carriage. The abundance of reported incidents like the ones quoted above in newspapers and journals suggests that despite the fact that the railway was viewed as a democratic – equally accessible to all – form of transport, women's occupancy of the technologically advanced spaces of transit was, quite often, fraught with dangers and threats which compromised the emancipatory potential of high-speed travel. Just like men, women on trains were very often victims of robbery and even murder; but the sexual component of the physical attacks against women on trains suggested that the railway compartment was also an erotically charged space which generated unregulated, and often unwarranted, desire in men who asserted their sexual authority over physically weaker women. The narratives of these sexual attacks within a public space, which – regardless of whether they had occurred in comfortable first-class carriages or in second- and third-class ones – had been considered monitored and secure, shocked the public and excited the Victorian imagination. The second epigraph narrates the most publicised case of the well-respected Colonel Baker, who in August 1875, for the actions described in the extract, was charged with attempted rape, indecent assault, and assault. Yet a simple search through the digital archives of Victorian newspapers and journals demonstrates that Baker's victim, Miss Kate Dickenson, was not the first woman to suffer the kind of sexually threatening behaviour Baker inflicted on her, and was not even the first to avoid rape by stepping outside the carriage door of a moving train, thus risking death.[1]

From the early days of the railway it became obvious that the architecture of the train with the corridor-less compartment – a site 'potentially, of a dangerous incarceration, an entrapment' (Beaumont, 'Railway Mania', 152) – was conducive to such crime, and journalism from the thirties onwards emphasised female sexual vulnerability within it, by consistently, and in an increasingly sensational manner, reporting the dangers of women riding on trains alone or even with their husbands or other male companion. What is particularly striking is the sexually explicit discourse employed in the accounts of such crime, discourse which opens up the abused female body to the public gaze, treating it as a text to be disseminated by the media and interpreted by legal authorities. According to a variety of reports, ladies were subjected to embracing, kissing, fondling, molesting, violating, and beating, or, in milder cases, to language described as disgusting, disgraceful, indecent, or brutal by passengers deemed maniacs, ruffians, drunkards, or scamps. But the sexual detail of the descriptions rendered the writing porno-graphic and constituted the readers of common newspapers and journals voyeurs of criminal sexual conduct:

A short time after the train left Warmley station the prisoner put his hands into her lap, and said he should have a New Year's kiss. She resisted him, but he thrust his hands inside the bosom of her jacket, after which he forced her against the back of the compartment and, against her will, kissed her. Owing to the resistance she offered the buttons of her jacket were broken. (Anon., 'Charge of Assaulting a Lady in a Railway Carriage at Bitton', 1878)

It is no wonder that such descriptions, as well as the Colonel Baker case which generated extensive and sensational publicity, inspired the publication of the anonymously printed pornographic book, *Raped on the Railway* (1894), which focuses on the victim's alleged sexual pleasure in being raped. As it has been widely argued in studies of female urban pedestrians, increased mobility and exposure were associated with prostitution or with a woman's supposed sexual dissipation, and by offering the mechanical means of increased and accelerated mobility, the railway was assumed to facilitate woman's sexual degeneracy. On the one hand, as Ana Parejo Vadillo has shown, 'From the early origins of the transport system women were targeted as passengers' (18); on the other, it seemed that as women were getting more comfortable in their new role, they were encountering more social prejudice and moral scepticism, to the extent that, as in our day, sexual crime was in many cases deemed inevitable or even provoked. *Raped on the Railway* proposes with conviction that Baker's victim was in reality the victimiser:

Most people now living, who have passed life's meridian, will recall the famous case of Colonel Baker and the Fascinating, Finely-made, Talkative, Coaxing, Venturesome, Frightened, Inquisitive, Warm-blooded, Voluptuous, Cock-teasing, Young lady, whom it is reported, he attempted to ravish. The gallant Colonel, no doubt liked, what is called, 'a bit of skirt', or in other words, was, an ardent woman-hunter, and took his pleasure wherever he could find it. But many men, who knew Baker intimately, did not believe in his guilt. There are many girls, especially those of a fashionable, know-all kind, whom a little healthy slapping on the lovely, plump buttocks, would do infinite good; who delight in working a man up to a pitch of erotic paroxysm, and when he draws his sword to strike, shrink back in terror at the sight of the gleaming blade. Be all this as it may, we are happy to record that other cases have come before the Courts, where the woman was a willing, consenting, and most delighted victim. (n.p.)

As women increasingly stepped out of the confines of the home and sought practical ways in which to participate in the fast pace of life in the Victorian times, their exposure to complex and untried mobility systems or networks, and, at the same time, to unpredictable human agency, made them the weaker link in this race towards the modernisation of city and country. As Lynda Nead has argued, 'The modern city was a world devoted to the production of constant motion and was inhabited by a new, ideal citizen: "locomotive man"' (54). But, as the examples of sexual crime demonstrate, to what extent could women participate with impunity in the mechanised mobility of their times? Transport offered woman pleasure but also moments of adversity and danger, and her contemporary socio-cultural discourses seemed divided about her right to such spaces, given not only her assumed physical weakness but also her anticipated incompetence to deal with the intricacies of urban or national networks. Focusing on the latter, numerous are the articles, illustrations, and short stories in journals which make fun of women's supposed ineptitude, verging on stupidity, as they are depicted unable to deal with simple tasks such as buying tickets, managing their luggage, and boarding the right compartment.

Older women and spinsters were especially targeted in such farcical discourse which emphasised their incompetence, while younger women were often shown as too naïve and trusting, yearning for male patronage during the train ride. The following extract from a short story entitled 'Ruby Denzel's Travelling Companion' (1881), by Marcia Whiteside, is typical of such attitudes which stressed feminine weakness:

> When the train arrived at Millberry and she looked out on the crowded platform, her heart sank within her. There was hardly standing room, as it appeared to her. Heaps of luggage lay piled up here and there; porters were rushing hither and thither; the crowd, composed principally of factory hands, as she could easily see, swayed from side to side as the train stopped; children screamed; women shrieked; men grumbled and swore; and as she tremblingly opened the carriage door and prepared to step out she felt as if the crowd would carry her away and that any search after luggage was an impossibility. (553)

In such stories women readily and even gladly acknowledge their inability to deal with the mental or physical challenges of travel, having successfully internalised a version of femininity socially constructed as weak and vulnerable. Plots devised around scenes such as the following,

> [Ruby Denzel] was borne along by the hurrying crowd to the end of the platform, and nearer and nearer to its edge [. . .] 'Help me! – I am falling!' she cried, in a broken voice; and in another instant she would have been on the rails, and under the wheels of the engine, had not a strong arm seized her, and dragged her back, scattering the crowd that surrounded her, and leading her to a place of safety [. . .] 'You are not hurt, I trust?'
> 'Oh no!' panted Ruby; 'thanks to you. But if you had not caught me I shudder to think what would have been my fate.' (554)

served to immobilise women, if not physically, since long distance travel had become routine, then, beyond doubt, ideologically within the rigid

A LITTLE FARCE AT A RAILWAY-STATION.

Lady. " I want One Ticket—First ! "
Clerk. " Single ? "
Lady. " Single ! What does it matter to you, Sir, whether I'm Single or not ? Impertinence ! "

[*Clerk explains that he meant Single or Return, not t'other thing.*

Figure 1. 'A Little Farce', *Punch* (16 July 1859): 23.

boundaries of the stereotype of passive and pliable femininity. As a result, most fictional women in train stories seek and even enjoy the patronage of male companions or co-travellers, asking them to get refreshments and look after or load their luggage, thankful for the anchoring that this dependence on typical masculinity effects on their new drifting identity as travellers at high speed. In their analysis of the production of gender in railway spaces, Sabin Bieri and Natalia Gerodetti point out that

RAILWAY MORALS.

Guard. " Now, Miss! Are you going by this Train?"
Miss Rebecca. " Yes! But I must have a Carriage where there are no Young Men likely to be Rude to One."

Figure 2. 'Railway Morals', *Punch* (17 September 1864): 116.

while social discourses served the useful purpose of warning women of the potential difficulties and dangers to be faced in such spaces, at the same time they were responsible 'for the construction of young women travellers as utterly unprepared, frivolous and unaware of the dangers of life outside the private sphere' (226). Women were thus 'perceived as flighty, negligent and sometimes as possessing diminished responsibility' (226), physically, intellectually, and emotionally incapable of mastering technology or braving the threat of mere rudeness or, more seriously, assault.

The 1870 fictional story of a middle-aged Mrs Gandy, who needs to travel by underground in London, stresses her lack of orientation and inability to fathom the public function of such transport and its differ-ence from privately-hired cabs, due to her bossiness, impertinence, and presumption, all of which render her unfit for the railway. Moreover she dreads every stage of the rail travelling process:

> Tunnels were things of fear; the screeching of steam-whistles was shocking to her tympanum as well as to her nerves; the obtaining of a ticket was a feat to which she had to 'bend up' all her faculties, mental and corporal, and in nine cases out of ten it was a wrong one; while its preservation to the end of her journey was a matter which to say was problematical, would be to indulge in very inadequate phraseology. (Anon., 'Of a Respectable Couple', 56)

The narrator concludes that Mrs Gandy would have been spared such troubles if she had just assigned all these mystifying and confusing duties to her husband, even though he is thought to be a meek and inefficient man. At the end of her railway adventure, after having boarded the wrong train and met with a frightening man, she finds herself lost in the dungeon-like tunnels of an underground junction, as a 'wanderer' (63), and experiences a change of personality, as she is tamed by the intricacies of technology. Helpless and subdued, Mrs Gandy acknowledges the superiority of her husband, who, 'with a briskness and alacrity, and with a capability of penetrating the mysteries which seemed to come to him by intuition', takes charge of their railway travelling and fixes the destination. Such stories proposed that men, by intuition alone, were more fit to use public transport, whose intricate structure seemed to be aimed at supposedly masculine powers of orientation, organisation, and self-discipline. And yet, as we shall see in the next part of this chapter, many heroines of sensation fiction went against this stereotype, exhibiting, as Henry James remarked of Mary Elizabeth Braddon's Lady Audley, a remarkable familiarity with the use of the railway ('Miss Braddon', 593).

Rude or otherwise irritating middle-aged and older women were often the butt of the joke in such stories of the period from the fifties to the seventies, which capitalise on the annoyance of men when finding themselves sharing a carriage with them. These women, nevertheless, are often presented as well prepared to evade and even ward off the masculine threat to their physical integrity. In an 1855 *Household Words* story, 'The Railway Companion', 'Aunt Dorothy', who hates the lack of exclusivity and the democratic conditions that trains foster, manages to neutralise the threat of a too-forward, seemingly low-life man by staring at him fixedly. Unable to meet her gaze, the man gradually loses his supposed aggressiveness and is subdued. The case is one of mistaken identity, as it turns out that the man is an elderly baronet awkwardly testing the new familiarity in the semi-private space of the railway, and Aunt Dorothy's fear is thus misfounded, a product of an over-suspicious disposition fed by the mass hysteria about the dangers of railway travelling. By 1864 the eponymous heroine of 'Aunt Tabitha's Railway Adventure' has prepared herself even better for railway travelling by practising self-defence at home through rehearsed attacks and defences and carrying with her a dagger and a gun. In the carriage she first threatens an innocent man who narrowly escapes by climbing out of the flying train, and secondly shoots the ticket inspector, fortunately without killing him. The story focuses on her paranoid behaviour and exaggerated suspicions generated by the media's descriptions of attacks on women on trains. At the same time women are rendered unable to discriminate between the motives of male co-passengers. Thus, in both stories, while women are shown actively to take control of their body and the penetrable setting, the narrators consistently deride and under-value their self-defence mechanisms by hinting at their failing faculty of reason – the former is described as deaf and senile and the latter mad. Nevertheless, such women's behaviour was compatible with the counsel provided by manuals such as *The Railway Traveller's Handy Book* (1862), which recommended various means of managing the unexpected dangers of the journey. For example in describing rides through tunnels, the *Handy Book* advised potential travellers 'to have the hands and arms ready disposed for defence, so that in the event of an attack, the assailant may be instantly beaten back or restrained' (Anon., 94).

Older women's behaviour on trains was deemed not only annoying but also dangerous. In 'A Railway Adventure' published by *Chambers's Journal* (Anon., 1875), a man's encounter with an elderly woman on a train transforms him for life, from light-hearted and cheerful to dejected and grave. The cause of this change is his female co-passenger, who during the journey mesmerises him with her gaze and later tries to kill him; apparently she had recently escaped from a mental institution, having been committed for murdering her own daughter. Dangerous women were not infrequent, and this story demonstrates how a close encounter in a carriage could compromise the safety of men at the same time that it could shatter their sense of superiority and identity. In this particular story, the hero, Jack, is unable to defend himself and is saved only when the train crashes, killing the woman. Moreover, on discovering her identity, he is scarred for life as it is revealed that she was actually his mother, considered dead for twenty years. The story, though relying on an improbable, sensational plot, centres on the psy-chological effects of the railway adventure on both parties, while the train accident is explored for its paradoxical dual role. It releases the man from the deadly grip of the insane woman but at the same time it further immerses him in shock and trauma as he comes face to face with his own double susceptibility to contingency, to the precarity of identity and the unreliable mechanical function of trains.

More frequently, dangerous women on trains appear as accomplices of male robbers. Ellen Wood's 'Going through the Tunnel' from *Johnny Ludlow: First Series*, in which a squire's pocket-book with fifty pounds is stolen in a first-class carriage, makes use of the train compartment not only as a *locus suspectus* (Beaumont, 'Railway Mania', 129) but also as a theatrical space which facilitates the performance of roles associ-ated with specific social classes. In the particular story, the duplicitous couple pretend not to know each other, the man pretending to be a lord, 'exempt from suspicion' (125), and the woman generating doubt about her person on purpose, first by being too fashionable in terms of hair and make-up and second by letting loose her little dog while they are travelling in a tunnel in order to cause a distraction and allow the real robber, the 'lord', to get away. Her enigmatic appearance and behaviour make her look like a 'Jezebel' to the passengers (126), who judge her according to class and gender expectations. But when, after the fake lord has descended, she readily submits to being searched, she is exonerated and deemed an innocent witness to a crime which in reality she in partnership committed. At the end it is proved that the woman and her accomplice had been acting a carefully thought out performance which involved the manipulation of gender and class roles and the trading of social identities. The story finally shows that no first-class compartment could safeguard class codes and manners within its boundaries, which were after all penetrable. Such carriages, in which interaction was necessarily brief and temporary, were targeted by criminal women and men who could play-act a variety of social roles, thus de-essentialising the categories of class and gender with their successful imitations. In Wood's story, the train produces the conditions for the victimisation of the upper class whose members are easily duped by a man masquerading as one of their own and a woman with an effective flexibility of mind. Within the breached compartment the distinguished passengers become 'lambs between two wolves' (132).

Moreover, the railway is presented as providing opportunities for lower-class women, especially, to make use of their sexuality for questionable or even criminal purposes, endangering the life or honour of men. Such dangers for men on the train, which provided the germ for many fictional plot lines, included being duped by cunning, fraudulent women, who would feign vulnerability in order to appeal to the romantic or sexual inclinations of men and then swindle them. One such story published in *The Englishwoman's Domestic Magazine*, 'A Railway Adventure' (Anon., 1872), recounts the adventures of a London clerk, who, during a business trip away from the smoke-filled city and his busy lawyer's office, falls victim to a beautiful conniving woman in a carriage, who uses demure charms, confessing to being a sorrowful, penniless widow, only to gain his trust and rob him. With her veiled appearance, her enigmatic past, and her alluring yet at the same time prohibitive sexuality, she draws out his dormant romanticism, to the extent that he seems to shed his practical, professional attitude, assuming instead the persona of a poet in love. The restful time on the accelerating train, paradoxically, invites him to adopt an upper-class leisurely attitude which counteracts the speed of his everyday business transactions. His observation that 'Thousands of grasshoppers – dark brown, drab, and pale sea green – were singing their joyful song, leaping high into the air, and falling heels over head in every direction' (214), is just one in a series of meditations on nature which suggest his rejection of urban velocity in favour of a more humble life, one that is impervious to the pressures of rigid time-tables. Hinting at a gender – and class – reversal, feasible in the transitory space of the train carriage which fosters, in return, the flourishing of transitory identities, the story suggests that his retrogressive – conventionally feminine – attitude makes him careless enough to allow the more practical woman to steal his valuable cheque. The story unambiguously contrasts female agency and male passivity, pointing at the dangerous consequences of the immobility experienced inside the train carriage, where men, used to exhausting mobility, find opportunity for repose, while women, whose movement has been traditionally restricted, become aware of favourable conditions for active agency. Nevertheless, in the end, the woman, who is proved to be the accomplice of a forger, gets caught and is duly disciplined for her transgression. The social threat produced by the contrast between men's emasculation by too much railway travel, which promotes leisure, and woman's confident riding of the rails in search of sexual escapades or upward mobility is most famously explored in Mary Elizabeth Braddon's *Lady Audley's Secret*, where the heroine, after a series of train trips which successfully obscure her identity, is, in the end, immobilised, as Daniel Martin has observed, incarcerated in a mental institution, markedly away from railway traffic: she is removed from 'the transportation grid of the nineteenth-century railway system' (Martin, 'Railway', 149).

On account of women's potentially dangerous liaison with criminal men, their annoying habits, their assumed incapacity to deal with the practicalities of travel, but also their tendency to falsely accuse men of rape – as we shall see in Chapter 2 – 'one cannot avoid the general feeling', Ivor Smullen contends, 'that women on the railway remained a nuisance to all concerned' (81).

During the same period, in short stories in journals, young women passengers are usually the targets of either amorous or criminal intentions. Men are often depicted scouting the train and choosing a carriage with a beautiful young woman already on board with the intention of flirting with or harassing her. Railway technology and the unavoidable intimacy it produced, cultivating a new custom of brief interaction among strangers in cramped spaces, raised opportunities for temporary or in some cases more permanent romance, as an 1846 story in *Chambers's* tried to prove: 'when our ideas get time to adapt themselves to the hurry-skurry of the rail, adventures, we have no doubt, will be picked up at every station, and denouements found at every terminus' (Anon., 'Railway Romance', 314). Numerous stories recount such brief encounters during which young women are rapturously stared at, flirted with, or feverishly pursued from carriage to carriage. Often romance results from opportunities for men to rescue woman from either crime or train accident. The train is repeatedly treated as a libidinal space which created opportunities for romantic or erotic encounters, legitimised by the unavoidable proximity between men and women in sealed compartments that were at once private and public. As Christopher Matthews argues in his study of mid-Victorian visual art and short narratives, 'the railway promises to secure vast new territories for erotic circulation and consumption' (446); 'The railway might even be considered a material prerequisite of Victorian love at first sight, producing the social and technological conditions of unplanned meeting and exhibitions of spontaneous emotion' (442–3). The nearness of bodies in the compartment, together with the journey's rigid temporal boundaries within which romance could be cultivated, generated and accelerated the speed of the attraction between men and women, who more freely hastened to express it. As the fictional production of such stories in journals was prolific, it seems that railway romance was a favourite plot line, according to which young men fall madly in love on trains, sometimes succeeding in winning the lady's attentions and even marrying her, but also, oftentimes, becoming disappointed when despite the achieved intimacy, it turns out that she is engaged to another. Such stories tested the new conditions of interaction between men and women in spaces of transit, welcoming the increased opportunities for intimacy but seldom going against the moral standards which required women to be demure and reticent, despite the intense wooing. In fact it is chiefly such modest young women who usually enjoy a happy end in marriage, while more forward or overfamiliar ones, who have been too comfortable with railway flirtation, are either jilted or mocked.

Nevertheless, the train ride also incurred dangers for women, as the journalistic accounts in the epigraphs of this chapter demonstrate. While short stories seldom or never described such crime in the sexually explicit way in which the media dealt with real cases, the horror of the assaults captured the imagination of many writers who did not refrain from describing violent physical attacks on women. Particularly striking is a short story published in *Dublin University Magazine* in 1867, entitled 'A Night in a First-Class Railway Carriage', which describes the experience of a young woman on her wedding tour, who, while on the train, falls victim to a man dressed up as a woman, who manages to physically separate her from her husband with the intention of extorting money and other valuables from him. The story indulges in profuse examples of masculine verbal and physical aggressiveness, as the villain, by means of invidious abuses, openly tells his victim that she, as woman, is not entitled – nor does she have the ability – to defend herself. Realising that the woman has been merely feigning sleep in order to protect herself and prepare for a potential assault, he abuses her for daring to fix her furtive gaze on him instead of submitting to his violent attempts to put her to sleep via a cordial: 'Diablesse! Treacherous cat!' he cries; 'So you have been awake and watching me. You spy on me, do you? Twice you have circumvented me [. . .] this pistol will make quick work of you, and your body thrown out in this dark night will tell no tales' (422). When, on the other hand, as a helpless victim, she begs for mercy, he decides to spare her life, on the condition that she never again transgresses from the feminine ideal. As woman she must never give in to 'infernal curiosity' and never act against his wishes: 'You have no one to blame but your own infernal curiosity [. . .] that feminine propensity,' he tells her (422), turning the tables and making her gender responsible for her plight; vulnerability is essentialised as a natural feminine trait. In another instance, the villain suggests that women's submission and loyalty to a man should apply in all settings, private, like the home, and public, like the train, and in the context of all heterosexual relationships, whether marital or not, like the one here between a criminal and his victim. Gazing, normally a man's privilege, unsettles this trust and transforms woman into a demon with selfish ambitions. Even though at the end of the story the villain does not succeed in his ultimate aims, the woman is never vindicated. His threat to silence her ('your body [. . .] will tell no tales' [422]) comes true, initially, as she suffers from brain fever and lies unconscious for weeks, and later, as her story is questioned even by her husband who 'thinks the man was right and the whole thing a *delusion*' (423). On the one hand, the murderous threat along with the unnecessarily sarcastic and scornful views of womanhood ('I hate your baby-face snivelling women. There, go back to your corner, and don't disturb me with your crocodile tears' [423]) would have successfully warned women of the dangers of independent mobility and the sexist prejudices encountered on the way. On the other hand, however, the fact that the story does not redeem its female narrator by offering a just resolution would not have motivated potential female train travellers. On the contrary, by questioning the reliability of the whole narrative and the woman's capability of retaining her sanity while alone on a train, the ending emphatically confirms women's weakness, dupability, and naiveté, all of which make them unsuitable travellers.

Thus, while news articles and short stories served to acquaint the public, and women specifically, with the dangers of mobility, at the same time they constructed a stereotype of womanhood which linked their physical exposure in public space with psychological (and not only physical) vulnerability. After an attack, women are presented as psychologically scarred for life, in a state of hysteria or unconsciousness.

'A Night in a First-Class Railway Carriage' demonstrates that in public spaces like the train women had to feign helplessness and vulnerability rather than self-assertiveness and confidence if they were to survive or even be considered respectable. However, 'Under the Cloak', by Rhoda Broughton, first published in 1873 and later collected together with other tales of mystery under the title *Twilight Stories* (1879), complicates the binary of self-reliance and submission.[2] It narrates the story of a woman who, while travelling with her maid by train to Paris to meet her husband, is robbed by two men, who, by means of an elaborate plan, get away briefly with her valuables: they have arranged the seating to their advantage, placing themselves in the middle seats of the car, thus forcing the women to sit in unwanted close proximity; one of them offers the women a drugged cordial to drowse them, and in the end ties up, gags, and places the maid under the cloak that originally camouflaged the second man, to incapacitate her. From the beginning Broughton, in her signature style of the first-person present tense, traces the emotions and sensations of this reluctant passenger as they move from an initial hatred of train rides to a hesitation to board, a defiance and later a dread of the strange male co-passengers, a drowsiness, and finally the horror of losing consciousness and waking up to a completely different reality. By concentrating on the female point of view, Broughton explores woman's ambivalent response to the train, revealing her uncomfortable appropriation of the new spaces of modernity. The female protagonist is particularly concerned about the blurring of the line between private and public experienced both in the train and in the station. As Amy Richter has shown, the homely aspect of trains – the beautiful interiors and comfortable furnishings, for example – succeeded in creating 'a type of "public domesticity" – a social ideal that was neither as private as a home, nor as socially unruly as a public street' (*Home*, 60). However, this 'public domesticity' had more disadvantages for women as it legitimised their becoming, during their most private moments, objects of an intrusive male gaze or even touch.

In Broughton's story, the female body is constantly at risk of being violated either by mere involuntary and unwanted touch or by actual physical manipulation. Before boarding, the heroine muses: 'I hate and dread exceedingly a crowd, and would much prefer at any time to miss my train rather than be squeezed and jostled by one' (206). This inability of the female body to retain a safe border of untouchability within public spaces is exacerbated in the actual train carriage, where she is forced to sit next to the villain, with his cloak touching her: 'I draw convulsively and shrinkingly away, and try to squeeze myself up as close as possible to the window. But alas! to what good?' (210). At another moment, while pretending to be asleep, she feels her own feet fingered and moved, as her box of jewels is stolen from under them. Broughton's story, however, daringly challenges the male prerogative with which the train has become a site facilitating the invasion of woman's private space and the manipulation of her body and subjectivity. The author constructs her heroine as strong-minded, bright, and wilful, prioritising the female gaze to show how by monitoring the space of the compartment for danger, a woman may develop powers of detection and defence. Nevertheless, the protagonist's confidence is tempered by a painful awareness of her inevitable physical inferiority, which makes her appear vulnerable and which invites exploitation. So, although she tries to outsmart the thieves, they manage to break her resistance by drugging her and rendering her unconscious. Thus Broughton presents us with a woman who falls victim not of her own folly or weak nature but of the railway system that provided men with opportunities to take advantage of women. In the story the men seem aware of the fact that it is only by enforcing sleep, a normally private activity, in which the heroine would never have indulged in public, that they can achieve their criminal goals. By causing the heroine and her maid to sleep, they impose a condition of defencelessness, brutally demonstrating their understanding that in these newly constructed urban or technological sites, like that of the train compartment, the boundary between private and public has been renegotiated to their advantage.[3]

Moreover, in 'Under the Cloak', the semi-private/semi-public nature of the train compartment causes the female passenger to experience the contradictory feelings that the *heimlich/unheimlich* paradox triggers, as explained by Freud in his essay on 'The Uncanny'. Freud writes that the meaning of *heimlich* – canny – 'coincides with its opposite, *unheimlich*' – uncanny – (934), when the former, the familiarity experienced in, for example, a site of privacy but also of concealment and secrecy, turns into fear of mysterious and hence unpredictable and even sinister or uncanny intentions that may lurk within. The train carriage initially promises familiarity and security, because of its likeness to a drawing-room and its secure confines which exclude the outer world, but eventually becomes uncanny because the random intimacies that it promotes may become uncontrollable and ultimately dangerous. In this story Broughton's heroine seems aware of the paradox as she initially tries to comfortably appropriate the familiarity of the compartment and the behaviour that it fosters as a site for socialising. Not liking her co-passengers, she decides to take advantage of their anonymity, which justifies her not having to talk to them: 'I give them up as a bad job,' she muses (207). However their inevitable close proximity, despite its impersonality, becomes uncanny, as she realises that the cosy enclosure, whose borders she thought would shelter to a certain extent her privacy, in reality conceals and secures their criminal intentions. The cloak, under which one of the thieves hides his body, further amplifies the feeling of uncanniness produced by the suffocating insulation of the compartment, generating in her imagination stories of horror that cause her to gaze in fear and wonder.

Fortunately, and unlike the case of the heroine in 'A Night in a First-Class Railway Carriage', this brave woman's gaze remains undetected and allows her to protect herself, albeit briefly, from the villains, who, like their counterpart in the previous story, resort to a drugged cordial in order to extinguish her consciousness. Anaesthetised, with all her defences completely neutralised and her jewels stolen, this passenger experiences 'a feeling of the most appalling desolation and despair' which 'vanquishes [her] utterly' (211). Broughton's diction highlights the totalising effect of the horrifying experience; nevertheless, what strikes the reader is not her anaesthetisation, but the 'despairing courage' with which, once awake, she attacks the cloaked villain, tearing the cloak, the mask, and the fake hands and feet in a frantic effort to unravel the mystery: 'It would be better to find *anything* underneath – Satan himself – a horrible dead body – anything, sooner than submit any longer to this hideous mystery. And I am rewarded' (212). So while the story ends with an appeal to the readers that sounds like a warning ('What I have written is literally true, though it did not happen to myself' [212]), its truth lies in her courage and confidence, which are not shaken despite the crime experienced. Not only are her jewels recovered, but also, at the end, the narrator humorously suggests that it is only her 'bad habit of travelling in company with [her] trinkets' (212) that she abandons, not that of travelling without a male escort. After all, from the start of her journey, the heroine showed a defiance of the assumed dangers of women travelling alone, preferring the hopefully livelier company of the *Fumeurs* compartment to that of the *Dames seules*, and focusing instead on its little discomforts rather than its risks:

> a little stuffy compartment, with nothing to amuse you if you keep awake; with a dim lamp hanging above you, tantalizing you with the idea that you

can read by its light, and when you try, satisfactorily proving to you that you cannot, and if you sleep, breaking your neck, or at least stiffening it, by the brutal arrangement of the hard cushions. These thoughts pass sulkily and rebelliously through my head [. . .] (205)

By the 1890s, young women – often New Women – are depicted as more assured on the trains and are thus entrusted with more important roles as detectives or even saviours of men or women in peril. In 'A Railway Carriage Adventure' (Anon., 1891), a male victim of two robbers is saved by a heroic woman with a pistol who hits the villains on the head. Predictably the crime plot turns into a romance plot, with the woman juggling two roles, one of physical prowess but also one of saving and healing the male victim from the brutal forces of society; the second role serves to correct the abnormality of the first, in accordance with Victorian gender ideology. More assertive and taking advantage of the railway not only as a means of speedy transportation but also as a setting which facilitates the keen observation of others, the professional female detective of Matthias McDonnell Bodkin, Dora Myrl,[4] fearlessly travels from place to place, coolly monitoring behaviours, unravelling secrets, and deducing solutions to mysteries. Dora Myrl is the successor of William Stephens Hayward's Mrs Paschal (1864),[5] who, by using the train as a vehicle that facilitates her work of detection, aligns herself with progress. As Mrs Paschal muses:

There is to me always something very exhilarating in the quickly rushing motion of a railway carriage. It is typical of progress, and raises my spirits in proportion to the speed at which we career along, now through meadow and now through woodland, at one time cutting through a defile and afterwards steaming through a dark and sombre tunnel. What can equal such magical travelling? (35)

By contemplating the processes of speed and simultaneity and the way perception is affected by them, the female detective becomes conscious of the continuity and significance of life in between points of departure and arrival, treating the journey not as an undesirable delay in the process of detection, but as this process's necessary part for it connects disparate spaces and moments. Thus 'magical travelling' and the thought processes it conjures become the equivalent of detective work during which Mrs Paschal links up the loose ends of a mystery that needs to be solved.

Grant Allen's captivating twenty-one-year-old amateur detective, Lois Cayley, in 'The Adventure of a Cantankerous Old Lady' (1898), keen on adventure, rejects a career in teaching in order to become an old lady's paid travelling companion. As such she exhibits a confident understanding of the practicalities of railway travelling as well as a sharpness when it comes to distinguishing the motives of co-passengers, thus overturning older stereotypes which showcased women's limitations in both tasks. Moreover, Allen differentiates his story from similar ones of the previous decades by having the old woman employ a young girl as assistant and protector, rather than expect some gallant male passenger to act as escort. Seeing through the polished appearance and ingratiating manners of their male co-passenger, who is in reality after the old lady's jewel box, the spirited Lois outsmarts the criminal by switching the inner case with a sandwich tin and arranging his arrest. As a New Woman, Lois joins in the chorus of young women of the eighteen-nineties who demonstrated self-reliance by defying the dangers of travelling. More specifically, emerging feminist discourses of the time tried to overturn the common belief in women's helplessness in the face of crime or disaster. For example, the founder and editor of the feminist journal, *The Women's Penny Paper*, Helena B. Temple, in narrating her experience of a railway accident in 1890, exalts the behaviour of the ladies who 'were very quiet, collected, and sensible', while the gentlemen 'were nervous and excited, and swaggered about in a very silly way indeed' (555). Such narratives and articles aimed at empowering women by commending their composure, intelligence, and agency.

With the rate of women travelling on the rise in the later Victorian times, it was important for women's texts on rail journeys not only to prepare women for the dangers they might encounter, but also to emphasise the pleasures of independent travel. 'Surely none is more excellent in itself and its results, than the power which has become the right of every woman who has the means to achieve it – of becoming her own unescorted and independent person, a lady traveller', wrote Lillias Campbell Davidson, in her 1889 *Hints to Lady Travellers: at Home and Abroad* (255). On the matter of railway travelling Davidson carefully listed potential dangers, such as having luggage fall on one's head and railway collisions, proposing useful protection measures. Yet the conclusion of the chapter on accidents emphatically re-establishes the journey as a source of pleasure and not of danger: 'Banish all sense of danger and all anticipation of accidents, if you want really to derive joy and advantage from your travels' (17). Much earlier, in 1852, in a letter to Cara Bray, George Eliot, whose journals are filled with the joys of independent travelling, had made fun of these dangers thus:

> I had a comfortable journey all alone, except from Weedon to Blisworth. When I saw a coated animal getting into my carriage, I thought of all the horrible stories of madmen in railways, but his white neck-cloth and thin,

mincing voice soon convinced me that he was one of those exceedingly tame brutes, the clergy. (Haight 2: 3)

Eliot's sarcasm through the animal metaphors, though strongly derived from her own views on religion, seems to a great extent also to suggest the constructedness of fear via the exaggerated sensationalism of journalistic accounts of unfortunate railway adventures.

These narratives of danger, fictional and journalistic, ultimately construct the train compartment as a space of liminality, one that defies the rules of the rigid transportation system that it serves. If the objective of the railway has always been to divide and chart space and time and to manage efficiently and reliably the movement of bodies, stories like the ones described above demonstrate the multiple ways in which its rational codes could be challenged and overturned, by either accident or crime and romance. Originally conceived as an integral part of an institution which runs by a set of restrictions, the compartment and the uses that it fostered seemed to escape the system's totalising power. As a penetrable space which could be used as a setting for disguise, assault, or flirtation, the compartment became, therefore, a space of transgression. Despite the divisions that the railway tried to impose on the organisation of its carriages – first-, second-, third-class, Women-Only, *Fumeurs* – these divisions seldom controlled or checked the disorderly circulation of bodies, for it was the circulation itself which obliterated the boundary between inner and outer, private and public, and which made the system permeable and vulnerable. Thus as a liminal space the compartment could not be attached to distinct social or gendered identities; instead it offered opportunities for destabilising social boundaries, for complicating and even overturning hierarchies. The cases of robbers posing as lords and men masquerading as women highlight the carriage's potential to unfix identity. The classification aimed at by the railway, this 'perfect actualization of the rational utopia', in which, as de Certeau describes, 'The unchanging traveller is pigeonholed, numbered, and regulated in the grid of the railway car' (111), is undone by the tendency of passengers to resist their compartmentalisation by reimagining and de-essentialising their subject positions. As a result train journeys become out-of-control experiences that destabilise the logic of ordered space. These contingent human interventions, which, as we saw, are either activated by or inflicted on women, disrupted ideological beliefs and challenged gender relations.

The short stories discussed also demonstrate the way in which the train compartment dissolved the safety/danger binary. They depict women who either cause this dissolution with their disguises and criminal intentions or are its victims. In both cases the compartment, which initially figures as a familiar, comfortable, and in some cases luxurious interior, is transformed into an *unheimlich* space, a *locus suspectus*, which, through the anonymity and arbitrariness of encounters, legitimises the exposure of secrets, repressed desires, or even criminal purposes. 'It is as if,' according to Matthew Beaumont, 'the train's mesmeric mechanical movement serves to detach the traveller's unconscious desires from his rational control' ('Railway Mania', 142). In such a space, in which the *heimlich* overlaps with the *unheimlich*, all identities are in flux, and all are, therefore, suspect; hence the occasionally unjustified fear or paranoia that women betray in carriages. Typical is the behaviour of all the passengers in Wood's *Johnny Ludlow* story already discussed, who hasten to prove themselves innocent to each other, knowing that their own social and moral position is indeterminate in the impersonal carriage. As Beaumont argues, 'The most disquieting aspect of these spaces is not that one might meet someone who seems dangerous but that one might meet someone to whom one seems dangerous oneself' ('Railway Mania', 130). This particular story, however, further illustrates a difference between men and women, for while it is the men who suffer most from this destabilisation of their social position and the ensuing speculative uncertainty, a woman may benefit from the neutrality cultivated on the train. I will now turn my attention to the genre of sensation fiction, which as Lyn Pykett has shown is pervaded by 'an anxiety about gender' (x), in order to examine the variety of ways in which the train participates in the production of sensation sometimes at the expense of woman, but at other times by having her embody transgressive subject positions.

Sensational Women and the Railway: Accidents, Risks, and Speculations in Ellen Wood, Wilkie Collins, Mary Elizabeth Braddon, and Margaret Oliphant

In his 1999 article, 'Railway Novels: Sensation Fiction and the Modernization of the Senses', Nicholas Daly sees the flourishing of the sensation genre as 'an attempt to register and accommodate the newly speeded-up world of the railway age' (464), and he identifies nervousness as the linking element between the novel and the train. As H. L. Mansel wrote in his 1863 review of twenty-four novels by numerous writers including Braddon, Collins, and Wood, the aim of sensation novels seemed to be to 'carry the whole nervous system by steam' (487), unfolding tales which aimed at 'electrifying the nerves of the reader'

(489). Sensation novelists used the railway not only as a setting in which they could develop original and modern plots, but also as a way of life, producing stories which appropriated its speed, fast transitions, and liminality. 'Velocity was a key component of the sensation novel,' writes Christopher Pittard, who relates the shocks produced by Collins and Braddon to those major and minor ones caused by the railway (38). Relying for its 'electrifying' effect on sudden episodic shifts, such novels seemed to imitate the complex function of the railway network, its connections and junctions, but also its broken lines and accidents. The railway was thus a literal part of the plot, speeding up the mobility of characters or involving them in tragedy. It may also be considered a metaphor for a newly developing narrative technique which relied on episodic incident, ephemeral connections, punctuality, spatial and temporal limitations, speed, but also shock. As Matthew Beaumont points out, in sensation novels 'the narrative's momentum, its sense of accelerating speed, is maintained by innumerable references to railway timetabling' ('Railway Mania', 136–7). In its double function, therefore, the railway became an important means of depicting the acceleration of daily activities and the regulated or unregulated mobility, nervousness, and trauma this acceleration entailed. It could very well be argued that sensation novels depended on the railway for the development of plot, character, and action.

Like the short stories described in the previous section, the novels of the sixties and seventies fictionalised journalistic accounts of sensational incidents, so their plots were not as improbable as their severe critics, such as Mansel and Margaret Oliphant, thought them to be. Yet they differed from realist novels of the same period in that they seemed to dissolve, too unproblematically, binaries between private and public, home and outdoors, safety and danger, angel and demon, upper and lower class. In other words, the sensation genre destabilised domestic, gender, and class ideology, shocking the Victorian audience with its alternative approach to character. As Richard Fantina and Kimberly Harrison point out, 'At the heart of many sensation novels lies the recognition of the fluidity of identity. Rather than embracing essentialist notions of class, gender, race, and religion, the sensation novelists often complicate and at times defy them' (xxi). As such, sensation novels intensified many social anxieties, especially when they targeted the upper and middle classes and the sanctity of the home. Flouting Victorian conventions, these novels exposed the permeability of the domestic by crime, vice, and even more shockingly by women's sexual deviance. According to Richard Nemesvari and Lisa Surridge, 'Sensation fiction played on the Victorian fear of scandal, especially scandal concerning women, and in so doing became scandalous itself by suggesting that improper female behaviour not only existed, but was widespread' (18). The transgressive behaviour of the sensation heroines who performed crimes such as murder, bigamy, and fraud just as easily as they tended to their domestic duties challenged Victorian hierarchies by exposing the artificiality of binaries. In other words, such women defied social and sexual stereotyping, not by adopting the opposite behaviour from that prescribed by social convention, but by blurring the boundary between the two extremes and ultimately defying categorisation. Mary Elizabeth Braddon's angelic/demonic heroines are the best examples of such women who cultivate ambiguity about their 'nature' up until the end of the narratives. As Lyn Pykett has shown, the complex machinery of the sensation plot usually requires heroines who combine various versions of femininity, questioning gender and class standards and complicating polarities (19).

As an ambiguous – semi-private, semi-public, safe, dangerous – setting, the railway may therefore be viewed as the space par excellence to be associated with the liminal types of femininity constructed in sensation novels. It will be argued that the uses of the railway articulate the complex intersection between gendered identities and physical space, the train facilitating both the blurring of identity on which the sensation plot depended and the consequent subversion of gender conventions through female transgression. The preceding analysis of short stories has already demonstrated the ways in which the impersonal compartment could be manipulated by or at the expense of woman, in cases where the carefully planned journey is rendered out of control by the contingency of the functions of the train and the alterity of bodies that circulate in it. Sensation novels provided more sustained studies of the paradoxes of railway travel, raising important questions about the limits of woman's mobility and her right to public space, to personal adventure, and to sexual or economic gratification.

In Ellen Wood's *East Lynne* (1861) and Wilkie Collins's *No Name* (1862) a train accident puts into motion the action of the novels and the transformation of their heroines. Train accidents were very frequent from the forties onwards, and as railway technology developed, the network expanded, and traffic became denser, accidents increased in number and in fatality. 'Unsurprisingly,' as Norris Pope writes, 'the speed and complexity of Victorian railways were thus sources of both pride and alarm' (440).[6] Accidents were proof of mechanical failure but also of human negligence or incapacity to catch up and deal with the demands of complex technology. In her eulogy to engine drivers, a short novel entitled *Mark Dennis; or, The Engine Driver. A Tale of the Railway* (1859), Mary Charlotte Leith compares the level of dedication of drivers, ascribing recklessness and immorality to those who are more interested in speed and record journey times than safety, and heroism to those who may risk their lives for the safety of passengers. Her hero, Mark Dennis, however, despite his dedication and sense of responsibility, is killed in an accident caused by another engine driver's lack of signalling. The text illustrates the complexity of the railway network, which relied for its safety on the accurate transmission of signals and a sense of interdependence among drivers. At the same time, it introduces the idea that collateral damage like the death of engine drivers, however heroic they may have been, is soon forgotten or even justified as being the unavoidable consequence of progress. Mark Dennis's life was primarily 'a life of useful service' to such progress, and thus, unhappily, his name and fate are read in public journals, 'carelessly, and soon forgotten, while few think of the affliction thus suddenly brought upon many, and the sorrowing hearts that are left behind' (182). Mark Dennis and 'his class' (182) are deemed mechanical parts of the technology they serve and are rendered anonymous after their death, losing the individuality that Leith has tried to bestow on them with her novel. Moreover, Leith's narrative suggests that the frequency of such railway accidents had already, by the late fifties, neutralised the feelings of media audiences who had got used to reading about them and for whom the horror of an accident lasted but an instant in their consciousness.

Dickens's December 1866 'The Signalman' and the article that had preceded it in October, also in *All the Year Round*, entitled 'The Hole in the Wall', dwell on the intense anxiety of switchmen, those vigilant 'sentinels' responsible for the lives of thousands of passengers.[7] 'The Hole in the Wall' vividly imagines numerous reasons that may lead to the human mistake, suggesting that technology with its demands, its sights, and its sounds may affect the brain, to the extent that the switchman may objectify and thus trivialise the lives of the passengers in his care. Detached from the fleeting passengers by virtue of his static position but also the glass and steel boundary dividing them, the switchman consigns the life of the passengers to silence and obscurity, viewing the passing train as an attractive show, 'the phantasmagoria of a magic lantern', which offers static vignettes of potential flirtation scenes taking place inside the carriages:

> It seemed a new view of one's fellow-creatures to see them as animated half-lengths, and, as shoal after shoal flitted by, the ease with which they might be immolated recurred again and again with terrible suggestiveness [. . .] when the touch of one of the instruments at our hand could consign them to immediate destruction. (Anon., 327)

The passage suggests, with a perverse attitude, the paradoxical power that the one may have on the many, and the precariousness of the passengers who, on the train, lose their individuality, and even their right to life, viewed by the omnipotent switchman merely as cargo, puppets, or half-length pictures. 'The Hole in the Wall' candidly expresses the fate of passengers who are at the mercy of a signalman and an engine-driver, who are, in turn, alienated from their own humanity by the technology that they serve. It implies that though constructed by humans, railway technology could not be controlled by them. It is no wonder then that the railway accident appealed to and horrified the Victorian imagination exactly because, in the words of Ralph Harrington,

> it denied its victims any chance of controlling their own fate; it crystallized in a single traumatic event the helplessness of human beings in the hands of the technologies that they had created but seemed unable to control; it was a highly public event that erupted directly into the rhythms and routines of daily life; it was no respecter of class or status; it was arbitrary, sudden, inhuman, and violent. ('Railway Accident', 36)

As a commonly reported and described everyday event with catastrophic effects on life and identity, one that could not be controlled or prevented, the devastatingly probable railway accident was thus the perfect means of developing a sensational plot based on the grim realities of the time. In Ellen Wood's *East Lynne*, Lady Isabel Vane, the transgressive heroine, who blinded by jealousy and sexual desire abandons her loving lawyer husband and children to live with another man who subsequently deserts her when her divorce is finalised, is involved in a train accident that leaves her scarred and disfigured. While the train accident is not described, it is nevertheless explored as the most detrimental of many contingent incidents in the novel that propel the plot and lead to the heroine's transformation. The reader is given a sense of its impact through the letter that Isabel writes to Lord Mount Severn while in hospital: 'It is written in the strangest style; syllables divided, and the words running one into the other' (376). Her handwriting, which offers a vivid sense of carriages separating and colliding, suggests the power of bodily and emotional pain to destroy language, causing deterioration and incoherence.[8] Subsequently, Isabel's loss of control of the body and its means of articulation leads to the unmaking of her personal and social identity. Realising that she is thought dead by her former husband and her relatives, since she is misidentified as another lady passenger who died in the accident, Lady Isabel decides to accept this erasure and live in obscurity: 'She longed none knew with what intense longings, to be unknown, obscure, totally unrecognized by all'

(380). If by dissociating her name from her body the accident obliterates her social identity, by disfiguring her it also forces her to erase her sense of self as a sexually desirable and desiring subject. This transformation takes place on two levels, first as she tries to bury her passions underneath a particularly unattractive appearance that she constructs for herself and second as she transposes all inner longings to childcare by becoming a governess, initially to an unknown girl and next to her own children in disguise. Thus she effects a double erasure, physical and social. The thick veil, spectacles, and bonnet that obscure her face complement the position of social invisibility, of the governess, that she adopts. Andrew Maunder has argued that after the accident 'Isabel's tortured and disfigured body [. . .] becomes both the site of punishment for her transgression and a marker of her wrong-doing' (65). However, I believe that the accident is more than just a means of chastisement or nemesis. If as Marlene Tromp argues, 'Lady Isabel symbolizes the loss of clear class demarcations through her liminal position as the aristocratic wife of a middle-class lawyer' (163), the train accident further explores the social liminality that a woman is apt to experience as a result not only of economic disgrace and social estrangement but also of chance. Yet, as will also be seen in the following analysis of Collins's *No Name*, liminality leads to risky choices. 'What is it that would keep me away?' Lady Isabel asks herself measuring the risks of being exposed working as a governess in her former house. 'The dread of discovery? Well if that comes it must; they could not hang me or kill me' (455). The text focuses not only on Isabel's efforts to tame her desires in order to enter her former husband's home and tend, unrecognised, to her children, but also on her extraordinary ability to defy many emotional and physical hazards. It could be argued that this strength is derived from living as a spectral presence in the fringes from where she can indulge, unnoticed, in transgressive observation and mothering. So through this position of invisibility Isabel attempts to claim, not her husband and not her former social position, but a new sense of personal identity which is derived from the destabilisation of ideological boundaries concerning gender that the train accident incurred.

In Wilkie Collins's *No Name*, a railway accident that kills the father of Magdalen and Norah Vanstone is the incident that causes the fatherless and nameless condition that afflicts the heroines. The accident appears as an inexorable force which destroys the plans of the Vanstone parents to provide for their daughters after realising that their restorative act of marriage cancels out previous wills, disinheriting the children born out of wedlock. The accident, which demonstrates the malfunction of the most advanced expression of technology in the Victorian period, thus annuls intentions and promises and mocks class presumptions and even legal action. As a result the Vanstone girls are left with no fortune and no name, the accident having dissolved their social identity and rendered their whole future precarious. Subsequently, chance, contingency, and trauma, which are represented by Mr Vanstone's fatal accident, prove to Mrs Vanstone and her daughters that their body, too, is uncontrollable: the widowed mother and her newborn baby die from grief-related complications and Magdalen, who in the beginning of the novel brims with energy and confidence in her health and who after her disinheritance is able to manipulate her appearance to fulfil her desires, at the end loses command of her mobile body, just like her father, whose aberrant behaviour the train accident punished. Moreover, Magdalen's restless mobility as she feverishly pursues disparate causes and distractedly changes course, swiftly substituting one goal with another, resembles railway traffic and the frantic mobility that it promoted. Magdalen embraces her position as a displaced subject and moves in the margins of private and public, middle and lower class, taking advantage of the ambiguity that her liminal status affords her in order to subvert social conventions which render her classless and invent for herself a position she believes she deserves. In other words, the crisis of identity triggered by the railway accident finds expression in the multiple roles, disguises, and positions that Magdalen adopts in her attempt to restabilise her personal and social identity.

In *No Name* the railway makes only a few direct appearances. The most damaging intrusion on the lives of the female characters, the accident, is merely reported. But it is the railway, literally, that tears the sisters away from their family home, detaching them forever from the domestic, class, and gender privileges that their upbringing had bestowed on them. Moreover, as Norah writes in a letter to Mr Pendril, the railway station which enables their displacement already represents the loss of their sense of belonging and their alienation from society:

> There was not a soul we knew at the station; nobody to stare at us, nobody to wish us good-bye. The rain came on again, as we took our seats in the train. What we felt at the sight of the railway; what horrible remembrances it forced on our minds of the calamity which has made us fatherless – I cannot, and dare not, tell you. (178)

As 'Nobody's Children' (138), Norah and Magdalen are no longer part of a high society admired and stared at by both their peers and the lower classes. At the station they become part of the anonymous crowd, enjoying neither distinction nor care, receiving, instead, a taste of the social invisibility and friendlessness that their loss of place and ensuing liminality enforce.

If the railway is a damaging force for the sisters, it is a space of opportunity for Captain Wragge. In spite of the fact that he has been ruined
by ill-fated investments in the 'railway mania' of the late forties, Captain
Wragge acknowledges other economic prospects that the railway offers
as a speculative enterprise: 'When it is one of a man's regular habits
to live upon his fellow-creatures, that man is always more or less fond
of haunting large railway stations' (187). Captain Wragge views the
station as a conduit which attracts persons in a state of vulnerability and
foresees that Magdalen, who is believed to be pursuing a career on the
stage, will want to take advantage of the invisibility that the masses in a
train station offer. Indeed in trying to speculate where Magdalen might
be found, the Captain mentally places her in a variety of places of transit
that would represent her homeless and nameless state – a thoroughfare,
a waiting-room, a hotel, a cab – only to finally find her loitering on a part
of the 'Walk on the Walls' just beyond the York train station, literally
on the border between spaces, decisions, and identities. And yet, though
the Captain figures as the predator let loose in the station, the narrative
does not fit Magdalen into the role of his potential victim, and she soon
turns the tables on him, having him admit that he is swindled by her
(253). Magdalen's transgressive behaviour intensifies as she tries out
different roles and settings, alternating identities and taking risks, as her
initial posture on the York Walls suggested. As Andrea Kaston Tange
has argued, Magdalen takes her liminality 'as a sign that she is author-
ized to occupy any place she should choose. If she belongs nowhere in
particular, she reasons, then she might as well move anywhere she likes
across and between multiple identities at will' (215).

In a world overrun by contingency – manifested in the novel by the
arbitrary railway accident which rendered the Vanstone girls' identity
unstable – Magdalen appropriates precariousness as a way of life and
adopts speculation and risk in order to win back her socio-economic
position. As she confesses, 'Whether I succeed, or whether I fail, I
can do myself no harm, either way. I have no position to lose, and
no name to degrade' (182). Daniel Martin relates Magdalen's risks
to Captain Wragge's speculative activities during the railway mania,
which 'contain the possibility of *future* rewards (whether financial or
social), but they are the result of calculations that rely on probabilistic
patterns of normativity' ('Collins', 190). Fixated on financial and social
rewards, Magdalen 'run[s] her risks to the very end' (Martin, 'Collins',
191), taking chances and swiftly exchanging one speculative activity
with the next. While Captain Wragge believes that he is 'the architect
of her fortunes' (*No Name*, 247), in reality her fortunes are determined
by her own calculations bent on immediate and future economic gains.

As Wragge himself admits, 'she has become as anxious to make money as I am myself [. . .] I don't like this change in her' (246–7). The novel juxtaposes the attitude of the two dispossessed sisters, of Norah who initially strives to earn economic independence through earnest work and of Magdalen who seeks easy money through speculative actions, but with an ambiguous stance concerning the latter's course. Magdalen is struck by illness in the end and her plotting fails, but she is nevertheless rewarded with a marriage and the recovered social position. Her risky investments in playacting on stage and in life are unsuccessful, but they seem to imitate acceptable speculative practices by women of the mid-nineteenth century, regularly recorded in fiction by Elizabeth Gaskell and George Eliot, among others.[9] In Aytoun's *Norman Sinclair* (1861), ladies are described as particularly prone to the lures of market speculation:

> Even the fair sex did not escape the infection, for ladies of high rank and position placed themselves in direct communication with sharebrokers, and bought and sold in the market more recklessly and greedily than their lords. (II, 33)

Though not investing in the business world, Magdalen treats life like business, making the bold speculative leaps that Captain Wragge and Michael Vanstone, that 'bold speculator' (244), have structured their lives and fortunes around. Her decision to embrace a morally suspect life of risk exposes the problems arising from women's lack of direct access to money and the prejudices that they encountered if they decided to take short cuts. At the same time Magdalen seems more conscious of the uncontrollability of life, exemplified by her own misfortunes via the railway accident, and of the artificiality of class and gender constructions; she thus calculates more possibilities for women than the ones afforded by Victorian gender ideology.

As Martin argues, in *Armadale* (1866), Collins experimented even more with a transgressive heroine who not only embraces risk but also stages 'accidents' which are aimed at ameliorating her socio-economic position ('Collins', 193). Yet, like in the case of the fortuitous railway accident in *No Name*, Lydia Gwilt's unsuccessfully fabricated accidents of a shipwreck and a gas poisoning only serve to further displace her and destabilise her identity, as she too, having become a Mrs Armadale, participates in the doubling of Armadales that preoccupies Collins. In this novel the railway helps to illustrate Lydia's confident risk-taking, which is exemplified in the scene during which she uses the architecture of the carriage to her advantage, as a means of restricting Allan's mobility and harming his reputation. Wearing a thick veil to protect herself from potentially 'rude' male co-passengers (463) and professing to need an escort for her train journey to London, she forces herself on Allan Armadale, who is obliged to let her ride in a private carriage with him. The incident demonstrates Lydia's understanding of the erotic possibilities of the carriage but also of the assumptions that the eager public ('dealers in small scandal' [486]) may make at the sight of a couple entering a private carriage. So by causing Allan's entrapment she is not so much employing her sexual power over him as manipulating social convention, and ultimately rendering him incapable of refuting the tales that circulate about this incident. '"She's got him, hasn't she?" "She'll come back 'Mrs Armadale', won't she,"' are only two of the scandalous rumours that circulate at the station after their departure (465), rumours culminating in the wild speculation of 'Mr Armadale's scandalous elopement, in broad daylight, with Miss Gwilt' (483). Despite the agency attributed to her, as a woman in pursuit of a man ('She's got him'), the carriage incident secures Lydia's position as that of a vulnerable and ultimately compromised female subject, one whose honour has to be restored through marriage. Ironically, this has been her aim all along, and her risks and speculations pay off. Lydia's own description of the event in her diary demonstrates this ambitious woman's ability to reverse power relations by initiating the assault and thus challenging Allan's proprietary perception of public space. Indeed it is Allan who is uncomfortable in the carriage, while Lydia appropriates the public/private space with ease. 'Little by little I tamed my wild beast' (486), she writes, yet it is she who poses the threat from the start with Allan being the innocent victim of her machinations and not the beast. Further defying convention, Lydia causes the safety/danger binary to collapse in the train: the speeding carriage, this impenetrable capsule whose contents and happenings no witness may verify, instigates murderous thoughts in her as she considers how easy it would be for her to extinguish the life of the man who naïvely travels with her:

> As the time wore on, I began to feel a terrible excitement; the position was, I think, a little too much for me. There I was, alone with him, talking in the most innocent, easy, familiar manner, and having it in my mind all the time to brush his life out of my way, when the moment comes, as I might brush a stain off my gown. It made my blood leap, and my cheeks flush. I caught myself laughing once or twice much louder than I ought; and long before we got to London I thought it desirable to put my face in hiding by pulling down my veil. (486)

The *unheimlich* effect produced by Lydia's veil, her fake laughter, and her thoughts of murder challenge public assumptions about a man's culpability in cases of railway assault. In presenting a potential murderess on the train, Collins corroborates the news stories which reported cases of fiendish or mad women trapping men on trains with the intent of murder or blackmail. Yet, despite her self-punishment at the end of the novel, Lydia remains, like Magdalen, a figure that threatens the ideal of middle-class femininity with her unpredictable mobility and flexibility, which find either literal or metaphorical expression through the railway.

In her determination to achieve a selfish goal through the manipulation of the spaces of the railway, Lydia Gwilt resembles the Janus-faced Lady Audley of Mary Elizabeth Braddon's *Lady Audley's Secret* (1862), a novel whose relation to the railway has been discussed extensively. The novel is structured around Robert Audley's attempts to track down Lady Audley who he thinks is responsible for the disappearance of his best friend, and who, nevertheless, constantly eludes him. Daniel Martin ('Railway') has read the novel in terms of the railway fatigue that plagues Robert as he compulsively tries to monitor her train routes and eventually arrest her movements, while Louise Lee has preoccupied herself with Lady Audley herself and her extraordinary 'proficiency at channeling modern invention' such as the railway and telegraphy (135). While the novel connects railway travel with idle masculinity, as Robert's leisurely journeys with George Talboys demonstrate (Martin, 'Railway' 138), it also points to a woman's more purposeful and fatigue-less use of the train. As Lee argues, Lady Audley seems 'proactively in control of modernity, whilst men seem merely reactive' (138). Though related to masculinity and to social institutions aimed at subordinating women, the railway has been mastered by Lady Audley better than by Robert Audley.

What is particularly suggestive in this novel is the narrative means by which Braddon handles her heroine's mobility. While Robert's journeys, as he tries to tail Lady Audley, are described in detail by reference to timetables, points of departure and destination, Lady Audley's remain unrepresented, only guessed at by both Robert and the readers. Thus the heroine eludes, via the railway, the surveillance techniques not only of her hunter but also of the Victorian (and contemporary) audience which cannot easily reconcile her sweetness with the diabolical motives that Robert ascribes to her. The railway is both visible and invisible in this novel, and Lady Audley's undescribed attempts always to remain one step ahead of Robert with her railway journeys sustain the narrative mystery as well as the sensationalism of her ambiguous, double-faced persona. Because even the ending, with its revelation of Lady Audley's secret insanity, is equivocal and does not satisfactorily account for her actions. If the train has been her means of escape from an unhappy marriage and from the suspicions of her foe, it has also been her means of juggling multiple identities. As it has already been argued, the train enabled women who found themselves in liminal positions to take advantage of the anonymity and ephemeral connections it fostered, falsifying identities or inventing alternative ones. Confessing to hereditary madness, Lady Audley seems to be once again manipulating her identity, consciously adopting yet one more role which, to the satisfaction of Victorian gender expectations, would account for her deviant mobility as well as ascribe her murderous inclinations to mental illness rather than feminine dissatisfaction with the limited choices offered to women. And while her conveyance to a madhouse seems to collude with Victorian practices of disciplining aberrant female behaviour, Lady Audley's new role seems once again to mock and undermine these practices. After all, her final words in the novel exemplify her extraordinarily sane ability to manipulate legal and moral codes:

> 'You see I do not fear to make my confession to you', said Helen Talboys; 'for two reasons. The first is, that you dare not use it against me, because you know it would kill your uncle to see me in a criminal dock; the second is, that the law could pronounce no worse sentence than this – a life-long imprisonment in a mad-house. You see I do not thank you for your mercy, Mr Robert Audley, for I know exactly what it is worth.' (313)

Her final abode, the madhouse in Villebrumeuse which 'lay out of the track of all railway traffic' successfully halts Lady Audley's deviant mobility (304). Nevertheless, as 'Madame Taylor', Lady Audley, 'the wretched woman who had borne so many names, and was to bear a false one for the rest of her life' (344), once again eludes the narrative and confounds the reader. Her railway mobility seems restricted, but not the complex management of identity that this mobility enabled. Ultimately, Braddon's claim at the close of the novel, 'I hope no one will take objection to my story because the end of it leaves the good people all happy and at peace' sounds quite ironic (355). For the person most at peace (even in death) seems to be Lady Audley, completely out of the gaze and control of the men whose dissatisfying or threatening actions instigated the multiplication of her identity through mobility.

Likewise, equivocal female identity is linked to railway mobility in Margaret Oliphant's *Salem Chapel* (1863).[10] In her sole sensation novel,[11] Oliphant makes use of the railway in order to obscure the fate of two abducted women and at the same time to develop a detective plot which speeds up the pace of the narrative and incites nervousness. The protagonist, a Dissenting minister, Arthur Vincent, is forced to neglect his clerical duties when his sister, Susan, and the young daughter of the enigmatic Mrs Hilyard are thought to be abducted by Susan's fiancé, a dishonest man with a false name, Fordham. Worried about the future but also the reputation of his sister, Vincent embarks on a series of train journeys seeking clues to their whereabouts. The train is the means of speedy abduction and efficient concealment for the captor, participating in the dishonouring of Susan who has 'go[ne] astray' literally and figuratively (157); it also becomes the means of her recovery. However, the narrative insists on the confusion that the complex railway networks may cause, as Vincent and his mother desperately travel backwards and forwards from Carlingford to Lonsdale and London, fearing that Susan and they have been travelling on opposite lines, thus missing each other. Focusing only on Vincent's futile journeys and not on Susan's, the narrative builds up mystery and suspense, while showing Vincent's inability to adjust his thoughts and actions to the pace and routes dictated by the railway.

The railway, with its incarcerating and depersonalising effects, seems to serve the cool-blooded, double-faced criminals better than the overwhelmed and confused minister. The train protects the double identity not only of Fordham (his real name is Mildmay) but also of Mrs Hilyard, who is able to pursue her murderous vendetta via its routes. Unlike Vincent, who has been inept in structuring the fast-paced mobility of the railway in a productive way and in foreseeing the abductor's railway routes, Mrs Hilyard, who has vowed to kill the villain (in reality her abusive husband) that abducted her daughter, manages to track him down and embark on the same train as he, waiting 'with a horrible composure in her white face' as 'a conscious Death tracking his very steps': 'the doomed man and his executioner' (182). Mildmay's and Mrs Hilyard's inscrutability facilitates their plotting on the impersonal train which helps to conceal extreme passions. On the other hand, on the platform Vincent behaves like a 'maniac' when he catches a glimpse of the sought-after man, unable to suppress his feelings. To the extent that the railway literally conveys the sensation plot of the novel, Vincent thus seems unable to follow its pace. Once again he is left stranded on the platform, paralysed by the sight of the moving train, which figures as a setting for murder. Unlike other sensation characters whose railway mobility represents their comfortable appropriation of the complex signifiers of modernity, Vincent sits on a bench at the station, 'in utter exhaustion and feebleness, stunned and stupified' (183), suffering from the same railway fatigue that emasculated Robert Audley (Martin, 'Railway'). By showing Vincent struggling to keep up with the fast-paced Mildmay and Mrs Hilyard, the novel exemplifies the conflict between sensation, which relies on modern inventions and technologically enabled impulses, and romanticism which figures as a backward, idealistic, and sometimes unrealistic fancy.

Though 'diabolical' in Vincent's eyes (183), Mrs Hilyard, who in an effort to escape domestic abuse reinvents her identity, seems more in touch with her times and, being aware of the gender conventions that impose restrictions on women, she is not afraid to bend them. '[A] woman's intention is the last thing she is likely to perform in this world,' she gloomily tells Vincent early in the novel. 'We do have meanings now and then, we poor creatures, but they seldom come to much' (155). That Mrs Hilyard will defy this fatalism concerning women becomes clear when Vincent encounters her wandering unescorted in the streets at night, with a step 'firm and distinct, like the step of a person thoroughly self-possessed and afraid of nothing' (70). Railway mobility extends even further her subversive force, enabling her to shoot (but not kill) her kidnapping and almost bigamous husband. In presenting such a transgressive and sensational female character, Oliphant flirted with styles of characterisation and plot development that she had firmly denounced in her now famous diatribes against sensationalism in *Blackwood's Edinburgh Magazine* in the sixties. Yet the fact that in the end of the novel she returns Mrs Hilyard to her morally repulsive husband does not reduce her disruptive force as a character. On the contrary it demonstrates the limited legal possibilities that abused women had in those times, facing a binary of double incarceration: the prison or the home. Oliphant's fraught relation with the sensational and subversive impact of the railway on women is also explored in a later short story, entitled 'A Story of a Wedding Tour' (1898) which will be discussed in Chapter 2.

Death by Railway: Mary Elizabeth Braddon's *Wyllard's Weird*

While the stories and novels discussed so far have been preoccupied with the physical, emotional, and social implications of danger on the railway, none has actually dealt with the death of women, whether by murder or not. The plot of Braddon's overlooked 1885 novel, *Wyllard's Weird*, revolves around the death of an unidentified young girl on a train, a mysterious fall from the train that occupies merely the first few pages of the triple-decker novel, but one that is evoked throughout the story, instigating a suspenseful detective plot and intricate character development. The novel begins with an idyllic description of a serene Cornish valley traversed by a train, the narrative following the smooth passage of the train while at the same time pointing to the comprehensive view available from the window and the sense of simultaneity that the speed creates: 'Now the line seems strung like a thread of iron in mid-air above a deep gorge, *now* winds sinuous as a snake through a labyrinth of hills' (I, 2; emphasis added). The first pages of the novel insist on the pleasurable ways speed affects the traveller's perception of a landscape which is evidence sometimes of the smooth but at other times of the incongruous merging of nature and technology. For example, at the sight of a viaduct 'spanning a vale of Alpine beauty' an unfamiliar passenger 'is apt to look with some touch of fear mingled in the cup of his delight' (I, 2). Here the danger implied in the setting foreshadows the fatal fall that is to come. Thus the opening of the novel introduces a conflict between the sense of control passengers feel as conquerors of landscape and a sense of peril caused by unpredictable nature and chance. Yet it is human nature, and woman in particular, that is shown to be most frail and precarious in this novel, the one most at risk by this arrogant dominance of man over nature and by the architecture of compartments which provide no safe way out. In a scene very much like the ones described in the beginning of this chapter, a girl exits the carriage and stands perilously on the footboard, 'hanging between life and death, a creature to be rescued somehow, were it at the hazard of a man's life' (I, 4). However, nobody has the chance of saving her as with a wild shriek she quickly becomes 'a fluttering form [. . .] whirling down the ravine, flashing white athwart the sunlit greenery, and [lying] half buried amidst a tangle of ferns and wild flowers at the bottom of the gorge' (I, 5). Her inexplicable death upsets the peaceful community of Bodmin while inciting pity, fear, remorse, and obsession in its various inhabitants until the killer is exposed at the end of the novel. While the revelation of the killer is the ultimate aim of the detective plot of the novel, I would like to focus on the dead girl, Léonie Lemarque, who as an invisible protagonist haunts both the narrative and the characters and whose railway death is not just incidental to the plot but carries significant thematic weight.

Through the countless evocations of the falling girl throughout its pages, *Wyllard's Weird* seems to question the ethics of seeing reconfigured by the railway. The first person who sees the girl plunging to her death from the train is the parish doctor, who sitting idly in his carriage, experiences the numbing of body and mind caused by the lulling mechanical movement which disables physical exertion:

> He sat with his face to the engine, puffing lazily at his black briarwood, and gazing at the landscape, in that not unpleasant condition of bodily and mental fatigue, when the mind seems half asleep, and the external world is little more than a dream-picture. (I, 3)

Thus the movement of the train turns the scenery into a dreamy spectacle, blurring the line between what really exists outside and the vague panorama that one's abstracted perception constructs, but at the same time ensuring the passenger's detachment from that reality. When the girl steps onto the footboard she breaks this insulation of inner from outer, threatening to puncture the viewer's 'dream-picture', and involving him in the drama. However, none of the passengers is able to participate in her reality, and it could be argued that the 'dream-picture' that she unavoidably presents from the carriage windows is what all the characters consistently evoke with their multiple mental re-enactments of the girl's actions and reconstructions of her identity. For the shrieking girl on the footboard next becomes a 'mute' 'dead face', a 'piteous figure lying in a heap, like a limp rag', a 'poor dislocated form', unable to assert its own identity and history (I, 7, 10). The young woman's death thus becomes a mystery story, a narrative of murder or accident, constantly remoulded to the satisfaction of the curious community. Most characters indulge in speculation, providing her lifeless body with a nationality, class position, employment, psychological state, marital status, motive, and physical condition. Furthermore, the inquest aimed at illuminating the details of her death becomes a spectacle, an opportunity for gossip and entertainment for the Bodmin inhabitants. Thus the girl enters circulation, first as a consumable story and next as a photograph which participates in her multiplication and dispersal. The simulacrum replaces her real existence. The object of so much speculation and fantasy, the girl would thus risk remaining a sensational narrative of anonymous railway crime, were it not for the compulsion of one character to resurrect her identity. By differentiating between the various male characters' approach to her, the novel dramatises a conflict between the complacency of those who relegate her to spectacle and statistics, as the unidentified victim to be added to the numerous cases of unexplained death on the railway, and the impulse of one man to restore to her the name and history that define her.

However, Edward Heathcote, Bodmin's coroner, who decides to trace Léonie's origins and motives and uncover the killer, is not entirely free of the selfish intentions that have objectified the dead girl already. His investigation is prompted firstly by his love for two women, his sister who is engaged to the prime suspect and his former love, Dora, presently Wyllard's wife, and secondly by his thrill with amateur detective work. Moreover, his fixation with finding the girl's identity becomes almost fetishistic when he discovers that she is the niece of a famous French actress brutally murdered ten years earlier by a jealous lover, the man who he suspects has also killed Léonie. Thus both Léonie and her celebrity aunt, whose story and photographs also circulate, inviting speculation, are commodified by an audience which revels in the idols of mass culture. The train, a symbol of mass culture, has participated in the commodification of the lower-class female body, rendering it interesting only to the extent that it may satisfy mass curiosity and fulfil the demands of mass consumption. For in truth, though Heathcote via very successful detective work uncovers the killer, Wyllard, and proves that the 'assassins of our civilized era are high-handed gentlemen' (I, 58), no one is punished for the deaths of the actress in Paris and the young girl on the railway. Loath to wound his beloved Dora, by making her husband accountable for his murderous actions, Heathcote quite guilt-lessly consigns Léonie's identity and death to oblivion: 'I will not submit Mr Wyllard to the inconvenience of a trial. As for the episode upon the railway – we will try to think *that* an accident, an unlucky impulse, unpremeditated, falling considerably short of murder' (III, 239–40). Even Dora, who had initially shown great sensitivity and compassion for the dead girl, is ultimately unable to empathise with a lower-class foreigner at the expense of her loyalty to her husband: 'All her natural horror at his guilt was not strong enough to extinguish her love, or to lessen her compassion' (III, 242). Léonie does finally become a statistic, an anonymous girl killed by a ruffian on a train, and a spectacle of vulnerable femininity. Her class and gender seem responsible for this fate, a fate that has in turn ensured the maintenance of class stability.

The novel also presents differences in the gendered ways the railway is experienced. As in the case of the doctor already described, all male characters view the railway as an extension of their power and a means of satisfying selfish goals or desires; it reflects their self-assurance and sense of command over public space. So the train successfully up to a point conceals the sexual mobility of the main suspect, Bothwell Grahame, who is secretly entangled with the wife of his general in Plymouth. It also facilitates the plans of the actual murderer, Julian Wyllard, who lures the girl on the train in order to obtain from her incriminating letters which prove his culpability in the murder of the actress ten years before. For the girl, however, who has lived in dependence all her life, the train and the railway station are threatening spaces, full of practical and psychological obstacles, spaces in which she struggles to assert her identity while becoming in reality the object of speculation, manipulation, and crime. In his confessional description of the fatal train ride, Wyllard makes clear how his masculine will and physique as well as his social position and reputation render her identity insignificant and ultimately expendable throughout the journey. Not expecting her to have a will of her own, he draws up several plans about her future, modifying her journey and destination in accordance with his wishes, and considering her a gullible and manageable protégée, perhaps a commodity like her aunt: 'I anticipated no difficulty in getting [the incriminating letters] from her' (III, 234), he says, as he lures her into her final space of confinement. Her unexpected resistance, however, stimulates his buried murderous drives and uncovers the real face behind the mask of gentility, the face she identifies as her aunt's killer. Her vain threats, however, 'I will tell people what you are!', 'You shall not escape' (III, 236), reveal the impossibility for honest women to use the carriage as a space of discipline for criminal men. And though Léonie tries to frame her aunt's killer by exiting the carriage, the architecture of the carriage, whose only way out leads to death, emphasises the futility of the struggle.

> While she stood wavering on that narrow ledge, her life hanging by a thread, the train rounded the curve and passed on to the viaduct. The stony gorge was below, deep and narrow, like an open grave – tempting me – tempting me as Satan tempts his own. One sudden movement of my arm, and all was over. I had held her, for the first few moments. I had tried to save her. Had she been reasonable, I would have saved her. But there was no middle course. Ruin, unutterable ruin for me, or death for her. One motion of my arm, and she was gone. Light as a feather, the frail little figure fluttered down the gorge. (III, 236–7)

The carriage therefore becomes the space of gender and social conflict with Wyllard's sense of dominance and entitlement to space obliterating the girl's sense of justice and struggle to survive. With self-assurance, derived from his sense of being beyond suspicion in public space, Wyllard effortlessly escapes notice and, for a long time, ruin: 'I had my railway-key ready before the stoppage, and did not lose an instant in getting along the off-side of the line back to the compartment I had left' (III, 237). The railway-key, which is proof of privilege and possession and which guarantees his freedom to ride any carriage, secures his innocence. In the end of the novel, even though Wyllard's moral guilt has been established through solid evidence and his own confession, legal guilt falls on an irrelevant-to-the-case miner, who is convicted and hanged for another murder nearby: 'although he confessed nothing, and died a hardened impenitent miner, it was believed by every one in the place that his was the pitiless hand which had sent the French girl to her doom' (III, 251). 'Thus having identified somebody as the murderer, Bodmin was content' (III, 252). The novel ends by confirming the unredeeming aspect of the railway as a geography of fear. However, the ironic tone of the ending and the sympathy raised for the poor victim of class and prejudice, both of which the railway helped to sustain, offer an indictment of woman's ruthless and unpunished victimisation. At the same time the novel anticipates an important modernist concern which was often associated with the railway: the assimilation of the subject by industry and technology via the extinction, literally and figuratively, of his or her individuality.

Notes

1. See incident reported in the *North Wales Chronicle* and *Liverpool Mercury* between 13 and 16 July 1864, entitled 'Outrage on a Lady in a Railway Carriage'. See also *The London Review*, 'The Murder in a Railway Carriage', 16 July 1864. In the last part of this Chapter, I discuss Mary Elizabeth Braddon's *Wyllard's Weird* which figures a girl in the same perilous position.
2. See also my discussion of Broughton's story in *Critical Survey* (2011).
3. The introduction of the side corridor in train carriages gradually alleviated the feelings of isolation and incarceration experienced by women such as Broughton's heroine. See also Schivelbusch, 196.
4. See McDonnell Bodkin's 'How He Cut His Stick' (1900).
5. See Hayward's *Revelations of a Lady Detective*.
6. Pope reports that the London *Times* ran a total of 113 articles reporting railway accidents in the short period of six months before and after the famous Staplehurst accident in 1865 (438–9). Moreover, it should be noted that the opening of the Liverpool and Manchester line on 15 September 1830 was marred by the first death by train of William Huskisson, MP, who, unable to calculate the speed of the approaching train, the *Rocket*, was crushed to death. From its first journeys, therefore, the train was associated with peril and violence.
7. 'The Hole in the Wall' is attributed to Joseph Charles Parkinson (Pope, 437n7).
8. Elaine Scarry has argued that 'A fifth dimension of physical pain is its ability to destroy language, the power of verbal objectification, a major source of our self-extension' (54).
9. Nancy Henry lists a number of successful lady speculators found in the fiction of Gaskell and Eliot, comparing the financial independence gained by these women to the vulnerability of others who are ruined by their husbands' financial losses (124). Henry also discusses the difference between speculating and investing, arguing that though the former was charged with a negative moral sense on account of the risk involved, novels of the period obfuscate the difference between the two, showing that investors sometimes took equal risks as speculators (120).
10. In its use of a female character who changes name, identity, and occupation in order to escape her husband and of a detective plot in which a man compulsively follows, by railway, the villains, *Salem Chapel* bears an uncanny resemblance to *Lady Audley's Secret*, despite Oliphant's negative views of Braddon.
11. See Tara MacDonald for an overview of the critics who have discussed Oliphant's foray into the sensation genre with this novel.

Chapter 2

Railway Speed

Fast and Forward: Women and Railway Manners

> Better the quietest parliamentary train, which starts very early in the morning and carries its passengers safe into the terminus when the shades of night come down, than that rabid, rushing express, which does the journey in a quarter of the time, but occasionally topples over a bank, or rides pickaback upon a luggage train, in its fiery impetuosity.
>
> Mary Elizabeth Braddon, *Aurora Floyd* (1863) 280

The above description from Braddon's very popular 1863 sensation novel rather than referring to the dangers of fast trains, in fact juxtaposes, through metaphor, two types of women that men felt they had to choose from in a period of strained gender relations. In the particular extract one of the novel's characters, Talbot Bulstrode, justifies his choice of marriage to Lucy rather than Aurora, by pinpointing the risks that marriage to an impetuous, fast woman like Aurora might incur and employing the familiar discourse of danger, violence, and death that the accident prone train had generated in the press and popular fiction. At a time of railway speed, when numerous daily and weekly articles in the press heatedly debated the practical, social, and medical dangers and benefits of high velocity, and when urban activities of business and leisure were often visualised as following the dizzying tempo of 'the railroad of life', it is not surprising that the speed of trains was applied as metaphor to young women of the upper middle class who rejected the slow pace of domestic existence and who strayed from the ordinary path of feminine delicacy, modesty, and self-effacement. Compared to the pale and angelic Lucy, who at another point in the novel is fantasised by Bulstrode as an aestheticised dead female body, Aurora Floyd, the bigamous and violent heroine of Braddon's fiction, is the epitome of speed.

Speed and haste had since the early Victorian times entered the discourse of social texts that described the lamentable effects of urban life – of the increasing work-related urge for continuous literal mobility and rapid business manoeuvres – on masculinity and urban or professional relations. Fastness in girls, however, which had little or nothing to do with business, industry, and professionalism, came to describe a less than desired evolution in their manners and morals, equivalent, if not comparable, to the literal speed of commercial deals and transactions that dominated the male public sphere. Allegedly eating, drinking, and smoking in public, talking slang, heartlessly flirting with men, and pitilessly scheming against their own sex in order to conquer fashionable society, such 'fast girls' seemed to partake rather superficially of modern, urban living in its accelerated form:

> The *summum bonum* of existence of the 'fast' young ladies is to get as much pleasure out of life as possible [. . .] They enjoy eating and drinking, and are not ashamed to do either, publicly or privately. Indeed they rather delight in setting the ordinary usages of society at defiance [. . .] Such girls shine for a few years [. . .] But they do not marry. They are passed over for less extravagant and quieter creatures [. . .] Defend us, then, from 'fast' young ladies, and may their numbers become less. (Anon., 'Fast Girls', 196)

Not suited for marriage, like Aurora in the eyes of Bulstrode, fast girls were certainly not as criminally dangerous as the sensational heroines of Braddon's or Collins's fiction; yet in their association with speed they challenged conservative views on women's nature and anticipated transgressive forms of femininity and sexual behaviour that flourished especially in the modern city.

Between the 1860s and 1870s women debated their alternatives, often defending the choices of the fast girls. In 1869 *Macmillan's Magazine* printed an article, subsequently much quoted and commented on in other journals, which claimed that due to the lack of consistent higher education and misguided goals, 'adornment, comfort, and amusement of the great idol Self is the only duty' of girls of high society (Harrison, 324). Young ladies become 'fast' because they are deprived of other alternatives: 'It would be easy to prove that in the present day there is scarcely any alternative for a girl in fashionable society, between reckless dissipation and a convent life' (324). For such girls, whose aspirations for education, self-cultivation, or charity work have been thwarted by overprotective parents or by the lures of a glittering fashionable life, 'society is odious, but a quiet life is unendurable' (326). Fighting the 'listless torpor' of domesticity (325), the fast girl gives herself up to the pursuit of popularity through dancing and flirting – 'cling[ing] the more desperately to the only excitement with which she can kill time and smother conscience':

Hence also the wretched extravagances of tasteless fashion (whose only object is to attract attention), and, worse still, the low tone of morality which all agree in declaring to be daily gaining ground. The affectation of schoolboy slang which was in vogue ten years ago is fast being superseded by conversation of a far more dangerous type, and she who would earn the reputation for being fashionably 'fast' must stifle every feeling of delicacy and amuse herself by making good men blush while bad men laugh. (Harrison, 326)

Many articles in a like fashion suggested that such behaviour was the only means by which girls could 'kill time', withstanding the boredom of a slow life at home. Often, illustrations in periodicals such as *Punch* would link the metaphor of fastness to literal speed, depicting 'fast' women driving carriages and hansoms or boarding trains. One illustration from 1857 shows a 'fast young lady' in a railway carriage, shocking an elderly gentleman by nonchalantly asking for Lucifer matches to light her cigarette, thus challenging the norms by unexpectedly supporting the cause to allow smoking in trains despite the abundant complaints voiced by mostly female non-smoking passengers (see Figure 3).

At the same time, however, hinting at the moral depravity supposedly reflected in such conduct, and caring to uphold Victorian domestic ideology on which the Empire depended for its socio-economic progress and success, articles like the *Macmillan's* quoted above acted as deterrents to a life of reckless speed. Fastness in a middle-class girl, like fallenness in a working- or middle-class girl, could only lead to ruin and ultimately despair: 'So much for the fast young lady. If her course was dazzling and brilliant, like the meteor's, it was quite as brief, and went out suddenly in eternal darkness' (Anon., 'The Fast Young Lady', 523). Or even more vividly detailed:

> the Fashionably-Fast Young Lady is nothing if not flashily notorious. It is, in fact, her object to become a Comet of Society, in order that she may (literally) 'take the shine out of' all other stars.
>
> She is perpetually letting off her conversational fireworks, and lives in a state of chronic bang. She is, however, often the rocket of feminine pyro-techny, and, by aspiring to distance all her friends with a brilliant and swift ascent in the world, comes down to her level again, a poor, burnt-out, used up little stick. (Anon., 'Young Ladies of the Period', 180)

Fast behaviour was, moreover, considered sexually forward, and fictional stories, aimed at discursively regulating the sexuality of women, targeted fast girls, whose unrestrained flirtation in public spaces like the railway threatened to extinguish the feminine ideal of reticence and incorruptibility. Laura Fillingham, who describes herself as 'a little fast' in 'An Expensive Journey' (Anon., 1867), and who is proud of her talent of 'pick[ing] up' random young good-looking men for companions in

Fast Young Lady (to Old Gent). "HAVE YOU SUCH A THING AS A LUCIFER ABOUT YOU, FOR I'VE LEFT MY CIGAR LIGHTS AT HOME !"

Figure 3. 'Fast Young Lady (to Old Gent)', *Punch* (29 August 1857): 92.

railway carriages (36), is robbed on the train by a sleek, very handsome young man with whom she becomes infatuated and to whom she readily divulges information about her jewels. In the end, and a few weeks after the incident, the thief, in a condescending gesture, returns an insignificant locket which he has stolen from her (containing a photograph and a lock of hair of another man she has flirted with), which functions as a bitter reminder of the unpleasant results of 'fastness': 'as the reader may imagine, [in my next train ride] I did not look out quite so eagerly for handsome travelling companions', Laura muses, accepting the regulation that her experience has imposed (40). While the train, like other urban spaces, fostered such freedom of manners in young women who made the most of the dead time on the train by striking up conversation or flirting, cultural texts of the period punished them for init_ating romance, forcing on them the disadvantages rather than the advartages of this sexual freedom. In 'A Trip by Rail; or, the Third-Class Passenger' (Anon., 1864), a young first-class lady passenger, who is described as 'one of those modern monsters – a fast girl' (213), is contrasted to a shy and dutiful, lady-looking g_rl, travelling, for mysterious reasons, third class, who, after finding herself in a 'perilous position', from which she needs to be saved by masculine intervention during a railway collision, wins the heart of the beau of the story. As a result, the fashionable but too fast and unpleasant girl, who had unashamedly flirted wit; the man throughout the journey, is given up: 'The fear of remaining an old maid, after all, had given her, towards gentlemen, an eagerness which defeated her own object, and was far from procuring her the respect of the opposite sex, whom her good looks attracted' (213). Though not fallen or sexually corrupted, fast girls are consigned to the same fate as their unfortunate counterparts, since flirting is associated with deviant sexuality which cannot but thwart a fast girl's hopes of marriage: 'Men like her as the partner of the dance, but none had proposed to the "fast girl" to become his partner for life' (213). Such train stories, with their insular settings functioning as microcosms of society, become the means of contrasting 'fast' and 'slow' – or static – types of womanhood, and in all cases examined, as Deborah Epstein Nord has written in a different context, 'the ascendancy of uncorrupted womanhood can only follow the expulsion of debased womanhood' (85).

In a much more subtle, but no less threatening way, the remarkable heroine of George Meredith's, *Diana of the Crossways* (1897), Diana Warwick, describes the fate of a married woman who defies convention and who chooses speed and independent mobility thus:

> We women are the verbs passive of the alliance; we have to learn, and if we take to activity, with the best intentions, we conjugate a frightful disturbance. We are to run on lines, like the steam-trains, or we come to no station, dash to fragments. I have the misfortune to know I was born an active. I take my chance. (64)

By combining metaphors of technology and grammar, Diana pinpoints the paradoxes and conflicting expectations that were testing Victorian domestic ideology at the fin de siècle. Meredith captures the main dilemma that women had to confront in the late Victorian period, called upon to choose between active visibility in the public sphere and passive obscurity within the home, between speed and leisure, mobility and immobility. The metaphors that Diana uses, women as verbs or trains, suggest that while women were increasingly located within contexts of agency and settings of mobility, they were, nevertheless, expected to follow the prescribed routes of passivity or linearity. Like passive verbs, women were subject to rules which ensured a predictable and rigid pattern of behaviour as well as an obscured or thwarted agency. As trains, in rapid transit, they had to run on lines, lines undoubtedly laid out by men who had engineered their straight, cast-in-iron paths. Women, on the one hand, because of their newly acquired freedom of movement, are related to the most powerful emblem of speed and transitoriness in the nineteenth century, the train, but on the other, it is suggested that their speed and direction have to be prescribed and monitored: they are expected to follow rather than forge new paths. Otherwise, as Diana says, by being uncontrollably 'fast', they run the risk of breaking up, dashing to fragments.

The ideological tensions arising from women's 'fastness' may also be detected in a much discussed painting by Augustus Egg, entitled *Travelling Companions* (1862), which, like Diana's metaphor, focuses on speeding women, only to blunt their purpose and neutralise their potential for transgression through mobility (see Figure 4).

Two identical looking young ladies occupy opposite seats in a com-

Figure 4. Augustus Egg, *Travelling Companions*. 1862. ©Birmingham Museums Trust

partment of a railway carriage which is travelling at full speed across a sunny coastal landscape. The painting has been celebrated for its symmetrical treatment of the face, clothes, and posture of the two travelling companions, while their different occupations, one reading, the other sleeping, have elicited interpretations which attribute innocence and virginity to the former and sexual awareness or indulgence to the latter. Indeed, despite their massive identical travelling clothes which aim at obscuring their figures, the woman on the left may be construed as the invidious, for the Victorians, reflection of her 'companion', with her body more suggestively exposed, hands ungloved, neck extended, and one button undone. And yet the painting, with its lighting contrasts, between the bright exterior and the drab interior, and the general sameness of its two protagonists, in my view, succeeds not only in representing the two conflicting yet oddly complementary types of femininity but also in addressing and abating male fears about women's potentially conscious sexuality, which partly resulted from their embrace of boundless mobility and their gradual mastery of such radical, for 1862, means of transportation as the train. The borders of the carriage, so clearly marked through detailed depiction of walls, corners, and side shadings, serve to frame the purpose of these women's voyage within rigid gender boundaries and to slow down their rapid movement by suggesting their lack of interest and participation in the speed that only the tassel above the carriage door actually indicates. With eyes closed or half closed (even the reading woman is presented with heavy eyelids), both women are represented by Egg as oblivious to the beautiful view rushing past them outside and to the bright sunlight in which their faces and dresses inevitably bask, while speed seems only to lull or drowse them. The painting succeeds in containing and thus domesticating its fast travelling women, suggesting that even when in transit, women conform to the ideals of domesticity, to pastimes appropriate to the homely private spaces that this carriage resembles. With their grey, uniform-like clothes, they have conquered all temptation to look outside, helped by the comfortable interior which has lulled them to lethargy and fulfilled their desire for quiet repose and safety. At the same time the women, enjoying their seeming privacy, are oblivious of the presence of one more travelling companion sitting comfortably in the shaded opposite corner of the carriage – the invisible spectator, whose powerful, inquisitive, and voyeuristic gaze may construct and reconstruct their sexuality at will. Thus contained, such women docilely 'run on lines' and will, for sure, come to the desired station.

Despite the thirty-five years that separate Egg from Meredith, their work expresses a similar cultural anxiety lest women should assume the active agency available to them through the opportunity of train travel and through their overly comfortable occupation of spaces of transit. The discourses of the latter half of the Victorian period seem, on the one hand, to accept the transformation of the train compartment into a libidinal space, one that fosters sexual desire as well as pure love in men; on the other, however, as a symbol of technological advance, science, and business, the iron horse was not meant to be appropriated by women for their own emotional fulfilment or economic and sexual advantage. Examples of such dangerous women, described as fiends or *femmes fatale*, who, ready to rob or seduce men in train carriages, embody male roles, have already been examined in the sensation stories and fiction of the sixties in Chapter 1. But fastness in girls, which had no criminal incentive, was often taken for indecent behaviour or relaxed morals, provoking in men confusion, sexual urges, and sometimes violence. And while, as we saw in Chapter 1, many of the rape cases reported in the news were true, the media also printed numerous stories of false accusation, emphasising the unexpected dangers of the railway not only for women but also for men, and especially 'the liability which every man incurs of being charged with indecent assault' (Anon., 'Other Dangers of the Rail', 106). Women's new freedoms in public spaces thus blurred the line between decent and indecent behaviour, and, in cases where women's incentive proved to be blackmail, they threatened to emasculate men, traumatising their male pride. Confined within the hermetic borders of a railway carriage, in which their word did not necessarily prevail over that of their female fellow passengers, men found themselves to be the victims of overactive women who employed their sexuality, either through flirting or through feigned timid glances, in order to gain economic advantages through marriage or theft. As a result the railway was considered an unstable space, not only for the criminal aims that it sheltered, but also for the incompatibility between men's and women's intentions, manners, and morals in the age of the fast girl.

Fastness, which was linked to the middle-class mores of bored society girls who claimed possession of urban public spaces through their superficial freedoms but also sexual licence, may thus be seen as challenging the insularity of middle-class gender limits. And though there was a vast difference between the fast young ladies of first-class carriages and the shop-girls or streetwalkers who had mastered the means of transit of the late Victorian metropolis, the urban freedoms of both classes of women exemplified a sexual restlessness that gradually upset the clear divisions between middle-class and working-class sexuality. The train compartment, which was conducive, as we have seen, to the dissolution of binaries of class and private/public, was the site of such gender trouble and a site in which women and men tested sexual freedoms sometimes reciprocally but at other times not. For accusations of true or false sexual assault and rape came from all carriages and all classes. Attributing these dangers of social intercourse arising from the railway to the freedom with which women unreservedly occupied all carriages on a train (and not only the *dames seules* compartments), the authors of articles which discussed false accusations recommended that all travelling women were confined to a 'railway gynæceum' ('Other Dangers of the Rail', 107). Segregating the sexes by restricting women's (and not men's) choice of train compartment and forcing them into a prison-like gynæceum would become the means of containing the burgeoning sexuality of women which had proved to compromise the sexual prerogative of men.[1]

Such a gynæceum would have saved the reputation of Everard Barfoot in George Gissing's *The Odd Women* (1893), who, in his account, is trapped in a railway carriage by Amy Drake, allegedly a promiscuous girl with devious intentions:

> Amy managed to get me into the same carriage with herself, and on the way to London we were alone. You foresee the end of it. At Paddington Station the girl and I went off together, and she didn't get to her sister's till the evening. (107)

MAKING THE BEST OF IT.

First Passenger (horrified at seeing the other burst into the carriage while the train was in motion).—GOODNESS, MAN, YOU'VE HAD A NARROW ESCAPE!
Second Passenger.—I HAVE. THERE WAS A SOLITARY LADY IN THE COMPARTMENT I SCRAMBLED OUT OF.

Figure 5. 'Making the Best of it', *Funny Folks* (14 August 1875): 44.

The episode casts a shadow on both participants, on Amy for initiating the sexual liaison and using it for blackmailing purposes and on Barfoot for callously taking advantage of the sexual offer and compromising the working-class girl. Manipulating sexuality and mores, both Barfoot and Amy take part in an intricate social intercourse fostered in spaces such as the railway carriage, which becomes the setting most conducive to casual sex. However, despite Gissing's sympathetic account of the struggles and new freedoms of working-class girls, his text is loath to unreservedly endorse women's urban circulation. His shop-girls, who have 'ready knowledge of London transit' (51), have difficulty negotiating respectability with the image of sexual looseness that they project in their urban wanderings. Insecure about her self-image, Monica Madden, the impoverished middle-class girl, is reluctant to form the acquaintance of Widdowson in the streets of London, and later she is apprehensive of the coincidence of meeting Barfoot at Sloane Square Station and travelling by Underground with him. Both meetings prove disastrous. Similarly, her sister Virginia is filled with trepidation and shame on entering Charing Cross Station to quench her desire for alcohol. Acknowledging their compromised image as potentially loose women in search of illicit pleasures in railway spaces, the sisters are thus linked to the fallen Miss Eade, their distorted double, who accosts men at Victoria Station. In Gissing's novel, therefore, spaces of public transport become settings of moral and sexual ambiguity, where men and women are attributed the role of sexual predator, in some cases justifiably and in others not. For example, for his past morally dubious act of seducing or accepting to be seduced by Amy Drake on the train, Rhoda Nunn cannot trust Barfoot, so when she catches sight of him innocently talking with Monica at Sloane Square Station, she immediately implicates them in a sexual liaison. Rhoda's inability to dissociate spaces of transit from illicit desire in Gissing's text of the nineties demonstrates that gender normativity was too deeply ingrained in the conscience of writers and characters. And despite the progressive impulse of male-produced texts such as Gissing's, sexually straying women with unrestricted access to spaces of transit end up being contained.

Trains to Perdition: Transgressive Transit in Rhoda Broughton, Dora Russell, and Margaret Oliphant

The tensions surfacing in railway stories which negotiate sexual impulses with social convention reveal acute sexual anxieties, the pathologies of a modern culture that was struggling to accommodate gender transgression or deviance in women. At the same time these adventures in the micro-settings of the train suggested that a major threat to the sense of exclusivity and immunity of upper- or middle-class patriarchy, epitomised by the first-class railway carriage, came from the most unlikely candidate: woman of all ages and classes. Despite the regulatory role and disciplinary impulse of those narratives which repeatedly punish the straying women, railroad culture pointed to the discrepancies of gender ideology and the artificial boundary between private and public space, girl of the hearth and fast girl. In the narratives that follow by Rhoda Broughton, Dora Russell, and Margaret Oliphant, the train offers the erring heroines a chance to fulfil sexual desire or to escape from abusive marriages. In all three cases, however, the heroines are made to confront the disciplinary force of the railway as an institution, a force which counters its liberating potential. The texts thus voice the anxieties of women who choose transgression via the train but who are thwarted by the conventions and prejudices that associated women's mobility with social and emotional perdition.

In the novel, *Not Wisely, but Too Well* (1867), Rhoda Broughton's narrator describes the volatile and often vacillating heroine, Kate Chester, as a girl 'in a state of transition, though transition to what remained to be proved' (138–9).[2] Indeed the novel traces Kate's emotional, moral, and spatial shifts in the course of many years, laying emphasis not so much on her ultimate moral reform as on the significance of perpetually testing new experience, the formative value of trial and error. By tracing Kate's transitional and transitory states of being as she traverses a variety of settings and is overwhelmed by a wide range of emotional crises, Broughton emphasises, as Pamela Gilbert has shown, her heroine's liminal position: 'Both morally and physically, [Kate] inhabits a borderland'; 'she moves among the margins of the suburbs, of society, of the river, of life itself' (121, 123). Kate's liminal position may be said to reflect to a certain extent Broughton's own ambivalence as an author who, as Tamar Heller has observed, constructs narratives 'split between radical and conservative elements, at once critiquing women's lack of autonomy within Victorian culture and serving as a cautionary tale about the dangers of female appetite' (88). Broughton's fascination with woman 'in a state of transition' found expression in the use of imagery and metaphor drawn from the railway which served to represent her heroines' literal and emotional transit, their tentative and ultimately dangerous journey, during which the final destination is indefinitely deferred, changed, or cancelled. In many of Broughton's novels we encounter women roaming the streets, participating in the public life of cities through visibility and exposure. However, her texts treat the railway as a more complex, challenging, and ultimately bewildering setting than the street, as it combines privacy and publicity, movement and stasis, and provides the author with opportunities to experiment with the new ways of socialising cultivated in spaces of transit. The author shows an intriguing awareness of the way in which the train's constant mobility, speed, and temporariness of encounters impinge on the subjectivity and everyday routine of women, and she incorporates its effects in her plots but also, most originally, in her style.

Broughton, a relatively neglected writer today, was favourably received in her time, with extensive reviews in periodicals like *Temple Bar*, *Blackwood's*, and *London Society* which often praised her 'flesh and blood' heroines (Anon., 'The Novels of Miss Broughton', 208). Edith Simcox, reviewer for *The Academy*, goes so far as to claim that 'Miss Broughton's talent [. . .] if taken care of [. . .] might develop into something standing in the same relation to the highest form of humour as that in which Charlotte Bronte's works stand to the highest kind of tragic fiction' (85). Rhoda Broughton distinguished herself from other female popular writers of her day, paradoxically, through her commonplace, domestic plots which dispensed with sensational material. Her plots were vivid and fast moving, but without, as Pamela Gilbert has noted, the aid of the kind of extraordinary events that propelled the plots of Wilkie Collins and Mary Braddon (89). Moreover her heroines were direct and engaging without being voluptuous beauties; nor did they have to resort to unnatural sensuous raptures and exaggerated gestures. 'Whilst we glance through her pages,' one reviewer remarked, 'we feel we are being told of no mere puppets evoked from the writer's imagination, but of real flesh-and-blood people who have lived and loved and gone to their rest like the myriads before them' (Anon., 'New Books Received', 93).

While not making use of extraordinary events in her plots, Broughton contributes to the genre of sensation fiction in a more provocative way, by focusing on the swift and unpredictable alternation of sensations in woman. In an article in *Blackwood's Edinburgh Magazine* in 1867, Margaret Oliphant complained that her contemporary women novelists were too preoccupied with 'sensuous raptures', representing 'this intense appreciation of flesh and blood, this eagerness of physical sensation [. . .] as the natural sentiment of English girls' ('Novels', 259). Broughton, however, whose work is somewhat reluctantly included in Oliphant's list of 'second-rate women's books' (266), is not so much interested in those 'revolting', in Oliphant's phrasing, 'burning kisses and frantic embraces' (259). Oliphant herself is at great pains actually to pinpoint what it is that she finds so objectionable in a work (*Cometh up as a Flower*) that 'is not a stupid book' (265) and a heroine who 'is not revolting, nor yet nasty' and whose sensations are 'not unnatural' (267). It is the diction that Broughton uses to describe her heroine's emotions and sensations that repels Oliphant – 'speeches about shrinking bodies and sexless essences' that are 'disgusting in the fullest sense of the word'. 'There may be nothing wrong in all this, but it is curious language, as we have said, for a girl,' Oliphant complains (267). Inadvertently Oliphant is suggesting that Broughton is ahead of her time, daring to forge a language of physical sensation and desire that women may admit to and employ, defying socio-cultural codes that attributed such bodily consciousness to immorality and eventually fallenness. Oliphant herself admits that, after all, there is nothing immoral about Broughton's 'free-spoken' heroines (258): 'intense goodness follows the intense sensuousness', albeit quite implausibly, in this critic's view (269). In that sense, by contesting the Victorian equation between female sexuality and immorality, Broughton provides the reader with a woman's complex, inside view of 'fastness' in girls, one that defies its superficial representation found in the popular press. Moreover, as Helen Debenham has argued, Broughton's texts challenge Victorian assumptions 'that the intensity of feeling associated with female sexuality has no place in ordinary middle-class life and is not a proper object of "creative art"' (12). Broughton's heroines, as one reviewer in *Temple Bar* wrote, are 'unruly, rebellious, "fast", and at times even what is called "slangy"' (Anon., 'The Novels of Miss Broughton', 204); her 'particular species of girl' is a 'wilful, perverse though by no means shrewish, mettlesome, wayward, warm, sensuous creature, that walks, lolls, looks beautiful, flirts, is epigrammatic, and makes love half-way through her pages' (206); but, as the same reviewer remarks, in an age of women's rights and emancipation, such girls are 'so much on the increase that they have become interesting' (205). In a sense, then, her heroines' fastness is a manifestation of their 'state of transition', sexual awareness being perhaps the most important stage in the development of a young girl.

In her article on *Not Wisely, but Too Well*, Heller illustrates the novel's sexual explicitness, with which Broughton 'contest[s] her culture's emphasis on female disembodiment' (89), and explicates scenes which suggest the female protagonist's 'intense capacity for sexual arousal' (90). However, as Laurence Talairach-Vielmas has argued, throughout the novel Kate Chester 'shifts between the positions of desiring subject and desired object' (100). In settings of literal transit, public expectations clash with women's private desires, threatening to extinguish the burgeoning bodily awareness that Broughton's heroines experience. Having adopted mobility as a means of self-definition, advancement, and sensual gratification, Kate suffers, within these transitory spaces, the thwarting of her agency, as she is manipulated by men who view her as a desired object. In this way Broughton exposes the paradoxes of gender ideology, suggesting that women's free mobility, though encouraged, was perceived both as an invitation for covert or overt abuse and as an indicator of immorality. In *Not Wisely, but Too Well*, Broughton's impulsive heroine is encumbered by many characters who associate her physical mobility with dangerous or unacceptable emotional transitions or sexual desires. Her craving for autonomy, represented through her solitary walks in remote country roads and slums and through her boarding of trains, is constantly questioned, and her decisions are overturned by male characters who force on her stereotypical definitions of Victorian womanhood.

Early in the novel, Kate's elaborate erotic fantasy of Dare Stamer, a fantasy linked to the sensual gratification derived from her walk through nature, is interrupted by Dare's sudden appearance, which, on the one hand, fulfils her romantic expectations, as he arrives, Rochester-like, on horseback – 'he pulled his horse up sharply, so sharply as to bring it almost upon its haunches' – but, on the other, also indicates the objectifying and ultimately disorienting potential of his gaze: 'an ill light flashed over his face as he turned towards her – a light bred of earthly exhalations – a will-o'-the-wisp, potent to lead astray – a light that came, not from heaven, and which brought no blessing to the woman on whom it fell' (29). As the ominous, gothic imagery foreshadows, Kate soon finds out that Dare's desire is stimulated by much more sinister motives than her fantasy had allowed: he wants her to abandon her family and to flee with him while he is already married. While her sensual desire is celebrated by the narrator as innocent and natural – after all it is corroborated by nature which participates in her ecstasy – his selfish desire aims at distorting her attraction for him and tempting her to accept a life of fornication and adultery. As a 'fast' girl, Kate is lured to immorality not by her own impulse for sensual gratification but by patriarchy itself incarnated in the person of Dare Stamer, who, enjoying the benefits of Victorian double standards that did not label adulterous men as 'fallen', misconstrues the motives of the flirty young girl, deeming her a right candidate for disgrace and marginalisation.

Later in the novel, during the period of her charitable district-visiting in the slums of Queenstown, Kate's longing for independence and self-definition through social work is again challenged by a bargee outside a public house, who, regarding her as an available object of desire, blocks her way and treats her like a prostitute. Her right to occupy public streets is questioned not only by Dare and the accosting man, both of whom interpret her impulse to walk alone outdoors in terms of their own sexual desires, but also by the secretly-in-love-with-her parson, James Stanley, who, in this second instance, meets her in the street and initially casts doubt upon her perception and her sanity, treating the whole violent incident as an illusion: 'Are you quite sure you have not been dreaming,' he asks her (91). Compelled to confront the dangers of visibility, and the objectification her need for independence has subjected her to, Kate suffers a triple disorientation: physically and socially she is lost, as the bewildering streets and the offensive man confirm; and mentally too she might be lost, as the doubting James insinuates.

Finally, the most subtle but most devastating abuse that Kate suffers is on a train during her final attempt to join Dare in London where they plan to live in sin. In this scene the train comes to resemble a disciplinary institution, in which normalising tactics are applied to the transgressive woman. In fact from its inauguration in Britain, the railway was strongly linked to discipline, as it was staffed by police officers and ex-military men who either patrolled the stations or held other positions of responsibility.[3] As in the previous cases, in this scene Kate's personal fantasy of finding sensual and emotional fulfilment with her lover is once again distorted by James Stanley who, combining principles of Victorian gender ideology and Christian theology, disrupts her path, follows her on the train, and forces her to change her destination. By unfolding horrific details of 'the abyss that was yawning at the very feet of this wretched woman' (134), James first imposes a spatial and temporal disorientation on Kate, by drawing her attention away from the here and now of the train of pleasure towards the timeless setting of hell which is beyond the scope of the lived experience that Kate is fulfilling with her actual journey. Kate, who has knowingly chosen the 'train [. . .] to perdition' (128), after having almost died of unquenched desire, and who is conscious of the irrevocable social effects of her bold transgression, is manipulated into forgetting the temporal in favour of the eternal. Moreover, anticipating her disregard for her own fate and turning her strong devotion to Dare against her, James manoeuvres her into believing that she has to suppress her longing, not for her own salvation, but for Dare, in order to save *him* from eternal damnation:

> 'If you do love him, I say,' went on James emphatically, 'if his good, his welfare, are of any moment to you, give him up. Don't you see that you are the bait with which Satan is angling for his soul? As long as you are before him, a stumbling-block in his path, he has not a chance of ever coming back to the light.' (136)

James Stanley's imagery ironically reverses a series of scenes in the novel during which men have functioned as 'stumbling-blocks' hindering

Kate's path. Yet it is suggested that as a woman in transit, figuratively and literally, Kate cannot offer stability and nourishment to a man who is naturally prone to corruption. Only by giving up fastness and mobility – and him – can she secure Dare's social and spiritual salvation, restoring the order that has been disrupted with her actions. Ironically, the ending of the novel that showcased a young woman's potential for ardent sexual desire confirms the alternatives of women as they were voiced by the writer of the 1869 article in *Macmillan's Magazine* discussed earlier: 'reckless dissipation' or 'convent life'. Kate chooses the latter, not being able to negotiate a middle ground in which she would be able to continue living fast but without being socially stigmatised.

It should be pointed out that before entering the train Kate imagined herself immune from social influences, bodily identifying with the potent symbol of the iron horse and its speed. However, within the hermetic and inescapable borders of the carriage she had imagined private, her energy is drained and her impulse extinguished by James who invades her space treating it as a suffocating confessional, in which she must be converted. The train ride, which was supposed to make possible the fulfilment of Kate's sexual desire, inadvertently, through the insulation and incarceration that it effects, facilitates James's normalising purpose, numbing Kate to the point of unconsciousness:

> There she sank down, motionless, nerveless, almost senseless [. . .] All the way back, Kate sat staring, vacant-eyed, apathetic, out of the window, at the quick-passing landscape, not seeing one inch of it – like a woman on whom a stunning blow had just fallen, numbing her senses, like one whose last hope in this world was extinct. (137)

On the train, James targets her presumed physical strength and invulnerability, introducing her to the idea that she might die young and in sin, and hinting, perhaps, at the dangers of the transportation medium itself, the train, and its potential to crush the body in a accident, leading to premature death:

> 'Don't talk of dying,' cried Kate, shivering, 'I'm young and strong; why should I die?'
> 'Is it only the old that die?' inquired James very mournfully. 'Ah, no; any paper you take up will tell you differently.' (135)

James is right to fear that 'in saving her soul [he had] killed her body' (137). While he does indeed rescue her from the social plight of fallen womanhood and the sexual objectification she is certain to suffer in the hands of Dare, he, at the same time, numbs her potential to desire and find sensual gratification, which, from the beginning of the novel, are seen as a vital process of Kate's self-definition: 'By his words he vanquished and subdued her utterly' (137). By bracketing experience within an unspecified geographical space, the train initially represented an indistinct nowhere, a space detached from its social surroundings – impervious to the laws of morality and convention – nourishing in Kate the illusion of escape not only from her family but also from society. However, as a setting which while in motion has no outlets, a no way out, the compartment becomes an insular microcosm in which Kate's moral shortcomings are exaggerated and her imminent torments in hell made to appear more ominous. The train thus becomes a space of physical and spiritual vulnerability, ultimately crushing Kate, forcing her to deny the body and mortify the flesh. Like the heroine of Broughton's 'Under the Cloak',[4] Kate is anesthetised on the train, forced to confront the dangers of her mobility and to adopt the social and religious identity imposed by the expectations of Christian patriarchy.[5]

As Heller has pointed out, Broughton's narrative is 'ideologically double-voiced, celebrating Kate's exuberant fleshiness on the one hand, but, on the other, making her do penance for her transgressive desire' (88). While the literal crossing of borders that train travel performs is an image suggestive of Kate's potential for the bold transgression of social codes, Kate is unable to see this transgression through, finally dying – 'gladly', the narrative insists – in early middle age, worn out by exhausting social and religious work in total self-abnegation – the course of these years described in less than half a page (176). A novel which similarly explores the limits of female transgression but which allows its heroine to finally enter a marriage that fulfils sexual desire is Dora Russell's *Footprints in the Snow* (1877). A much neglected author, who nevertheless enjoyed popularity and economic success, Russell was viewed by many of her contemporary reviewers and critics as comparable to Collins and the heir of Braddon as far as sensational plots and suspense were concerned.[6] Reviews of her work were mixed, combining a critique of her adherence to an old-fashioned (for the late seventies and eighties) sensationalism with a somewhat embarrassed interest in her plots and characters. A reviewer of *Footprints in the Snow* in *The Saturday Review* remarked that 'its moral is almost, if not quite, as bad as the old-fashioned abduction and seduction plots of the books of a past generation, which are now regarded with pious horror', but at the same time he or she singles it out among the mass of railway novels published in the same year for its 'tolerably exciting plot' and the 'amusement without fatigue' that it offers (Anon., 150). Though her novels are rarely read nowadays, I would agree with Janice Allan in that Russell, with her particularly sensitive portrayal of femininity, 'effectively foregrounds the limitations and inequities of women's roles both within and beyond the domestic sphere' (368). In *Footprints in the Snow* her transgressive heroine, Elizabeth Gordon, chooses a life of precarious mobility outside the marital home, and the treatment of her attempt at autonomy anticipates later presentations of (New) Women's tenuous relation to urban public space and public transport.

Elizabeth Gordon, after discovering her detested husband's guilt in killing her admirer Harry and incriminating her real love, Jasper, decides, in the middle of the night, to leave him and move to London where she can hide from him. In London, however, her life gets entangled with a lecherous, harassing man, Mr Wilmot, who sullies her reputation by spreading lies about her character and conduct, thus complicating and delaying her final reunion with Jasper. I would like to concentrate on the function of the railway in this novel for it becomes the setting which best illustrates Elizabeth's precarious position as a displaced subject striving to retain a balance between transgression and respectability. Her escape to London by train dramatises this struggle for it depicts the ways in which female independence is encumbered by ingrained anxieties and insecurities, practical difficulties, and social prejudices. On her way to the train station in the darkness, Elizabeth's inner determination clashes with her fear of the unknown future embarked on but also with the outer image that she knows she projects as a woman walking alone at night, a woman gone astray. Thus in the eyes of a patrolling policeman, she is not very different from the drunken and homeless woman encountered by Elizabeth in the street who pines for her imprisoned husband. But at the same time, for Elizabeth this woman prefigures the disgrace and degradation that she is apt to suffer as one who has abandoned the home and embraced risky mobility. Similarly, at the train station Elizabeth confronts another version of her potential future when she forms an empathic connection with a working-class woman whose daughter has just died and who stands for the loneliness and alienation that Elizabeth's life in London might generate. Thus the street, the station, and the carriage that she enters, having ensured the company and protection of this kindly, motherly woman by buying her a second-class ticket, become spaces of realisation for Elizabeth as, through multiple mirrorings, they demonstrate to her the thinness of class barriers and the universality of female precariousness: 'Wrapped in our garments of respectability (real or imagined), we shake the dust off our feet, and refuse to admit our relationship – alas! perhaps, were the the [sic] garments gone, our close resemblance – to the sinner and the lost' (103), the narrator remarks, in free indirect discourse voicing the thoughts of Elizabeth. The heroine's experience in the spaces of transit, the street and the railway, where she identifies with the two displaced and degraded women, exposes the false assurances of class and the superficiality of feminine refinement. Only an accident of birth has saved her from squalor in the past, but her birth right will not protect her from the potentiality of mortification in the future. The second-class carriage, therefore, breaks the barriers of class and brings together the two different cases of female displacement and alienation, which, however, Elizabeth recognises as interchangeable. So much does she identify, in terms of emotional pain and economic and moral insecurity, with this rough-looking stranger that in the carriage she is even able to fall asleep, experiencing the homely comfort and motherly protection that only a kinswoman, friend, or relative could provide.

The second-class carriage, therefore, expresses Elizabeth's liminality as she wavers between her middle-class upbringing and the working-class or fallen future that awaits her. But as a middle space it is penetrable from both sides. For it is not only the deprived female stranger who gets to share Elizabeth's more privileged space; as soon as this woman disembarks, the carriage is invaded by a first-class male passenger, Mr Wilmot, who declines his rightful first-class place on the train in order to spend time alone with the beautiful Elizabeth, whom he deems static and malleable as a work of art:

> He was an admirer of beauty this intended traveller – an admirer as some men admire wonderful works of art, and rare pieces of sculpture, and as his cold steady eyes rested on Elizabeth's face, he was struck by its regularity, the nobleness of its expression, its rare and peculiar type. (104)

Exemplifying the authority of class which grants access to all spaces and of gender which privileges the male gaze, this man provokes uneasiness and fear in Elizabeth who is trapped by the rigid borders of the carriage and the intrusiveness of his gaze. But while Elizabeth cultivates an air of respectability and unavailability in her limited interaction with him, her occupancy of the particular carriage, the darkness of the hour, and the fact that she is travelling unescorted suggest otherwise to the man who treats her as a sexually promiscuous woman of indeterminate and thus insignificant social and personal bonds. In fact, it is her reticence and obvious anxiety that most arouse and challenge Wilmot, for they demonstrate a social vulnerability that may be easily taken advantage of in the context of metropolitan anonymity and vastness: 'her reserve only tended to amuse her travelling companion, and make him the more desirous to break through it' (106). With his indiscreet questions and 'scrutinizing gaze' Wilmot exerts sexual authority over the exposed and unprotected woman, who by placing herself in a dubious public space has, in his view, forfeited respectability. By having her heroine treated as a prostitute, even though trains were legitimate means of women's participation in urban and cross-country circulation, Russell thus illustrates a common impasse facing women passengers. Not only does Wilmot forthrightly acknowledge his sexual attraction to her by admitting that it was her face that lured him into the carriage, but he also tries to make her feel guilty for her beauty by blaming her for a possible attack of rheumatism that may afflict him after travelling in the cold and uncomfortable second-class carriage (105–6). In fact this is the second time Elizabeth is made to feel guilty for her attractiveness, as before her escape, her husband had blamed her for his murderous deed which was prompted, in his view, by the jealousy she aroused in him. Russell's text thus raises crucial issues related to violence against women, suggesting that women were made to feel responsible for the aggression or abuse they inspired in men. Whether in the home or the semi-private space of the carriage, Elizabeth has to be immobilised as punishment for negatively mobilising men, even though she does not actively provoke sexual desire.

Elizabeth's adventure in the train, which signifies her passage from the domestic sphere to the public space of work, underlines the dangers that exposure and visibility incur for the woman in social transit. Elizabeth's boldness as she embraces speed, anonymity, and independence of movement is curtailed by social and gender prejudices that the vehicles of transit perpetuated with their permeable tripartite class structure and unstable rules of interaction. The carriage which is the means of Elizabeth's flight from her husband, makes her realise the limits of her transgression, for her longing for freedom is hampered by previsions of class degradation and sexual abuse. Thus Elizabeth's means of access to London also becomes the means of her entrapment within an urban setup in which women's relation to spaces of transit is tenuous and fraught with prejudice and danger. In fact, just as in the station and carriage, in London Elizabeth is monitored by the various policemen who eye her suspiciously as she walks the streets looking for employment and by Wilmot who has ordered his servant to follow her and track her every move and every house she enters. At one point she has to stay indoors for six weeks in order to avoid detection as Wilmot has vowed to hunt her down personally and through the police. Institutional disciplinary policy thus colludes with male gazing tactics in order to read and misrepresent Elizabeth's motives as an urban subject exposed in public space. Moreover, Wilmot manipulates her aims and reputation even further by telling Jasper that she has been passing as his wife since she came to London, hinting that her train escapade and London wanderings prove her sexual looseness and degradation.

However, Russell distinguishes Elizabeth's streetwalking from her sexual desire, legitimising both in their different contexts and locating the latter not in spaces of transit but in private spaces in which Elizabeth exemplifies sexual agency. After her husband dies she does not refrain from giving in to the temptation of a sexual embrace (potentially intercourse) with Jasper, even though he is engaged to be married to another woman, Eva. Interestingly, the novel punishes Jasper and not Elizabeth for their mutual sexual transgression but perhaps also for the fact that he wrongly and too easily conflated Elizabeth's mobility with promiscuity earlier in the novel when he was under the influence of Wilmot. A train crash cripples and disfigures Jasper, undermining his masculine vigour and authority but also releasing him from his engagement to Eva and enabling his marriage to Elizabeth. As Allan has pointed out, the train crash functions, as in Wood's *East Lynne*, as a form of 'retributive judgement' meant to expiate sexual transgression (371). But rather than denying her heroine further sexual desire or satisfaction, 'Russell refuses to countenance any further sacrifice or punishment' (Allan, 371). In fact, Elizabeth is shown to finally fulfil her sexual and emotional desire for Jasper, despite his disfigurement: 'Jasper's handsome face was marred and changed for evermore. Not in Elizabeth's eyes though. The scarred visage to her was more beautiful even than the young lover's had been' (272). With its two train episodes the novel has demonstrated the vulnerability of both sexes when given up to transgression, for the train that victimised Elizabeth on the run from her marriage next punishes Jasper for betraying his vows. By being the epitome of permeability and uncontrollability but also the representative of institutional power, the railway entraps the heroine, the erring wife, in a space of compulsory monitoring and visibility which endangers her ethical and social position; it also mocks the false assurances of Jasper who travels to return to his betrothed after his passionate encounter with Elizabeth. Even though the railway's warnings of fallenness and death do not get fulfilled, at the end of the novel the protagonists are shown to have limited their mobility, Jasper because of his crippling and Elizabeth by choice. The novel returns Elizabeth to the domestic sphere and re-establishes her ties with the middle-class, which had been strained. Yet she recoils from assuming the confident position of visibility that her social status requires. 'Why don't you go out oftener, dressed as you are now? Every one would admire you, Lissa,' remarks her husband (298). For Elizabeth mobility in public spaces has proven the porosity of class barriers and the concomitant disadvantages that the ensuing liminality entails for women. Although the text does not elaborate on the heroine's preferred invisibility at the end of the novel, the fact that she avoids aimless mobility and exposure in the circles of the rich suggests her need to avoid the status of spectacle. On the other hand, she prefers a more purposeful mobility – she becomes 'a very frequent [visitor] among the poor and needy' (298) – where her agency is not subverted and her visibility more meaningful to herself and others.

A third text which associates railway speed with a woman's escape is Margaret Oliphant's short story, 'A Story of a Wedding Tour' (1898), which, by moving its setting to a non-urban, almost Edenic landscape of a French seaside town, partly succeeds in working against the social construction and labelling of gender norms in the metropolitan spaces of transit.[7] Despite her reputation for being a conservative writer, Oliphant provides the reader with an alternative story of a rail experience and its subversive effect on female subjectivity and agency. In Oliphant's story, which uses relentless irony to expose the hypocrisy of charitable high society and to revise the popular Cinderella tale, the trope of the train journey becomes a narrative opportunity for the exploration of a woman's transgressive impulse and for testing the limits of her mobility. The story involves a beautiful orphan girl, Janey, who is adopted by her dead father's business partner and his wife, who lovelessly dress her in cheap clothes and send her to various boarding schools around the world in order to distract their son from her beauty and to enhance 'her commercial value' as a future governess (426). Burdened by her state of financial dependence and tired of the precarious mobility of her home-lessness, she accepts a marriage proposal by an insensitive man who has seen her but twice – the first time briefly on a train – and who is attracted to nothing but her external appearance. Like Kate Chester's in *Not Wisely*, Janey's sensual responses are intense; yet in her case they express the repulsion at being touched by a man who is completely insensitive to her inner self: 'he overwhelmed her with caresses from which she shrank in disgust, almost in terror' (427). During her wedding tour in France and by a twist of fortune, she is left alone on the train and decides to escape from him forever, by changing trains and getting off to settle at a remote seaside town where he is unlikely to look for her. Ten years later, while on the railway platform of the town, together with the son that she didn't know she was carrying on the day of her escape, she sees the long-lost husband rushing past in the express train. Their startled glances meet, but he, being a very nervous and irritable man, suffers a stroke caused by his fury and, fortunately for her, dies before he has the chance to confront her. 'This is how the train brought back to Janey the man whom the train had separated from her ten years before,' Oliphant writes. 'The whole tragedy was one of the railway, the noisy carriages, the snorting locomotives' (439).

Oliphant explores in detail the oppression felt by Janey during the tête-à-tête with her new husband on the train, tracing her fear of the possessive and unresponsive man whose company she is forced to endure within immoveable borders. The train compartment normally locks its occupiers in a mutual gaze which limits the privacy of the woman. In this case, however, Janey's privacy is violated not by his gaze, but by his complete indifference to her emotional needs, an indifference expressed through either unsolicited sexual contact or gratuitous rage, provoking anxiety in Janey and prefiguring the abuse and lack of privacy she would have to suffer in his home. The train's incarcerating effect – it is likened to a cage (433) – foreshadows her submissive imprisonment within the confines of a rigid marriage. However, the train's scheduled motion inadvertently gives Janey the opportunity for independent agency and action. The story acknowledges the paradoxes of train travel – the rigidity of schedules contrasted to human errors, unexpected transitions, and endless unforeseen possibilities: a guard wrongly calls for a twenty- instead of a five-minutes' pause and the husband is accidentally left on the platform while she is still comfortably sitting inside.

> Was it possible that she was alone? Was it possible that for the first time since that terrible moment of her marriage she was more safely by herself than any locked door or even watchful guardian could keep her, quite unapproachable in the isolation of the train? Alone! (428)

From a suffocating space of indifference and abuse, the compartment becomes a liberating setting of female subjectivity, which in this dependent and timid woman triggers 'a mingled sensation of excitement and terror and tremulous delight' (428), eventually turning into a 'sudden acceleration of the movement of her heart' (429) comparable to the acceleration of the locomotive that races her off to freedom. Appropriating the speed of the train Janey becomes a 'fast' woman in a double sense: for society, she is fallible, or even fallen, as a few months later she gives birth to a son, while her marriage is unverified and mis- believed by the new French community she establishes herself in; for herself, the unanticipated acceleration experienced brings emancipation; the mechanical fastness of the train and the fastness of her decisions have enabled her independence.

Being left on the *rapide* alone, and despite the fact that she is an experienced traveller, Janey for the first time has to take control of her own mobility, deciding where to get off and where to resituate herself. Ironically, even on her wedding tour Janey had not been consulted or informed by her husband as to the destinations or hotels of their journey. Therefore, contrasted to the inflexibility, punctuality, and orderly mobility of the world of trains and timetables to which Janey has not been privy, her decision to 'plunge into the unknown' (432), board the next random train, and choose a destination constitutes a case of feminine transgression, one that challenges and even annuls the rigid decisions and routes forged by her husband and which the railway as a patriarchal institution promotes. The woman's need for freedom from confining, prescribed roles is fulfilled through the randomness of the journey and the contingency of the whole incident. 'She did not want to know where she was going' (433), the author writes to emphasise Janey's identification with the haphazardness, fleetingness, and transitoriness of the spontaneous train ride. She moves, however, 'with a quiet assurance and decision', having appropriated the dynamic movement of the train with confidence (432).

As an orphan with ambiguous origins herself, Janey identifies with the randomness of people and identities encountered on the slow train that she next boards, adopting such a random identity herself and deciding to create, from the instability of her unexpected position, a new self which fulfils her emotional and physical desires irrespective of society and the ties which had been imposed on her through unwanted adoption and marriage. As a matter of fact, by welcoming the opportunity for instability, transition, and risk, she rejects the fixed positioning inflicted upon her by her marriage. Disorientation and homelessness become desired states: 'Left home! And she had no home now anywhere, no place to take refuge in [. . .] But Janey did not care!' (433). Oliphant suggests that the train may become the means of women's self-realisation, pleasure, and even reinvention. By fostering temporary meetings and mingling ambiguous, even interchangeable, identities, the train might give a woman the opportunity to acquire a new self or, as in the case of Janey, retrieve a long suppressed one. Relocation via independent mobility may activate rebirth:

> as she looked at herself in the glass [she] encountered the vision of a little face which was new to her. It was not that of Janey, the little governess-pupil; it was not young Mrs Rosendale. It was full of life, and meaning, and energy, and strength. Who was it? Janey? Janey herself, *the real woman*, whom nobody had ever seen before. (emphasis added, 431)

Emerging from the train, unlike Broughton's Kate Chester, Janey is not anaesthetised. Her new identity, 'the real woman', breaking through the restraints of the social constructions of governess and bride which had successfully buried her desires, is derived from the train, whose potency she now emulates. The 'real woman', then, is this transgressive, fast, woman, who would prefer 'to leap from the window, to throw herself into the sea, than to fall into [the] hands' (434) of the man who would, no doubt, once again impose on her silent immobility and denial of life, of energy and strength (431).

Janey's potential for independent and unfettered mobility is rendered in the description of her decisive second journey via the slow local train, which ironically activates her imagination and fulfils her need for escape much more than the *rapide* that she and her husband travelled on. While in the first train the window pane had revealed nothing but the darkness of the night during which they travelled or of the tunnels through which they sped, in the slow train, the window pane becomes the means through which Janey can enlarge her vision and her experience, as she views an array of mountains, villages, and rocks as well as the boundless sea, all of which come to stand for the limitless range of possibilities she may embrace. In the second-class compartment of this train occupied by non-intrusive fellow passengers, Janey's thoughts also reflect a sense of safety and privacy that were not experienced in the former carriage. The suggestive view and the privacy experienced elicit her determination to fix a new destination – 'I will go too' (433).

Her willpower is contrasted to the ineffectuality of her husband, who is forever subject to the restrictions of rigid timetables and set destinations. After all it is the train's scheduled departure that is to blame for his loss of Janey. For all his power as a man of business, he is unable to use the train to his advantage, as a means of regaining his control over his wife. Moreover, contrary to Janey's desire, which finds expression and outlet on the train towards an unspecified location, her husband's desire is contained and denied by the motion of the train. First he is left stranded on the platform while the train with the object of his desire, Janey, in it races off. And secondly, towards the end of the story, in a reversal of the previous scene, he is exasperatingly enclosed within a tight compartment of a rapid train, while Janey, this time the object of his wrath, is standing on the platform. In both cases the train and the platform signify freedom for Janey, while they stand for helplessness and unwilling submission to technology for the husband. The story further elaborates on the man's frustrating inability to go against the regulated mobility of trains through its imagery of motionlessness. During the first train ride, before Janey's escape, the husband is constantly asleep, and, ten years after the incident, passing by in the express, he is sitting with his foot supported on a cushion, suffering from immobilising gout, while he is also depicted by the narrator as a lifeless 'apparition' (435), an image foreshadowing his death. On seeing Janey on the platform he roars with anger, but his roar is muffled by the tunnel into which the train inexorably plunges (435), thwarting his desire for immediate revenge, and triggering, we assume, a stroke which turns him into a 'great inert mass' (439), a still corpse to be carried out of the train.[8]

And yet the story does not end in triumph, even though Janey is forever freed from her brutal husband and even though her son is acknowledged as the dead man's heir:

> She had not blamed herself before; but now seemed to herself no less than the murderer of her husband: and could not forgive herself, nor get out of her eyes the face she had seen, nor out of her ears the dreadful sound of that labouring breath. (439)

In these last words of the short story, the transgressive woman sees herself through the eyes of society as a *femme fatale*, a murderer, whose unsubmissive acts have brought atrophy – consider the gout – and death to the man she was supposed to nurture as a wife. Reminded of the wifely obligations and the angel-in-the-house role that she renounced in order to pursue her desire for independence, she internalises the guilt that society expects her to feel, becoming fully possessed and restricted by the memory of the dead man brought out of the train. His helplessness, compared to her – selfish – strength, serves to indict her as a woman who has criminally dared to reverse gender relations, with tragic results. Not unlike Broughton's story, then, Oliphant's, on the one hand, celebrates transgression and independence for women, but, on the other, does not let its heroine disengage herself completely from the deeply ingrained moral implications of such deviant behaviour. Like Kate Chester and Elizabeth Gordon, Janey has to do 'penance for her transgressive desire' (Heller, 88). The ending unambiguously declares, 'The whole tragedy was one of the railway' (439). The railway – representative of random encounters, coincidences, and accidents – which helped to conceal her identity in the first place, is the one which in a similarly random fashion re-establishes her social identity at the expense of the fantasy she had given life to during the ten years of her stay in France. In this sense her happiness in the Edenic St Honorat could not have been anything but ephemeral. Bracketed within this remote part of the world, her desire found fulfilment only to the extent that chance (the railway) permitted it. Tainted with the moral stigma of a woman who has reprehensibly appropriated mobility to her selfish advantage, Oliphant's heroine, at the very end of the story, has to pick up from where she left off, reactivating a life which seems not worth telling.

Urban Speed: Women and Traffic in Henry James's London Underground

Chastising or hiding themselves at the very end of their stories, the heroines of Broughton, Russell, and Oliphant seem to negate their life-giving mobility, choosing – or being obliged – to step back from the liminal space of possibilities into the familiar locus of conventional gender relations. The railway as a site of social and sexual licence tests the limits of their potential, though their experience of speed tends to represent not a practice of everyday life, to use de Certeau's terms, but a chance in a lifetime, a temporary opportunity to resist gender constraints – a destination chosen but ultimately abandoned or deferred. In his complex portrayal of women who famously choose the difficult path, Henry James also made use of the liminal spaces of the railway. It could be argued that in his exploration of the relationship between subjectivity and space, James rejects the gendered mapping of the spheres, challenging the idea of the spatially and socially bound female interiority. In this sense the railway, even more than other urban spaces such as the street or the park, with its mobile and indefinite geography, its contingent and tentative social codes, and the ambiguous identities that it propagates, allows for a subtle study of women's sexuality in the famous Jamesian style of writing that relies on indeterminacy, omission, and silence.

Trains feature in many of James's novels, stories, travel writing, and essays. They appear not only as rapid conveyances, carrying his characters to and fro, but also as metaphors suggestive of continuous motion, speed, discomfort, containment, and even periodical literature. In his essay entitled 'Criticism', first published in *New Review* in 1891 as 'The Science of Criticism', the train and the railway station are used to illustrate the devaluation of literary criticism by the multitude of periodicals which fill their pages with crude and vulgar reviews, like a train whose seats are filled with 'dummies' just because it is not allowed to leave unless every seat is occupied:

> A stuffed mannikin is thrust into the empty seat, where it makes a creditable figure till the end of the journey. It looks sufficiently like a passenger, and you know it is not one only when you perceive that it neither says anything nor gets out. ('Criticism', 260)

Produced for and consumed by the masses and threatening to stifle and eventually fully replace quality literature, like dummies replacing passengers, these commodified reviews, like cargo, are part of an industry aimed at speedily conveying the public towards a predictable and predetermined destination – a railway station, the epitome of publicity and financial exchange: 'we blunder in and out of the affair [the critical sense] as if it were a railway station – the easiest and most public of the arts' (263). James's metaphors convey his abhorrence of publicity and mass circulation at a time when profit and popularity had entered the scope of literary production, and male and female authors had successfully made writing a profession, earning their living from periodicals which published their serialised works. Their success depended to a large extent on the market system and their income on the popularity of their stories. James followed their example by maximising profit through the writing profession, but his narratives often express the conflict he must have felt between mass production and his own high standards of writing,[9] a conflict often articulated in his stories of celebrity writers, like himself, who are forced to negotiate a private consciousness with a public persona. The contradiction between James's dense and inaccessible – private – style of his late career and his attempt to achieve success with a more popular medium, the stage, in the same time period, signifies that the writer found publicity as alluring as it was threatening. His interest in the erosion of boundaries between public and private space, detected in his plots which involve the railway, may, therefore, have arisen from his own experience as a writer who was forced to juggle aspirations to literary uniqueness with an intense gratification at the material rewards of his talent. The conflict between James's insistence on quality, on the one hand, and his delight in mass entertainment, on the other, exemplifies exactly the power of publicity to encroach on the private self.

Writing at a time when women were increasingly repudiating the domesticity of the private sphere, James often preoccupies himself with the porosity of the boundary between private and public space and with the social, sexual, and moral consequences of women's physical exposure in spaces of transit. However, James is not interested in facile labels which would mark his mobile women as fast, fallen, or immoral, but in the ambiguity of identities that proliferate in such settings. In this section I will look primarily at James's use of the London Underground, a means of transportation that he rarely used himself,[10] but which seems to have fired his imagination in the cases of two important texts, his 1888 story 'A London Life' and *The Wings of the Dove* (1902). In the words of David Pike, 'The first-class Underground could be simultaneously a space of propriety and one of transgression, by turn private and public', a setting in which characters would typically struggle 'with their own middle-class values' (46).

One of the most memorable scenes in *The Wings of the Dove* is the chance encounter of Kate Croy and Merton Densher in the London

Underground – a chance encounter following their first meeting at a party, during which they had experienced a brief yet paradoxically sustained moment of sexual chemistry: it had not 'simply [been] that their eyes had met; other conscious organs, faculties, feelers had met as well' (38). Until their second meeting in the Tube six months later, Kate fixes that moment in her memory in terms of a vivid image which combines the magnetic effect of each other's gaze with the sensual elevation simultaneously experienced:

> She had observed a ladder against a garden wall, and had trusted herself so to climb it as to be able to see over into the probable garden on the other side. On reaching the top she had found herself face to face with a gentleman engaged in a like calculation at the same moment, and the two inquirers had remained confronted on their ladders. The great point was that for the rest of that evening they had been perched – they had not climbed down; and indeed, during the time that followed, Kate at least had had the perched feeling – it was as if she were there aloft without a retreat. (38)

It is quite ironic and perhaps sadly prophetic, therefore, that their next 'lofty' and most significant meeting, which 'had been the real beginning – the beginning of everything else' (39), takes place in the abysmal depths of the London Underground, the setting of the 'sewer' or the 'sardine box' railway, as it had been dubbed by *Punch* since the 1860s. In his description of the carriage, consistent with many depictions of the Metropolitan Railway as an infernal Hades filled with fumes emanating not only from the engine but also from the pipes of the smoking passengers, in the 'British habit',[11] James insists on its darkness and the smokiness of the atmosphere. And yet, Kate and Densher 'looked across the choked compartment exactly as if she had known he would be there and he had expected her to come in' (39). Despite its public function and the arbitrariness of encounters on the train, the Underground, with its out-of-view location and the enclosing effect of its carriages, fosters private meetings which are described as predictable and habitual visits to each other's homes. Kate's almost blasé reaction to Densher's sudden appearance aims to convey to her co-passengers, and to a certain extent, to Densher as well, that the Underground is part of her everyday routine, and, therefore, there is nothing extraordinary in her unexpected meeting with him. The narrative, however, suggests that the fortuitousness of their encounter, evidence of the Underground's capacity to generate coincidences, bestows on their meeting a fatality which is treated with a pregnant silence concealing sentiments and sensations inappropriate to air in public. As the train moves through the tunnels and beyond the various stations on the way to Kate's destination, 'Queen's Road', Densher, by lengthening his own journey by a few stops, manages to shorten the distance between him and Kate, first moving to a seat exactly opposite her and finally, when opportunity arises, to the seat next to her.[12]

But though the free seating allowed on the Underground offers Densher such opportunities for stealthy moves facilitating romance, propriety still did not. The couple's timid yet suggestive glances are met with the regulating stares of the fellow passengers, and Kate is more than conscious of the critical gaze of the young man opposite her who appears to have detected her more than welcome reception of Densher's approach. On the one hand the Underground train, like other urban spaces, offered anonymity and freedom of movement, fostering the paradoxical isolation experienced in the midst of an unknown crowd, but, on the other, it did not free its passengers, especially female passengers conspicuously belonging to the upper middle class, of restricting rules of interaction between men and women imposed by domestic ideology and social etiquette. As Amy Richter has argued, trains created 'a type of public domesticity', which 'attempted to bring the cultural associations and behaviors of home life to bear upon social interactions among strangers, to regulate public interactions and delineate the boundary of Victorian respectability' (*Home*, 60). As a result, 'Aboard the trains, [women] were subject to dual expectations: to maintain their private roles and to learn and conform to the rules governing much of public life' (*Home*, 37). However, in the Underground, especially in the Tube that Kate most likely boarded, eye to eye contact could not easily be avoided as there was no view from the window towards which one could direct one's gaze, especially during such awkward moments as that experienced by Kate and Densher. [13] And yet it is precisely this tension between what is allowed and what not in the public space of the train that tantalises the particular couple of *The Wings of the Dove*, indicating to them both, and to the reader, the inevitability of their intense mutual attraction: 'this very restriction perhaps made such a mark for them as nothing else could have done' (39).

In the Underground train, despite the regulated speed and route of the journey, Kate and Densher experience intense, unregulated desire, expressed in terms of mobility and distance which lose coherence and geographical specificity:

> The extraordinary part of the matter was that they were not in the least meeting where they had left off, but ever so much farther on, and that these added links added still another between High Street and Notting Hill Gate, and then between the latter station and Queen's Road an extension really inordinate. (39)

Losing time and space, as the passage suggests, despite the invasive materiality of the suffocating setting and the inquisitive gazes of the fellow passengers, Kate and Densher, through furtive and discontinuous glances at each other, feel connected on the level of consciousness, 'as if they had come together in some bright level of the desert' (39), a space at once expansive and solitary, in which the performance of identity and desire may not be dependent on location. The particular physical setting of the Underground, therefore, with its dual impact on the characters, as an open and closed space, public and private, is connected, through James's dense, image-ridden prose, to transcendental spaces of consciousness – the top of the ladder and the desert. Rather than being an inert place, subject to timetables and regulated mobility, the railway carriage seems to become an interiorised, multi-dimensional, and even libidinal space which creates opportunities for romantic encounters, facilitated by the unavoidable proximity between men and women.

James himself was not particularly keen to witness public exhibitions of romance in railway spaces. In a memorable passage in *The American Scene* (1907) the 'restless analyst' or 'student of manners' (9, 8) at a Savannah train station cringes at the sight of bare-headed young women 'in the company of young men to match' who 'treat the place, in the public eye, that of the crowded contemplative cars, quite as familiar, domestic, intimate ground, set apart [. . .] for the innocently immodest ventilation of their puerile privacies at which the moralizing visitor so frequently gasps' (316). In James's words, there is no distinction between a 'place of passage' and a 'place of privacy' (166) in America, as modern urban spaces have effaced the difference between public and private. The blurring of this line has led to the lamentable, for James, erosion of manners, as intimate familiarity is now flaunted unashamedly at every setting, like the railway, which naturally mingles the modern economic concerns of a market society with personal interests and even secrets.

In *The Wings of the Dove*, however, which employs English and European settings, the question of manners in public spaces is intricately related to class. In terms of class, Kate occupies a liminal position, as the first pages of the novel make clear. Looking at herself in the dull mirror of her father's cheap lodgings, she wishes to mark her own difference from her vulgar surroundings which stand for her limiting class origins: 'personally, at least, she was not chalkmarked for the auction' (7). Yet her active participation in the everyday practices of metropolitan life is incompatible with the normative standards of proper feminine behaviour required by the upper-class circles that she wants to infiltrate. As her aunt Maud often remarks disapprovingly, Kate's public performances of familiarity with the opposite sex in various locations of the city compromise her access to high society and her potential for a noble marriage. However, Kate, having mastered public transport, is not merely an urban female pedestrian, a streetwalker prone to the ignominious labels attributed by social intolerance. For her the train has a twofold function: as a vehicle of modernity,[14] inextricably linked to technological advance and financial exchange, it makes her a dynamic part of the city's progressive practices. At the same time it functions as an antidote to the monotony of regulated – and anachronistic – upper-class social practices, providing instead opportunities for stimulating transgression. Kate is bored of stagnant salon life and desires sensual stimulation in urban settings which exemplify the social borderland that she inhabits. The subterranean area of the city that she seems so comfortable in, which until the building of the Underground railway was only inhabited by social outcasts,[15] and which was often linked to vulgar sexual desire, rather than associating Kate with her lower-class origins and restricted upbringing, provides instead freedom from norms. The ambiguous sexual relations cultivated in the liminal space of the Underground, which successfully obscures identities, contest the idea of stable gender hierarchies and rigid social and moral codes. It could be argued, therefore, that although urban mobility through transport is incongruous with her aspirations for upward mobility, for Kate it is a means of resisting immobilising class signification and of flouting artificial types of femininity which bind her to either end of the social ladder. Alternating comfortably between transitory settings, using their locational provisionality to her advantage by knowingly deploying her sexuality as a performance in accordance with the norms of each setting, Kate is able to both imitate and mock high society manners and morals. However, by resisting closure, the ending of the novel, which alludes to a disconcertingly ambiguous future for Kate, also points at the dangers of liminality, of constantly appropriating interstitial positions. I will return to these dangers of displacement that James's train narratives ultimately evoke.

Questions of propriety and public transport are also explored in James's earlier 1888 piece, 'A London Life', in which two American characters, opting to take the 'mysterious underground railway' from Victoria Station for their touristy ramble around town, contemplate the respectability of their actions: 'No, no, this is very exceptional,' Laura Wing tells her companion, Mr Wendover; 'if we were both English – and both what we are otherwise [young and unmarried] – we wouldn't go so far' (77). Her words, expressing Victorian standards of social and sexual propriety, suggest a conflation between extreme mobility and transgression – between going 'so far' physically, literally, by means of speedy transport, and going 'so far' figuratively, boldly going against rules of decorum which required of unmarried English girls to avoid the company of unmarried men in public. As Americans, however, used to more uninhibited interaction between the sexes, Laura and Wendover feel free to wander in the city together, taking advantage of the public means of transportation and enjoying the contingencies, 'the spice of the unforeseen' (79), that such mobility might offer. Nevertheless her remark exposes an internal conflict resulting from her liminal position between two nations and two norms of morality and manners, as, in the words of Merle Williams, Laura is 'integrated into English mores yet resistant to their wholehearted assimilation' (197). In this sense, Laura's urban journey constitutes a dramatisation of her liminality, as she freely and spontaneously alternates vehicles and means of transportation (the Underground, hansoms, walking), wilfully appropriating transitional settings. By embracing ephemerality in this way, Laura manages to defy the regularity of English life that she judges in moral terms: 'She had often before been struck with [. . .] that perfection of machinery that can still at certain times make English life go on of itself with a stately rhythm long after corruption is within it' (23). Underground technology, despite its mechanical motion, '*its* stately rhythm', and despite its being a closed system of transport, is treated by Laura as a space of infinite possibility, a means of liberating the self from routine, embracing contingency, and rejecting the regularity of the social 'machinery' which she finds invidiously disciplinary. For Laura urban mobility thus becomes an antidote to rigid social structures, to the extent that she momentarily even excuses Selina's – her married sister's – adulterous exploits:

> it might have been the same mere happy sense of getting the heavy British order itself off her back that had led that lady [Selina] to go over to Paris and ramble with Captain Crispin. Possibly they had done nothing worse than visit together the Invalides and Notre Dame. (79)

Entering and exiting the underground railway, Laura experiences a multiplication of identity, identifying as much with her puritanical American femininity as with the progressive European version of married womanhood that her sister has adopted. Her vertical movement as she descends and ascends, in the Underground and out on the surface, reflects her attempt to negotiate these moral potentials which traditionally have been hierarchised as relating to the depths of hell or to the heights of heaven.

The underground train journey which facilitates innocent sightseeing and spontaneous decisions, is, a few pages later, juxtaposed to another underground scene taking place in the basement of the Soane Museum in London, in which Laura, who has again descended, is confronted with Selina's blatant adultery. It seems that Laura cannot, after all, escape the corruption inherent in the social machinery she described in the beginning of the novella. Both spaces are dark and labyrinthine, favouring concealment. In fact Laura describes the museum basement in terms of a series of underground tunnels, 'of dim irregular vaults, passages, and little narrow avenues' (80), suggesting a continuity between her two underground adventures, both of which have taken place in settings at once private and public, out of sight and light but at the same time freely penetrable by the public gaze. During and after this scene, as Philip Horne has argued, a distorted mirroring between the two sisters takes place (xxii–xxiii). Selina, for whom the city's underground settings conveniently provide concealment and anonymity, subverts the logic of her sister's reasoning, telling Laura that it is the latter's behaviour that is irregular: it is Laura who defies a social machinery which tolerates adultery but not free mobility in young, unmarried girls: 'it was not your finding me that was out of the way,' Selina pronounces; 'it was my finding you – with your remarkable escort! That was incredible' (88). But in these scenes, with the two settings presented as interchangeable – the museum basement as the Underground and vice versa – it is the mirroring of the surroundings that produces this multiplying effect on the sisters. By being paratactically placed underground, in the setting that tolerates corruption and impropriety, the sisters are presented as interchangeable, with Laura's moral codes being levelled out with those of her sister. The succession of Laura's feelings in the two parallel settings, from the thrilling agency experienced in the London Underground to the insidious entrapment felt in the museum basement, exposes Victorian gender contradictions, as the new urban spaces supposedly open to women in reality served to maintain and sediment gender and social hierarchies, despite women's delusions of independent mobility. Unlike Kate Croy, who, created fourteen years later, is able to take advantage of the melding of private and public in the spaces of transit that she opts to occupy, the American Laura Wing is unable to negotiate moral integrity with social propriety and is crushed by the force of ideology.

The underground scenes, therefore, mark moments of undoing and rupture, moments during which codes of morality and manners fall apart or clash and are subverted. Rhizomatic by nature, establishing contingent connections just as much as they break them, the sprawling underground settings in James's fiction seem to embody Deleuze and Guattari's 'acentered, nonhierarchical, nonsignifying system [. . .] defined solely by a circulation of states' (21). With their rhizomatic, unruly expansion in all directions, the Underground and the basement foster arbitrariness and incoherence, nullifying beginnings and endings, offering, instead, opportunities for multiplication, as the interchangeability between the two sisters indicates. For Laura and Selina, the unexpected twists and turns of the literally rhizomatic setting reveal hidden realities about their motives and personal histories. The seeming symmetry of the two sisters' progression underground, as they have both pursued their selfish paths of desire, turns into a distorted doubling, which serves to challenge the moral hierarchies according to which each has moved. Because in the system of the rhizome, as Deleuze and Guattari argue, 'one can never posit a dualism or a dichotomy, even in the rudimentary form of the good and the bad [. . .] Good and bad are only the products of an active and temporary selection, which must be renewed' (9–10). James blurs the line between good and bad, between the two sisters and between the two settings, and although each sister follows a different social trajectory and different moral imperative, they are both exposed as belonging to this rhizomatic anti-structure, in which logic works against morality and (im)morality works against logic. After the rupture, the disastrous meeting of the two rhizomes – for Laura and her sister might also be viewed as rhizomes, in accordance with the Deleuze-Guattari paradigm – which threatens both sisters with exposure, the narrative again moves towards obscurity, treating the incident with mystification – having 'these wanderers', Selina and her lover, '[melt] away as it were, disappearing in the gloom or in the labyrinth of wonders. The whole encounter had been but the business of an instant' (81). The contingency of the meeting is complemented by the contingency of its dissolution. Michael Freeman has argued that underground journeys gave travellers an 'inchoate sense of space' as 'Underground lines offered a journey into spacelessness. There was no vista from the window, no cinematic encounter, no means of geographical orientation' ('The Railway Age', 27). The complex of underground locations, which defy the discipline of ordered, bounded space, having contingent links to each other and to the more geographically fixed surface, disorients Laura, making her too into a wanderer. Forcing her to confront her own liminality, these spaces of transition compel her to adopt, albeit reluctantly, the 'fast' profile imposed on her by her sister.

   In the pivotal scene taking place in the transitory space of the opera box, in which she is left alone with Wendover by her sister who runs off with her lover, Laura becomes conscious of her own respectability at risk by her sister's dishonour and by the fact that she has been intentionally abandoned in the theatre box, 'this little upholstered receptacle which was so public and yet so private' (112), in the company of a man who has no intention of asking her to marry him, although she very

Figure 6. George du Maurier, 'In the Metropolitan Railway', *Punch* (12 January 1878): 6.

ineptly tries to force the question out of him. Her experience in the dark box, which combines exposure and intimacy, is not so different from that in the museum basement and the underground train. James collapses the distinctions between these settings conceptually erasing the boundaries between them. Here again it is her wounded sense of security that takes over her vision, as once again Selina's unpredictable actions challenge Laura's sense of right and wrong, forcing her to voice her desire. The opera box, like the museum basement, has the same disorienting, nauseating effect of spacelessness, obliterating the actual opera being performed below, and suggesting to her the precariousness of her own integrity in the eyes of high society: 'the whole place about became a blur and a swim through which she heard the tuning of fiddles' (112). The underground train, the hansom, the museum basement, and the opera box are all liminal settings of great opportunity for the women examined. And yet as spaces of transit, as multiple plateaus, as Deleuze and Guattari might say, by functioning as distorted reflections of each other, they also point to the dangers of displacement, of moving in the margins of binary gender rules, and at the disorientation, or crisis of sexual identity, that ensues.

Women's disorientation is an obsessive preoccupation in James's writing. One again is tempted to evoke *The American Scene*, in which, in the same section on Savannah quoted from earlier, titled 'The Exposed Maiden', James contemplates the 'disconcerting' 'public behaviour' of young American women in a train station, who 'suffer from [. . .] the tragedy of their social, their cruel exposure' (317). Suggesting an affinity between the opportunities and prospects available, on the one hand, to these uninstructed, 'uncorrected' young women and, on the other, to the commercial travellers, the bagmen or drummers, who crowd the stations, James imagines one of the girls pleading: 'Ah, once *place* me and you'll see – I shall be different, I shall be better' (317). By not being 'placed' within the borders of such social and geographical demarcations which, in James's view, inspire mutual respectability not only on the level of manners but also of intellect, these hatless young women seem no less displaced and disorientated than the bagmen, the perpetually moving commercial travellers, whose way of life is defined by the contingency of the traffic in which they are involved. The bagmen are 'not relegated, shaded, embowered, protected' (316), James writes, in the sense that as representatives of commerce/business, the occupation that has overshadowed every other in American society, they have outnumbered other types of professionals, developing on their own, outside a more inclusive 'social landscape' that would allow their progress in proportion with other social or intellectual values or advancements. Similarly, in his depiction of the young girls who crowded the railway station and other spaces of transit, James is critical of their lack of social placement. While women's physical mobility is often seen as synonymous with their emancipation, in James's view, their swarming presence in the station becomes a measure of their social and psychological displacement (as in the case of Laura Wing) and proof of their participation in a commercialised sexual exchange (as in the case of Laura's sister, Selina). 'Isn't it too late,' the maiden asks; 'and am I not, don't you think, practically lost?' (318). The figurative limbo that these young girls find themselves in, rendered through diction and metaphors of place and non-place, finds its literal expression in the physical setting of the railway which stands for transit, vagrancy, and contingency. Similarly, at the end of 'A London Life', Laura is once again homeless, 'staying with distant relatives in Virginia' (146), 'lost', like her compatriots from *The American Scene*, not only in her social disgrace, but also from the scrutiny of the reader, as she loses her narrative position as a centre of consciousness – an enigmatic Jamesian stylistic move to which I will return at the end of this chapter.

Women in literal or figurative transit or vagrancy is a persistent theme in James, visualised best, I think, in *What Maisie Knew*, through his image of Maisie Farange, the young daughter of divorced and multiply adulterous parents, as the soaring 'feathered shuttlecock' (24) flying between mother's and father's house, 'rushing to and fro [. . .] changing of places' (76). Whether voluntary or involuntary, literal or metaphorical, movement seems to be the only constant around which female identity is oriented in James. One of the most heartbreaking scenes in *What Maisie Knew* takes place in the railway station of Boulogne, where Maisie, having tried out many parent figures ranging from her governess who becomes stepmother, to her two step-parents who eventually become lovers and to her final loyal governess, dreams of escape with her favourite step-parent, Sir Claude. The transitory platform here conveys not only the lamentable precariousness of Maisie's whole domestic existence but also her own liminality, between childish innocence and sexual knowledge, as she proposes to Sir Claude that he take her to Paris, forever severing the sexual attachment that he has with her former governess now turned stepmother. Maisie, having realised that she will always be the unwanted third wheel in families not biologically bound to her, tries to force a twosome, by means of a train ride, whose associations with elopements and illicit love affairs epitomise the blurring of the line between filial and romantic love experienced by Maisie: 'She knew how prepared they looked to pass into the train, and she presently brought out to her companion: "I wish we could go. Won't you take me?"' (235). The longed-for train, eventually not taken, represents her means of acquiring not only a stable parent/partner, but also agency, escaping the passivity and submissiveness of childhood in favour of transgressing, breaching the boundaries of forbidden adult knowledge which posits sexual desire as its most potent arbiter. For Maisie, then, the train becomes the aborted means of becoming an adult. The novel ends with Maisie, once again under the protection of a governess, on the steamer (another means of transit) on a voyage towards a new ineffable location, in between two worlds, England and France; the steamer becomes a symbol of the characteristic transitory position that many Jamesian women find themselves in, in the final pages of his novels.

In this sense, I would like to suggest that James's heroines, who roam the cities and appropriate its transitory pleasures, are located in the realm of what Homi Bhabha has termed the 'beyond', a conceptual space exemplified by a 'sense of disorientation, a disturbance of direction', 'an exploratory, restless movement', a 'here and there' (1); only I would like to slightly modify his description by rendering this 'in-between' space of women's occupancy as a *neither* here *nor* there', with the final destination indefinitely deferred, sometimes willingly, as in the case of Kate Croy and Laura Wing in their underground locations, and at other times reluctantly, as in the case of Maisie. The spaces of the city, like the railway station and the compartment, which have often been described as interchangeable with other settings under or over ground, and which combine a sense of privacy with the inevitable fate of exposure, emphasise the liberating but also dangerous consequences of this locational provisionality that James's women experience.

It might be argued that, roaming the exotic metropolis through its modern means of transportation, James's women experience a global, a cosmopolitan, not merely an urban, expansion. But to what extent does their urban cosmopolitanism offer them liberating detachment without reminding them (especially the American female characters) of their own uprootedness? And to what extent do the speed and transitoriness of the urban motion make them part of the vibrant metropolitan tempo without subjecting them even more to the fragmentation that swiftly changing and unbounded localities entail? If, as Judith R. Walkowitz has argued, in the late nineteenth century London's cosmopolitanism consisted in 'transnational forms of commercialized culture', 'foreign practices, bodies, and spaces that came to mark the central area of London's West End as a site of pleasure and danger' (430), it seems that James's American heroines are part of this international spectacle; they are seen either as exotic, a 'marked specimen of American freshness', like Laura Wing in 'A London Life' (6), or simply as 'a success', like Milly Theale in the London of *The Wings of the Dove*. In fact, Milly realises her limiting position as spectacle – commodity or even cargo – in the figurative space of a railway compartment in which she imagines herself having been mentally forced by Lord Mark:

> she was more and more sharply conscious of having [. . .] been popped into the compartment in which she was to travel for him. It was a use of her that many a girl would have been doubtless quick to resent [. . .] Milly had practically just learned from him, had made out, as it were, from her rumbling compartment, that [. . .] [s]he was a success. (104)

As in the previous examples of train scenes, the imaginary compartment here stands for the transitory space, the borderland, which serves to meld, in this case violently, Milly's private consciousness with the public function that her London friends impose on her. Contrary to the American girls in the Savannah railway station, who, as James lamented, had never been 'placed', in London Milly does feel 'placed' (*Wings*, 104), but placed within an invidious urban landscape that appropriates her subjectivity and thwarts her desire with its relentless social and economic strategies. Compartmentalised, Milly is thus categorised and defined, her love of risk, unpredictability, and invisibility (manifested in her love of steep precipices and urban labyrinths) thwarted by the calculating manipulation of those who forge her path and plan her route for her.[16]

In other words, while urban spaces, like the railway or Underground, have been traditionally viewed as sites of female emancipation, James, through his multiple distorted mirrorings of literal and figurative settings, seems to problematise women's 'triumph' in the city, by pointing our attention not only towards their success as independent, mobile subjects, but also towards the price of such success. In his illustration of women who seek spatial independence, James conceptualises the disadvantages of their ungrounded position at the fin de siècle, the feeling of unhomeliness that arises when his heroines realise their contingency within a precarious setting which epitomises motion and traffic. The novels and short stories discussed end with their heroines in transit, but James's endings refuse to provide us with their destination. The stylistic evasion by which James does not fix their future at the end of his stories, the disappearing act of Laura Wing, Milly Theale, Kate Croy, and Maisie Farange becomes his ultimate political gesture of corroborating the heroines' new understanding of their precarious place in the modern city. Paradoxically, the invisibility that James grants his heroines at the end of his novels, as he frees their desire from authorial control, and as they free themselves from the male hero's gaze and also from the readers' scrutiny, seems to be the only plausible freedom Jamesian women enjoy within urban culture.

Notes

1. In a number of short stories in British periodicals, not only are men not punished for flirting endlessly with or even stalking women in train carriages, but also they are rewarded for their persistence with marriage to the woman relentlessly gazed at or chatted up on the train.
2. See also my reading of Broughton's novel in *Critical Survey*.
3. See Freeman, *Railways and the Victorian Imagination*, 184.
4. See relevant analysis in Chapter 1.
5. The scene of Kate's reform on the train very much resembles a scene in Mrs Humphry Ward's novel, *Lady Rose's Daughter* (1903). In this novel, Julie LeBreton is intercepted at a Paris train station by her worthy admirer, Jacob Delafield who suspects her plan to elope with the unworthy Captain Warkworth and wants to save her from disgrace. So her sought after journey of pleasure is replaced by a train ride back home towards respectability. 'You are saved,' Jacob imagines himself telling her (345). Like Broughton's Kate Chester, in the carriage Julie experiences the suffocation of having to suppress sexual desire and is rendered helpless and motionless. Her deviant mobility has been successfully checked, and she now runs

on the right lines. Passivity and sacrifice of desire ensure her happiness in matrimony.

6. See Janice Allan for a comprehensive overview of Russell's reception and her publishing history.

7. See also my reading of Oliphant's story in Gómez Reus and Gifford's *Women in Transit*.

8. This motif of male immobility on the train is also used by Rhoda Broughton in many of her train scenes where men, whether criminals or friends, are described as hardly moving – pillar- or dummy-like. See my discussion of Broughton's *Nancy,* 'Under the Cloak', and *Second Thoughts* in Chapter 4.

9. George Eliot was also troubled by what she saw as the incompatibility between popularity or financial success (which were manifested in the plethora of novels figuring on the railway stalls) and literary merit. Still she acknowledges the importance of the railway vending spaces that had generated a new and important category of readers. In a letter to John Blackwood (11 September 1866), she wrote,

> And yet I sicken again with despondency under the sense that the most carefully written books lie, both outside and inside people's minds, deep undermost in a heap of trash. I suppose the reason my 6/ editions are never on the railway stalls is partly of the same kind that hinders the free distribution of [*Felix Holt*]. They are not so attractive to the majority as 'The Trail of the Serpent'; still a minority might sometimes buy them if they were there. (Haight 4: 309–10)

10. In a letter to his sister Alice, dated 10, 12 March [1869], James wrote

> This same underground railway, by the way, is a marvellous phenomenon – ploughing along in a vast circle thro' the bowels of London, & giving you egress to the upper earth in magnificent stations, at a number of convenient points. The trains are the same as above ground – [*blacked out bit*] but for cheapness. I went on Monday from the Nortons, in Kensington, to the Barings in the heart of the city, 1st class, for sixpence. As for speed, owing to the frequent stoppages, I should have gone faster in a Hansom; but I should have paid several shillings. Of course at each end I had a little walk to the station. (*Complete Letters*, 234)

11. According to R. D. Blumenfeld (qtd in Pike, 39). Pike elaborates on the trope of the infernal city applied to underground railway spaces.

12. David Welsh describes this scene as a 'musical chairs' game in 'the first novel to treat the [Underground Railway] system as a playground'. In his reading the Tube becomes 'a location of emotional fulfilment and engagement' (126).

13. Kate must have boarded the Central London Railway line, or the Twopenny Tube. But by the time of this novel a new train had been introduced by the City and South London Railway line, whose design had eliminated clear glass windows in favour of small narrow mirrors and tinted glass openings.

14. According to Vadillo, 'Mass-transport facilities were not just vehicles for moving across the different cartographies of London. They were vehicles,

tools of modernity, which the passenger used to inquire about modern life' (27).

15. See Rosalind Williams, 63. Also, as David Pike writes, 'Underground London in the nineteenth century was primarily represented as a negative, organic space, a space of cellars and rookeries, of disease and filth, of prostitution and crime' (105).

16. See Lisi Schoenbach for a powerful reading of the difference between Milly's refusal to categorise people and predict their actions, her embrace of 'freedom and incalculability', and Lord Mark's, Densher's, and Kate's calculated prediction of her actions: 'that Milly will fall in love with Densher and will, upon her death, leave him her fortune, which will enable him finally to marry Kate' (111).

Chapter 3

Breaching National Borders: Rail Travel in Europe and Empire

Women and Railway Tourism in Anthony Trollope and Henry James

Chapters 1 and 2 have concentrated on fictional representations of women's rail travel within national borders, in local narratives of adventure, fear, or romance in which women figured as domestic or transgressive figures braving the challenges of railway travel, that is, orientation, timetables, suspicious or abusive co-passengers, and heavy luggage. However, train travel was also women's means of acquiring an international geographical consciousness, and the aim of this chapter is to explore narratives which investigate wider geographical settings. In an age of heightened tourism the railway provided middle- and upper-class women with easy accessibility to the world, multiplying their opportunities for geographical mobility and intercultural knowledge, while at the same time making them part of an interconnected world rendered possible by the European rail networks which collapsed distances, creating the illusion of international connectivity among borderless nations. It has been widely argued that cosmopolitanism in the nineteenth century was mostly the privilege of men who had cultivated international artistic and literary tastes through travel and frequent relocation within Europe, and who, as James Buzard has argued, tended to establish a horizontal class consciousness, whose transnationality served to give men a shared sense of 'responsibility for the welfare of Europe as a whole' ('The Grand Tour', 40, 41). This humanitarian and political vision of cosmopolitanism which transcended national borders was not necessarily shared by women travellers who, apart from aesthetic cultivation and social facility in the international salon settings, had, due to social disenfranchisement, limited or no opportunity to partake of the exalted sociopolitical objectives of cosmopolitanism; nevertheless, the accessibility of Europe through the railway network allowed them to approximate in part this condition of intercultural cultivation and global consciousness which exceeded women's domestic or ethnically restricted realm. In the latter part of this section, I will return to the question of the extent to which international railway travel enabled women to embody classical and contemporary characteristics of the cosmopolite: i.e., freedom from restrictive cultural loyalties and prejudices as well as the ethical imperative of openness to the difference of the other.

However, to begin with, I would like to briefly address the more common fictional representations of women's international train travel, since it could very well be argued that the experience of the railway trained women in the tourist mentality, which many female characters exhibit as they roam through Europe on the grand tour themselves. To the extent that tourism has been theorised as an act of appropriation 'which converts the "culture" encountered through travel into exchangeable items, tokens of cultural accomplishment that are legal tender in the sign market of personal acculturation at home' (Buzard, *Beaten Track*, 225), the train window was the medium par excellence through which foreign places could be consumed. The tourist gaze partly consisted in the mobile and transitory glimpse of sites and landscapes briefly gazed at and swiftly exchanged with the next. Relating the development of the railway to the rise of the department store in the nineteenth century, Schivelbusch argues that the 'fragmentation and panoramic reconstruction of the railway journey's landscape *did* correspond, structurally, to the fragmentation and the pointillistic reconstruction of the appearance of the goods in the department store' (193). In other words, the physical speed of the train, which cultivated the mobile gaze, promoted the superficial, transient vision of the tourist, whose motive was to appropriate, consume, and quickly move on from one cultural curiosity to the next, just like a shopper. It could be further argued that the actual architecture of the train, with its wide carriage window panes, provided the prerequisites for safe tourist practices, for women especially, in that it guaranteed a transparent yet fixed boundary between themselves and the foreign territory which at times was considered dangerous despite its inviting beauty. From within their safe carriages, women could glance at the foreign landscape, marvelling at its splendour but retaining their safe distance from the unfamiliar view as well as their national insularity, often flaunting their own native codes of conduct during conversation with their fellow passengers of the same or different ethnic origin. Moreover, the frequency and regularity of trains ensured the ephemerality of international travel, since, as Kristin L. Hoganson has argued, 'Even as they crisscrossed the globe, tourists remained locals at heart.' The stance of the tourist was 'the aloof stance of the transient', the traveller with a return ticket, who did not plan a permanent stay in the countries visited (202). In this section I will examine the consumer mentality of female tourists by concentrating on the example of American women travellers in Europe. Hoganson maintains that 'The tourist [consuming] mentality taught Americans to regard the rest of the world as service providers, if only by providing the service of spectacle' (199), and my analysis will focus on the role the train played in cultivating this mentality in representations of American women by male authors.

Such women abound in novels and stories of the nineteenth century. In Anthony Trollope's *He Knew He Was Right* (1869), a train ride through the Alps is used as a means of introducing the audacious American female character who eventually propels one of the two marriage plots of the novel. Emphasising the American ladies' strong-mindedness but also adherence to nationalistic principles and ways of conduct, the narrator humorously elaborates on the expectations or 'perverse' presumptions of 'The ladies [who] were without other companions, and were not fluent with their French, but were clearly entitled to their seats. They were told that the conveyance was all coupé, but perversely would not believe the statement' (290). Treating the European coupé as though it was an American vehicle of transportation and exhibiting an arrogant inflexibility by not allowing for differences in custom and temperament between cultures, the Miss Spaldings manage to have their way, due to the comparable apathy of the French officials and the passive courteousness of their British co-passengers. The narrator's remark,

> A seat in a public conveyance in the States, when merely occupied by a man, used to be regarded by any woman as being at her service as completely as though it were vacant. One woman indicating a place to another would point with equal freedom to a man or a space. (292)

points not only to the American women's comfortable appropriation of means of public transport and the stereotyping of such aggrandising agency which erases manhood, but also to the insularity of the train which encouraged such techniques of distancing on behalf of the international passengers, who in this way were able to travel the globe without forsaking their national customs. In the first place, the proximity of relationships on the train facilitates the observation of such variations of conduct between women of distinct nationalities. For example in this novel, the narrator observes that 'with no women is a speedy intimacy [on a train] so possible, or indeed so profitable, as with Americans. They fear nothing, – neither you nor themselves; and talk with as much freedom as though they were men' (294). At the same time, the train became the means of constituting and perpetuating the stereotype of the American woman as different from her European counterpart on account of her audaciousness and lack of timidity or self-effacement in her interaction with men within the tight borders of the train compartment. The train, as a vehicle which crosses national borders, is appropriated (and represented by authors) as an ethnically neutral space which also ensures that these women do not have to change their manners while travelling as tourists. As Hoganson argues, for tourists, 'their travels fueled national pride' (203), and the Spalding sisters in *He Knew He Was Right* are certainly proud of their American democratic principles which they can exercise on the train, going against European gender and social expectations: 'for American ladies understand their rights', wherever they find themselves (Trollope, 290). The train thus gave rise to a 'The world is mine' mentality,[1] this sense of ownership being nurtured by the train's own invading power, imitated by the American women on board.

The train, however, is not always as ethnically neutral or malleable as the American sisters in Trollope's novel construe it. In Henry James's 'Travelling Companions' (1870), a train ride precipitates the marriage plot exactly because the protagonists cannot avoid the dictates of Victorian gender ideology, despite their American nationality and despite their being on Italian soil. Mr Brooke and Miss Evans, who meet during their travels in Italy, may thoughtlessly flaunt an American familiarity by deciding to visit Padua together by railway, but when they miss their return train to Venice and have to spend a night together at a hotel, the rigid rules of propriety, however hypocritical they may be, challenge the innocence of their spontaneous actions, obliging them both to consider their compromised relationship from a European perspective. Brooke, who has thought himself in love, but who has also considered the potential ephemerality of his feelings born out of the romance of Italy, is now forced to propose to Miss Evans, as Venice is scandalised by their actions. In this story which blends romance with travelling and sightseeing, the train, on the one hand, facilitates the characters' tour through Italy, creating opportunities for random meetings which spark romance, but on the other, the physical distance it creates between them, as they travel separately from Milan to Venice and then to Rome, mirrors the emotional distance that they both feel when apart. In other words, their feelings for each other seem to rise and fall according to the proximity or distance created between them by their mutual train rides. The railway, thus, seems to become the means of highlighting the difference between infatuation and love, as well as between the tourist's consumer mentality and an informed visitor's artistic appreciation. While both travellers share a deep appreciation of Italy and its treasures, in an unsuperficial, 'anti-tourist' way, according to James Buzard (*Beaten*, 242), they are, nevertheless, tourists, transitory visitors, exchanging one city for the next and one cultural attraction for the other. In fact Brooke constantly tries to reconcile his belief in the inherent quality of the cities and works of art with his own mediated response which is that of a consumer. In this sense, Brooke's infatuation with Miss Evans is as temporary as his temporary absorption in the various cities and works of art visited and admired; the transitory, consumer's, pleasures of tourism in Italy parallel the emotional fluctuations the two characters undergo. The fiery moments of infatuation he experiences whenever he is with Miss Evans, which accompany the moments of intense contemplation of monuments, are followed by moments of prosaic rationalisation when she is out of sight. Brooke, even after his first marriage proposal, readily acknowledges the 'unreality of [his] love' (695), admitting to the fleetingness of feelings aroused by temporary spectacles: 'Did I in truth long merely for a bliss which should be of that hour and that hour alone?' (686). Therefore, Brooke and Miss Evans cannot help employing the mobile gaze of the traveller, a gaze practised primarily on the train. As tourists they are trained in narrowing, expanding, and redirecting their gaze so that they focus on masterpieces or admire a view, and their feelings oscillate accordingly.

The title of the story, 'Travelling Companions', emphasises the contingency of their relationship, resulting from the ephemerality of their mutual mobility as travellers. The unfortunate train ride to Padua, the only incident in which they travel together at high speed, does not in reality deepen their feelings for each other, but its scheduled mobility – its rigid timetable to which they cannot adhere – makes them conscious of the fact that in the age of tourism, freely expressed, mobile, romance is untenable unless the parties involved observe the rigidly organised systems which make tourism possible in the first place. Neglecting the timetable, and the structured forms of touring that the timetable ensures, results in their becoming susceptible to moral criticism as their motives for going on a train ride together are no longer transparent. After all, tourism and railways are part of a complex social network of modernity which affects the way relationships are experienced and evolve. Tourism by train provided men and women with structured ways in which to interact, reconfiguring the terms and the intensity of emotional attachments, fostering a modern view of love based on transient feelings and fleeting impressions acquired by the mobile gaze. Indeed, at the end of James's story, the narrative still offers no guarantee of the permanence of either companion's feelings. Brooke's final wooing takes place as they stand before a Titian entitled 'Sacred and Profane Love', and James's characteristic, though early-career, indeterminacy, blurs the line between 'the passion that fancies and [...] the passion that knows' (697); one could very well surmise that the unfortunate incident of missing their train in Padua is one of the two sole reasons Brooke and Miss Evans find themselves married in the end of the story, the second being the passing away of her father, which leaves her without a protector during her tour, and which evokes in him 'an immense uprising of pity, – of the pity that goes hand in hand with love' (696). Brooke's first questions when he sees her in mourning are, 'Have you made any plans?' and 'How did you expect to make that weary journey home [on your own]?' (696) – both questions acknowledging once again her compromised position, in accordance with the unwritten laws of tourism. In other words, both marriage proposals come as a response to woman's presumed inability to cope with rigid societal imperatives, in this story both related to gender expectations applying to train travel. Indeed, Miss Evans finally accepts his proposal out of weakness. Unable to envisage the continuation of her tour, Miss Evans has been humbled by the death of her father (to the extent that she excites 'pity' in Brooke [696]), and like other fictional women in train stories, she seeks the 'patronage' of Brooke as a male companion and co-traveller (Parkins, 66), thankful for the anchoring that this dependence on reliable masculinity effects on her drifting identity as a sole traveller of long distances at high speed. As we have seen in Chapter 1, many popular stories of the same period showed women readily and even gladly acknowledging their inability to deal with the mental or physical challenges of train travel. James, in this early-career narrative, seems to partake in this tendency to confirm women's internalisation of a femininity socially constructed as weak and vulnerable.

As has been shown in the brief account of stories above, acculturation, which was the main incentive of women's travel within Europe, did not always result in ethical cosmopolitanism, that is, in freedom from national and cultural restrictions, or in the words of Amanda Anderson, in a 'cultivated detachment from restrictive forms of identity' (70). Nor are the female characters in their travels necessarily 'radically reshaped by the encounter with difference' (Agathocleous, 138), no matter how absorbed they may have been in the monuments and works of art contemplated. It would take Henry James ten more years of his own experience as a Europeanised American before he would produce a female character able to expand her mind and experience the permeable boundaries between self and world, thus embracing cultural relativism. Isabel Archer, of *The Portrait of a Lady* (1881/1908), who arrives in Europe for 'the purpose of improving [her] mind by foreign travel' (134) remains, nevertheless, quite unchanged for a large portion of the novel, as far as cultural understanding and transformation go. As her British admirer but also opponent, Lord Warburton, tells her early in the novel, 'You can't improve your mind, Miss Archer [. . .] It's already a most formidable instrument. It looks down on us all; it despises us' (134). It is not until the most formidable Jamesian narrative experiment in Chapter 42, in which James explores the gradual developments in her conscious-ness, that Isabel comes to experience, in the words of Homi Bhabha from his analysis of this novel, 'the estranging sense of the relocation of the home and the world – the unhomeliness – that is the condition of extra-territorial and cross-cultural initiations' (9). This expansion of Isabel's consciousness matures at the moment she recontemplates the ruins of Rome, 'for in a world of ruins the ruin of her happiness seemed a less unnatural catastrophe' (564). In this scene, unlike Miss Evans from 'Travelling Companions', her humility does not only result from a realisation of her own plight, but also consists in the ethical and secular perspective of sharing in the suffering of a polylingual and poly-cultural, global and diachronic community and of acknowledging the 'continuity of the human lot' despite national and cultural differences. As Rome 'interfuse[s] with her passion' (564), Isabel undergoes a true cosmopolitan fusion of cultures, histories, and ethnicities at the level of consciousness. Although physically restricted by her marriage, she acquires a humanitarian understanding of suffering and continuity that exceeds the boundaries of her limited and limiting position.[2]

And it is this understanding of human endurance that endows her with the strength to take the train alone, and cross many national borders, defying her rigidly conventional husband and the hypocritical gender ideology that he stands for, in order to visit her dying cousin, Ralph Touchett, in England. This journey is decidedly different from the grand tour she undertook earlier in the novel in search of cultural curiosities: 'the Pyramids', 'the broken columns of the Acropolis', 'the strait of Salamis' (376). Conversely, near the end of the novel, on her long train journey from Rome to London,

> her mind had been given up to vagueness; she was unable to question the future. She performed this journey with sightless eyes and took little pleasure in the countries she traversed, decked out though they were in the richest freshness of spring. Her thoughts followed their course through other coun-tries – strange-looking, dimly-lighted, pathless lands, in which there was no change of seasons, but only, as it seemed, a perpetual dreariness of winter. She had plenty to think about; but it was neither reflexion nor conscious purpose that filled her mind. Disconnected visions passed through it, and sudden dull gleams of memory, of expectation. The past and the future came and went at their will, but she saw them only in fitful images, which rose and fell by a logic of their own. It was extraordinary the things she remembered. (606)

As the fleeting view from the windowpane fuses with the fragments of her memory, it becomes transformed, reflecting her thoughts and feelings rapidly changing, fluctuating, in response to the rapid movement of the train across countries and landscapes. As a result, Isabel's mental season of perpetual winter replaces the spring which in reality enlivens the scenery flying past. Moreover, Isabel's borderless mentality is revealed in this description which highlights the heroine's freedom from cultural and national traits, as the terrain traversed is no longer there to be consumed as a spectacle of variable nature or of distinct civilisations but as a mirror of the bare, undifferentiated, human condition, its pathos-filled history – past, present, and future – and its potential demise. As she sits in the carriage, 'in her corner, so motionless, so passive, simply with the sense of being carried, so detached from hope and regret', she contemplates death – 'To cease utterly, to give it all up and not know anything more' (607) – as a means of release from societal, cultural, and ethnic demands which have dictated the 'unimaginable' unethical acts of Madame Merle and Osmond. It is this same pressure of the timeless suffering of the human lot, which she originally felt in Rome, that Isabel again grasps at Charing Cross station where 'The dusky, smoky, far-arching vault of the station [. . .] fill[s] her with a nervous fear'. She can no longer enjoy the London sites as 'part of a mighty spectacle' (608) in the tourist fashion, but she is humbled by an acknowledgement of her own insignificance within a huge world of common suffering that the station with its thousands of lives pushing forward, like the ruins of Rome, no doubt suggests to her.

James pays much more attention to this 'sightless' journey of Isabel's which betrays the expansion of her consciousness, than her touristy voyage to the East – Greece, Turkey, and Egypt – which is almost ineffable, rendered in a few dismissive sentences ironically alluding to the inability of such superficial travel to enlarge her mind. Whereas during that pilgrimage to the East, male-inflicted emotional restraints – Osmond's declaration of 'absolute' love – had in reality limited her intellectual mobility, her later journey to London, motivated solely by her own emotional needs, completely defies conventions of male companionship and patronage in travel. Besides, her former tour, despite its seeming recklessness, had been commissioned by Ralph, her patron, who had funded her whole future (in)dependent life. Now, with Ralph dying, and her husband disobeyed, the train becomes the means of independent and transgressive mobility, of escaping not the consequences of her past choices, but the hypocritical European conventions which have made her into a 'portrait', framed within the static 'picture of a gracious lady' (418). The novel's inconclusive ending, as James leaves Isabel's 'straight path' to Rome undescribed, and, arguably, even unverified, still further exploits the train journey as a means of reinventing the female self. This time with its unrepresentability, the train journey which ends the novel frees the female character from the most restrictive forms of identity-fixing: masculine narrative control – the structural borders of *The Portrait of a Lady*.

In its inexorable advance through vast spaces, the train, which is the locus of many international crossings within its very carriages, becomes the means of a cultural and moral, not merely geographical, conquest. What we see in Trollope's and James's early train-riding heroines is their tendency to immobilise the view, treat it as a static in-between surface on which they can impose their own trajectories oblivious to the different, albeit parallel, trajectories followed as much by their fellow passengers as by the space traversed. However, in Isabel's train journey to London we see the heroine struggling with the realisation of many comings and goings, many histories, and many different temporalities, some directly related to her and others completely irrelevant. As Doreen Massey affirms, one of the challenges of space is for the subject to become conscious of 'the contemporaneity of an ongoing multiplicity of others, human and non-human' (195). In considering the spaces of empire, next, I will look at the ways in which female characters (composed by women authors) negotiate the conquering impulse, granted to a large extent by the railway, with a more cosmopolitan understanding of travelling through spaces already and continually inscribed with history and multiple becomings.

Imperial Railways

While the first part of this chapter dealt with women's rail journeys within spaces of Western civilisation, as represented by male authors, in this section I will turn my attention to women's ventures beyond such spaces, in nineteenth-century Canada and India, which had few or none of the cultural associations that had motivated earlier travellers on the Grand Tour. Women's fiction set in Canada and India explores the impact of the railway on the consciousness of the female imperial subject. It is my contention that the train narratives to be examined exhibit the incoherence of national identity within settings of empire, and that women in particular, who occupy a peculiar position as, at the same time, colonists and disenfranchised subjects of empire, expose the impossibility of monolithic, solidly impermeable identities within this context. In such narratives the train becomes a metaphor for this permeability and is used as a vehicle for identity exploration. In this investigation I take my cue from important studies of Victorian travel writing by women and of colonial writing, though my analysis will focus solely on fictional representations of the railway in Canada and India by two understudied authors, Mrs Humphry Ward and Flora Annie Steel, whose use of the train offers important insights into the relationship between woman and nation.

It has been widely argued that the railway in the nineteenth century was a significant tool of imperial expansion. An 1846 book entitled *Indian Railways: as Connected with the Power, and Stability of the British Empire in the East, the Development of its Resources, and the Civilization of its People by 'An Old Indian Postmaster'* [W. P. Andrew], stressed the socio-economic, military, territorial, and administrative advantages of the project, which was to connect 'the seat of the supreme Government with its most distant provinces' (36), as well as the cultural importance of technology as a means of civilising the underdeveloped and 'primitive' Eastern territories. In his analysis of the commercial and political benefits of the project, Andrew quotes a native merchant of Calcutta who emphasises 'the civilising influence of steam' (28), which among other things would dispel fears, superstitions, and prejudices among the natives (28), bringing, in the words of Andrew, the favourable 'moral influence of improved intercourse' to India (27). In his discussion of the development of the railway in India, Christian Wolmar argues that its construction by the British was 'a nakedly imperial project' with tremendous political and economic impact (*Blood*, 50). When the first experimental line between Bombay and Thana was completed in 1853, the reports of its opening in *The Illustrated London News* made explicit the importance of the railway for the consolidation of Imperial power in the colonies: Britain's power 'was never so nobly exemplified as [. . .] when the long line of carriages conveying nearly 500 persons, glided smoothly and easily away amidst the shouts of assembled thousands' (Anon., 'Opening', 436). 'The railway was presented by the British as the embodiment of civilization', writes Wolmar, and at the same time as 'a great engine of economic growth, not so much for India as for Britain' (52, 58). Paradigmatic of the tendency of the British media to align the invasion of the train with discourses of evolution and progress is the *Illustrated London News* full-page image entitled 'Modes of Travelling in India' (1863; Fig. 7), which progressively, from top to bottom, portrays various natives (from tramps and pilgrims to wealthy travellers) and means of travel, by elephant, camels, horses, hand-held or animal-pulled carriages, and even creeping on all fours, before arriving at the image of the East India Company train, which, hailed by

Figure 7. Joseph Austin Benwell, 'Modes of Travelling in India', *Illustrated London News* 1222 (19 September 1863): 283.

crowds of gazing natives, seems to represent toil free, democratic, and reliable transport.

The railway in India represented a 'cluster of British concepts, practices, and institutions that had substantiated modernity [in Victorian England], including technology, capitalism, urbanization, individualism, secularization, instrumental rationality, alienation, and mobility' (Aguiar, 3). As such it no doubt came to exemplify the fraught relations between the two cultures whose contact would produce a hybrid civilisation. On the one hand, according to Laura Bear and Marian Aguiar, the railway was an important means of nation-building: 'Railway tracks became the skeleton that mapped territory and supported the corpus of the future nation, creating a dynamic social geography' (Aguiar, 7). On the other, by exemplifying, through its technical design and function, the blurriness of the line between private and public as well as the permeability of borders, the railway as a space of contact between peoples and traditions came to represent the porousness of ethnic identities and cultures, challenging the idea of nation-building. Moreover, even though the railways appeared to promise national progress and individual liberty in India, social distinctions and divisions, which, in theory, the railway had aimed to eliminate, prevailed, consolidating state authority and disciplinary tactics (Bear, 4, 37). As Bear shows, after the 1857 rebellion in India, despite attempts to divest all spaces of the railway, and the stations in particular, 'of all visible signs of the colonial state as an occupying force', still the railway was a space for the practice of imperial disciplinary powers and government control (39–42).

As a white settler formation, an outpost of the British Empire, Canada had obvious differences from India,[3] yet the railway, whose development was boosted in the 1850s, played an important role in promoting British economic expansion as most of the lines constructed were controlled by British interests. The railway enabled the economic exploitation of Canada's rich natural resources at the same time that it facilitated the territorial expansion of the colony. Although Canada became a Dominion governed by a federal constitution as early as in 1867, the British parliament kept limited political rights and control over Canada until 1931 when it gained full national autonomy within the British Commonwealth. The railway therefore, which, as a vehicle of British expansionism opened up to scrutiny and conquest the terra incognita of the Canadian wilderness, was, at the same time considered a means of bringing the country together as a discrete nation and of defining its new national boundaries which would confirm and safeguard its detachment from the rest of the American continent. The development of the railway coincided with the expansion of Canada into a transcontinental nation from the Atlantic to the Pacific. As Wolmar points out, the railway 'helped transform the disparate parts of the colony of British North America into the new nation of Canada' (143). Social cohesion, in other words, was achieved through the construction of transcontinental lines traversing the vast territory, but not without the upshot of consolidating British and, later on, federal control which functioned as a regulating force aimed at thwarting liberalising impulses (Wolmar, 228–9). The railway, therefore, was a conflicted space in which a shared, though often covert, imperialist desire of identification with the glorious British Empire merged – and at times clashed – with the settlers' pride of forging a new independent nation.

The Canadian Pacific Railway and Mrs Humphry Ward

Mary Augusta Ward visited the USA and Canada in 1908. In May of that year she was offered a private carriage of the Canadian Pacific Railway by which she journeyed across Canada, and the experience of that trip formed the basis of her 1910 novel *Canadian Born* (subsequently published as *Lady Merton, Colonist* in the USA and Canada), as the dedication, 'To Canada in memory of a happy journey May–June, 1908', explicitly states. The oscillation between two titles, which curiously, albeit justly, transpose the weight of the title role from the male, Canadian born, leading character, to the British aristocratic female protagonist, who also functions as a reflector for most of the narrative, indicates perhaps the conflict between the nationalistic and colonial sentiments the author attempts to negotiate and resolve in the novel. At the same time the two titles negotiate conflicts of gender and empire, with Lady Merton, in the US title, acquiring a triumphant role as colonist, not merely traveller, uprooted settler, or wife of the Canadian born man of the first title.[4]

    The novel, which traces the burgeoning romance between Lady Merton and the Canadian George Anderson during the former's railway journey through the prairies and mountains of Canada, was greeted on publication with conflicting reviews that, on the one hand, praised Ward's vivid accounts of Canadian scenery but, on the other, questioned the realism of her treatment of the very unlikely couple. Even Ward's son Arnold commented on the 'unnatural' relationship between the British aristocrat and the attractive yet unrefined self-made Canadian: 'you almost feel she is marrying a nigger – magnificently but against nature' (qtd in Sutherland, 307). A bizarre review in *The New York Times* (16 April 1910) starts by dubbing it 'The Premier Novel of the Year', which 'will doubtless be one of the most widely read, most earnestly discussed and, all told, most important works of fiction of the year', only to end up arguing that the novel 'is disappointing in its ineffectiveness and futility'. The reviewer's main objection centres on the implausibility of a woman who is nurtured in the luxury of the aristocratic country house, the heritage of traditions based on class, and the beauties of English landscapes abandoning 'the great house at home' in preference for 'the drudgery of life [. . .] the cooking, sewing, baking that keep man – animal man – alive'. Similarly, the reviewer is mystified by the refusal – or stubbornness – of Anderson, 'being a Canadian', to give up his primitive country, in which man is merely 'master of nature' with no ancestry and no established seat, for the motherland which has such social privileges to offer as would fit the husband of the wealthy and powerful Lady Merton. 'Love levels all distinctions and marriage comes in to break down the foolish relics of the old feudal system', the reviewer admits, but such marriages may only take place in heaven and in fiction, and such an unrealistic plotline would certainly make 'Balzac's eyes start from their sockets'. On the other hand, a review in the American *Bookman* by the US author, and granddaughter of Nathaniel Hawthorne, Hildegarde Hawthorne, praised the unconventionality of Elizabeth Merton, who 'drops all the unnecessary paraphernalia [. . .] chosen not so much by herself as by the exigencies of caste and breeding' in favour of 'something more vivid, more enduring, more intimately human than she has yet known [. . .] for all her wandering in France and Italy and the perfect surroundings of her ancient house' (308). The novel, in other words, despite its late date of publication well into the Edwardian era, was seen as a threat to Victorian domestic ideology, instigating discussion about whether woman by nature is inclined to prefer the stability and homely comfort provided by a rigid social structure or to give in to forbidden, transgressive impulses. In the words of Hildegarde Hawthorne, 'every real woman has a wild heart; a heart that the soft chains of civilized customs have smothered and controlled [. . .] but which, given the opportunity, will dominate her life and overthrow the careful building of the centuries in a moment' (308). Elizabeth Merton, who gives herself up to the thrill of her speedy train ride through Canada, seems to be just such a woman.

At the same time, the reviews reveal a colonial anxiety lest the ways of the new world should be seen to replace so easily those of the old. 'Canada is the rage just now,' admits one writer in *The Saturday Review*, but the fascination with its scenery is merely a temporary fashion, 'and Mrs. Humphry Ward must be in fashion', the article goes, belittling the force of Ward's treatment of the subject by relegating the novel to the baser category of easy, popular, or sensation fiction – of fiction that doesn't matter. On the other hand, in the American literary journal, *The Dial*, Ward's novel compels the reviewer, William Morton Payne, to acknowledge that

> the colonial note is destined to be heard with increasing insistence in the chorus of British fiction. The self-consciousness and the sentiment of local patriotism that are so rapidly developing in the far-off lands that owe allegiance to the British crown are rapidly making their way into literature, and are bringing with them a new coloring and a new imagery. This is all to the good; and the freshness of the new portrayals goes far to atone for that crudity they still exhibit. (394)

Why would an allegedly conservative British writer, who has subsequently been cast by critics as a nationalist with strong imperialist tendencies, write a novel that destabilises both gender conventions and colonial discourse of her day? In his negative rhymed review of the novel in *Life*, Arthur Guiterman, American author of humorous poetry, writes that 'The whole contrivance makes it look / As if, to risk a rash opinion, / This patriotic tourist book / Was writ to boom the great Dominion' (893). However, *Canadian Born* is far from a tourist book; and its patriotism (whose patriotism and for which country, Britain or Canada? Guiterman's choice of adjective is curious) is questionable. Ward's novel, in its depiction of the dilemmas confronting a prominent British woman of class, exemplifies the instability of narratives of gender and nation within the context of empire.

As the daughter of a railway speculator, one of the largest shareholders and founders of the Canadian Pacific Railway, Lady Elizabeth Merton cannot be entirely free of the imperialist discourse which justified capitalist and business connections between Britain and the colonies. In the first pages of the novel her observations blend a sensitive curiosity for the new country of Canada with the triumphant impulse for expansionism as she takes possession of the rich landscape rushing past from the train window or the observation platform. In her response to nature her voice parodies the imperialist rhetoric of a naturalist observing and naming trees and animals: 'what *are* those birds?' (10).[5] As she eagerly takes in 'hill beyond hill, wood beyond wood', she cannot help thinking of the commercial value of the land surveyed for its rich resources and the profit that her own brother is likely to make from mining and other business exploits (11). Picturesque romanticism evoked by untamed nature co-exists with a deeply-rooted understanding of her own dominant role, as colonist, as a representative of those who are entitled to appropriate, not merely as tourists, but as business entrepreneurs and as owners. Her attitude is that of the explorer, not only visiting land already inscribed in the geography books she remembers from her childhood, but making geographical discoveries of her own and conquering land. In a cartographic mood, she even imagines herself and her brother surveying, mapping, the land from above, discovering a new lake, and 'giv[ing] it a name – one of [their] names [. . .] and [their] name [. . .] would live for ever' (11). Elizabeth Merton is conscious of her civic duties, her active and enduring role as founder of a new nation, not only in the present, but also for the future.

Lady Merton's imperialist discourse is closely linked to, if not derived from, her consciousness of the train's tortuous, yet triumphant, movement through the vast territory, as well as her knowledge of the important role the railway played in the conquest of the distant and inaccessible parts of Canada. The infrastructure of Canada's economic development was largely dependent on the construction of the railway, and throughout the novel Elizabeth is at pains to reconcile the necessity of capitalist intervention with the lamentable destruction of nature: she particularly notices the burning down of the trees which line the railway tracks, a destruction, which, nevertheless, is rationalised as being part of the civilising work of empire. In this sense, Lady Merton's proprietary mentality, discourse, and gaze may be said to be not only aesthetic but also strategic. As many critics of women's travel writing have argued, by describing in writing their journeys through the spaces of empire, women, to a large extent, reinforced the ideological work of imperialism, sometimes unconsciously, but at other times proudly affirming their membership in the world's most powerful empire.[6]

However, Elizabeth Merton is not a complacent colonist. As she contemplates her travel arrangements, the luxury on board the train (the comfortable domesticity facilitated by submissive servants in liveries), and the insulation of the rich such as herself from the immigrants ('the blinds of the car towards the next carriage were rigorously closed, that no one might interfere with the privacy of the rich' [17]) make her painfully conscious of the exclusions that the European practices have already established in a country which is otherwise ignorant of social conventions and institutions, created, as it is, out of 'man's hard wrestle with rock and soil, with winter and the wilderness' (17). The train affirms social stratification, in spite of the fact that it is a shared space of travel which connects the lives of the passengers through common trajectories and destinations. Early on in the novel Elizabeth becomes aware of the equalising role of the train, carrying 'its freight of lives' (19), she being one of the indistinguishable lot, and she regrets, and is even embarrassed by, the increasing prevalence of British social standards which threaten to extinguish the natural equality of the new inhabitants of Canada, who depend on their hard labour, and not on heredity, for social advancement. Ultimately the train, a foreign, industrial product traversing the wilderness, functions as a contact zone, 'a space of imperial encounters' (Pratt, 8), in which different peoples, standards, and social practices meet and clash, destabilising hierarchies and reversing binaries.

One such conflict emerges through the comparison of masculinities in the novel. The Canadian born railway engineer, George Anderson, is compared to the two male representatives of Britain, Elizabeth's brother, Philip Gaddesden, and her eager suitor, Arthur Delaine, both of whom are characterised by a lack of interest in and enthusiasm for Canada, its natural beauties, and its social problems. While Anderson is distinguished for his ambition, self-driven success, and physical prowess as he stands for the force of the railway he has helped to construct, Philip is sickly and near death, constantly bored of landscape and physical activity, preferring the idle reading of books while on the train. For Philip time drags on sluggishly and uneventfully, while for his exuberant sister the passing of time is attuned to the fast movement of the train and to the fleeting impressions filling each minute and animating her blood with a new aspect of nature rushing past: 'so quickened were all her pulses, so vivid the memories of the day' (77). Delaine, like Philip, is uninterested in discovering Canada, indulging, instead, in critical studies of the classics, admiring a French Hellenist who discovered and identified the locations mentioned in the *Odyssey* (41). Discoveries of new land, by Anderson and Elizabeth, are contrasted to discoveries of ancient sites, the live language of progress to the dead language of the past. The text persistently juxtaposes the men of the story, comparing the feats of railway excavation initiated by Anderson, with the scientific, archaeological excavations that interest Delaine: 'Had she heard of the most recent Etruscan excavations at Grossetto? Wonderful! A whole host of new clues! [. . .] the whole learned world in commotion' (66); Delaine's vicarious participation in the reported 'commotion', through reading about such discoveries, is set against Anderson's (and Elizabeth's) active part in the present commotion of forging the future of a new country. In a letter to her mother, Elizabeth assesses the difference between the two men: Anderson 'in place here [. . .] where the world is moving' and Delaine 'a walking anachronism. He is out of perspective; he doesn't fit' (103). Elizabeth herself, despite the anchoring effected by her origins and social position, is enthralled by this metaphorical movement of the world that the train literalises: 'Here she was absorbed in a rushing present; held by the vision of a colossal future' (12). Anderson embodies the forward motion of the train – Canada's 'rushing present' but also its 'colossal future' – while Delaine represents the static and paralysing, even backward, European conventions that Elizabeth seems to defy in the wildness of spirit she has given in to during the train journey: 'Elizabeth's manner was really a little excessive', muses Delaine, unable to understand the self-expansion she is undergoing during this opportunity to extend her mind and vision to boundless landscapes and newly forming societies.

During this journey, Elizabeth escapes the hegemonic version of upper-class womanhood, overcoming the supposedly feminine traits of frailty, self-effacement, and, most importantly, the emotional attachment to home and country. The expanding, endless view from the carriage that she constantly reports corresponds to the limitless expansion of her consciousness, to the extent that she will eventually give up the security and stability of her luxurious home in England for the nomadic mobility of colonial settlers and the 'drudgery' of a farmhouse in unsophisticated Canada. Moreover, unlike her male compatriots, who passively enjoy their novels in the quiet of the carriage with the blinds pulled down, Elizabeth embarks on daring adventures, taking risks, physical and mental, and emulating the risk-taking that Anderson espoused during the railway construction through the dangerous Rockies or other challenging topography. While she accepts the patronage of Anderson, who becomes her guide, but also protector, the wild landscape gives rise to an inexhaustible exhilaration and freedom from convention; it becomes an arena for the expression of Elizabeth's self-transformation and empowerment, as she makes decisions regardless of the will of her brother and Delaine. In her examination of women's travel writing, Karen M. Morin has argued that some women's habitual 'resistance to adventure serves as a feminine standard against which their husband's or brother's active and adventurous male identities can be counterposed' (*Frontiers of Femininity*, 72). In this novel, the exact opposite takes place, with Ward projecting the British men's resistance to adventure as a distorted standard against which woman's aspiration for action is highlighted. In an intense scene, during their passage along a perilous track on the edge of a precipice in the Selkirks, a track that had apparently made a Grand Duchess faint with fear and which induces Delaine involuntarily to utter, 'It is a nightmare!' (168), Elizabeth leans over the narrow railing that divides the train from the abyss beyond, triumphing over social expectations of women's recoil from risk, but also, and most importantly, over the limitations of her own body – claiming mastery, not only of the view, but also of the self: 'Again the wildness ran through her blood, answering the challenge of Nature. Faint! – she was more inclined to sing or shout' (168).[7] Mastering the precarious cliff means mastering her own precarious position as a woman who defies convention – not only social but also sexual convention; but I will return to this point at the end of this section. While in the beginning of the novel untamed nature caused her to shiver and tremble in fear of its 'stealthy and hostile powers' (17), her experience on the train has made her identify with its powers.

It has been argued that in women's writing about the colonies, 'Modalities of self-empowerment and self-improvement worked through the impulses of empire' (Morin, 'Peak Practices', 493);[8] however, in *Canadian Born*, the self-empowered Elizabeth in the end of the novel does not cling to the authority and luxury that her position as an upper-class lady, and a colonist, grants her. Instead she assumes a position of relative social invisibility, in a house in the great, largely uninhabited Canadian outdoors, yearning for a Canadian citizenship earned through labour and not through economic and social privilege:

> 'If only I wasn't so rich!' thought Elizabeth, with compunction. For she often looked with envy on her neighbours who had gone through the real hardships of the country; who had bought their Canadian citizenship with the toil and frugality of years. It seemed to her sometimes that she was step-child rather than daughter of the dear new land, in spite of her yearning towards it. (248)

Up until the end, Elizabeth tests the limits of her body and spirit, not as a colonist, but as a woman longing for personal empowerment through the conquering of natural and social obstacles. The train, with which she identifies and which, in scenes like the precipice incident examined previously, seems to become an extension of her daring body, symbolises her strong will to appropriate her precarious position as a transgressive woman and a conflicted subject of empire. Her struggle for feminine empowerment becomes even more conscious when on her return to England she feels 'engulf[ed]' and 'entomb[ed]' within the rigid boundaries of her old house, of immoveable institutions that paralyse her (214). In contrast to the exhilarating mobility experienced in Canada during her train journey, Elizabeth now 'felt a miserable paralysis descending on her own will' (213–14). While the train encouraged not only physical mobility but also cultural relativism – in other words, the opportunity to envisage the self released from national anchors – her ancestral home imposes absolute stasis. Ultimately, the memory of the vast, limitless horizon from the train window is contrasted to, and even manages to '[wipe] out', the immobilising, artificial trappings of the 'restless scene [of] [. . .] diamonds, the uniforms, the blaze of electric light, the tapestries on the walls' and so on (228).

Elizabeth's experience, therefore, challenges the familiar tropes of women's place within a domestic and imperial context, and her role as a colonist is more ambiguous and even subversive than her compatriots', whose intolerance perpetuates binaries of imperial self and primitive other. In the first pages of the novel, in conversation with his sister, Philip dismisses the beauty of the landscape on account of its assumed lack of history, differentiating aspects, and human cultivation: 'And why you make such a fuss about the lakes, when [. . .] none of them has got a name to its back, and they're all exactly alike, and all full of beastly mosquitoes in the summer – it beats me!' (10). Similarly, Delaine scorns the empty landscape, unable to envisage its progress, as it is and will always be inhabited, in his view, by 'primitive earth-life', immigrants of no social standing and no socio-historical ties to place (47).[9] When he learns about Anderson's 'degenerate', criminal father,[10] he feels justified in his view of the difference between colonisers and natives.[11] For as Anne McClintock has argued, 'the distance along the path of progress traveled by some portions of humanity could be measured only by the distance others lagged behind' (46), and Delaine measures his superiority as a member of the civilised race in comparison with Anderson's supposedly inherited criminal potentials. To his utter distaste, Delaine finds that Elizabeth herself has deteriorated into a 'natural woman' (81), a woman who seems to be detaching herself from the institutional restrictions which bind identity in Europe.

Elizabeth's impressions and experience of self-expression and ultimately empowerment, on the other hand, destabilise such jingoistic assumptions by questioning the superiority of imperial civilisation. While the British men, in a typical colonial, chauvinistic, manoeuvre, cast the wilderness as primitive and anachronistic, threatening the imperial subject with regression and even degeneration, Elizabeth deems *them*, Delaine in particular, anachronistic. She also sees conscious evolution inscribed in the about-to-be peopled landscape, where the train has already overcome the challenging geographical difficulties, transforming the dull, dreary, monotonous, for the men, terrain into habitable space and into a burgeoning civilisation:

> 'When one thinks of all the haphazard of history – how nations have tumbled up, or been dragged up, through centuries of blind horror and mistake, how wonderful to see a nation made consciously! – before your eyes – by science and intelligence – everything thought of, everything foreseen! First of all, this wonderful railway, driven across these deserts, against opposition, against unbelief, by a handful of men, who risked everything, and have – perhaps – changed the face of the world!' (67–8)

Elizabeth is suggesting that there is more conscious progress and more resonance in this new history in the making than in the centuries' old European civilisation, and although one cannot deny that in her idealism she forgets or is self-deluded about the blatant role of colonists such as herself in the making of this new history, her rhetoric threatens standard imperialist discourse which equated new land with barrenness, emptiness, silence, and timelessness. While it is true that the unruly landscape has been tamed by the imperialist train, by the implanting of fixed lines which have created boundaries dividing the otherwise homogenised land, it is also true that the railway has provided opportunities for the social cohesion of the Dominion and for individual advancement. Anderson, who promotes a nationalist agenda, not without respect for the crown,[12] sees the spreading railway lines – for the construction of which he has distinguished himself as a future political leader – as a means of bringing the country together into a discrete nation. Elizabeth, too, after her experience visiting the crowded emigration offices, sees the train as the means of 'the new nation spreading, spreading over the open land, irresistibly, silently: no one setting bounds to it, no one knowing what will come of it!' (48). Her thoughts curiously cast the train as a force powered not by the capitalist and colonial impulses that built it but by the will of homeless, dispossessed people claiming a land of their own. Moreover, the railway, with its 'freight of lives' (19), '[speaks] to her in terms of human life' in the abstract and not in terms of ethnic or class identities (164). The railway is seen as the exulted outcome of man's efforts to make his presence and his technological progress visible in nature: 'For here man had expressed himself; had pitched his battle with a fierce Nature and won it [. . .] had made his purpose prevail over the physical forces of this wild world' (164). Although throughout the novel the narrative remains conflicted as to the dual function of the train as an imperial or a nationalist tool, Elizabeth also sees it in more Hardyesque terms, as a sign of the precarious balance between the romantic sublime and accelerating modernity. At such moments her discourse escapes political undertones.

Nevertheless, despite her occasional universalist impulse, Elizabeth's rhetoric is unavoidably affected by the blindness of the imperialist who does not consider the detrimental effects of this invasion on the Indian reserves that until now occupied the land and whose people will suffer the same dispossession that has driven the white setters' will to seize land.[13] While her stance as a colonist is conflicted and often embarrassed, until the end of the novel her belief in the settlers' entitlement to the land previously occupied by natives is never questioned. On the contrary, Elizabeth and her compatriots view first and second generation immigrants, like Anderson, as 'natives', and it is in their contact with *them* that othering takes place, with the settlers cast in the role of primitive other, in terms of their social obscurity and nomadism. However, the train, being a contact zone, 'the point at which [the] trajectories [of disparate peoples] now intersect' (Pratt, 8), becomes a space where the boundary between the self and other collapses. The novel traces the development of Elizabeth's gaze, which she uses in the beginning of her journey to satisfy her curiosity for the spectacle of Canada from the train window or of the immigrants on the train. The architecture of the carriage, its walls and windows, initially facilitates this division between spectator and spectacle while it ensures a safe distance between herself, the colonist, and the objects of observation, the immigrants – always already other, always already different from herself. But while for Delaine and Philip the train keeps this promise of separating the metro-politan self from the peripheral other, for Elizabeth it provides oppor-tunities for contact and for mutual transformation. The first moment of contact takes place when the train reaches a standstill and Elizabeth is faced with the prospect of entering the immigrant car in order to give a mother milk for her baby. The text juxtaposes the curious gaze of Elizabeth with the reluctant, even defiant, gaze of the Russian woman: 'The mother turned away abruptly. It was not unusual for persons from the parlour-cars to ask leave to walk through the emigrants' (27). Despite Elizabeth's genuine benevolence, the Russian refuses to be treated as a spectacle of race for the satisfaction of upper-class and imperial curiosity. Moreover, Elizabeth's charity, as she spares some of her surplus supplies for the relief of the plight of the poor, becomes a measure of her racial and class superiority against the poor and dispos-sessed immigrants. And in truth Elizabeth's rhetoric, this early in the novel, reveals an inability to see beyond the class and ethnic prejudices that differentiate her from the mass of indistinguishable others: she sees in the face of the woman 'eyes rather of a race than of a person, hardly conscious, hardly individualized, yet most poignant, expressing some feeling, remote and inarticulate, that roused Elizabeth's' (27). Similarly, in the emigration office, where she has the chance to interact with Yankees, Russians, Italians, and Frenchmen she is mentally engaged in an ethnographic project considering the ways in which these abstract ethnicities might cohere under a shared experience and a common aim. Despite her sensitive reading of cultural disparity and the economic necessities of the alterities that she meets, her discourse expresses the ethnocentrism of the imperialist who indulges in mere spectatorship and who self-deludedly presumes to empathise with the other: 'I am only a spectator. *We* see the drama – we feel it – much more than they can who are in it', she eventually acknowledges (49). Yet the dialectic of repulsion and desire, which seems to underlie her experience of finding herself in the same closed space as these unconstituted peoples, unsettles the imperial ideology and racial politics that inform her gaze.

Indeed, by the end of her journey, Elizabeth exhibits a consciousness of her proprietary gaze and she even regrets it:

> She fell into an angry contempt for that mood of imaginative delight in which she had journeyed through Canada so far. What! treat a great nation in the birth as though it were there for her mere pleasure and entertainment? Make of it a mere spectacle and pageant, and turn with disgust from the notion that you, too, could ever throw in your lot with it, fight as a foot-soldier in its ranks, on equal terms, for life and death!
> She despised herself. (165–6)

Her railway experience has tempered her imperial stance to the point that she exalts the life of toil undertaken not only by prominent Canadians like Anderson but also by Canada's 'foot-soldiers', the immigrants that she has seen on the train. The train has collapsed the distance between self and other, and eventually a mirroring takes place during which Elizabeth envisages herself as the other, as a labouring housewife and housemother in the service not of Empire but of the Dominion. No longer feeling a 'stranger', Elizabeth accepts that 'The teeming Canadian life had become deeply interwoven with her life' (199). Nevertheless, the text continues to waver between imperialist and Canadian nationalist discourse. In contemplating a life in Canada as the wife of Anderson, she imagines a necessary regression, as 'Life [on the prairie] returns, in fact, to the old primitive pattern' (166). However, in deciding to move permanently to Canada, she also aligns herself with progress, with the Canadian Pacific Railway and the experimental project of overcoming natural adversity and populating uninhabited land with people of different cultures and traditions. During her journey the train has synchronised the trajectories of old European customs and new Canadian potentials, and at the end of the novel Elizabeth acknowledges this collapse of binaries between notions of primitiveness and progress, regression and advancement, backwardness and forwardness: 'Old and new: – she seemed to be the child of both – gathering them both into her breast' (228). At the same time Elizabeth, by appreciating and even identifying with the nomadic life of the multicultural immigrants, embraces cultural relativism, defining herself not in opposition to but in solidarity with the other.

It has been argued that 'The evolution of Canada as a prosperous and peaceful community in the northern half of North America has been based on a tolerance of diversity, whether expressed regionally, politically, culturally, socially, linguistically, or religiously' (Riendeau, xix) To a large extent at the end of the novel, Elizabeth Merton has adopted this mentality. No longer place-bound, she exhibits a freedom from national

and cultural restrictions, deciding to marry Anderson whose national allegiance is different from her own and whose future is open and precarious,
not fixed. Through the train journey, a journey of self-discovery, Ward
has explored woman's negotiation of nation, world, and self, showing her
heroine struggling with deeply rooted and restrictive patriotism and imperialism. Ultimately her decision to move to Canada and become a settler
proves the artificiality and porosity of national and cultural boundaries
and Elizabeth's ethical receptivity and openness to the possibility of identification with the other, with difference. The train as a contact zone has
enabled these reciprocal, transformative encounters, manifested mainly
in the subversive relationship between Elizabeth and Anderson. After the
marriage, the couple settle in a farm in Canada, in the remote yet reach-
able-by-train region of Saskatchewan. One wonders if Elizabeth's new
home becomes a depository of domestic values imported from Britain, as
it has been widely argued that British women's role as settlers was more
often than not 'to transport British middle-class, domestic values to North
America' in terms of homemaking and the British class system (Peterson,
57, 63). Yet at the end of the novel, the old world – its standards, prejudices, and ideology – is envisaged by Elizabeth as an ominous 'shadow'
that threatens to obscure the prospects of Canada's unlimited possibilities
(250). Her new home, which, as a 'temple of industrious peace' (248–9),
is initially reminiscent of Ruskin's description of the wife's domestic space
as 'a temple of the hearth watched over by Household Gods' (Ruskin,
62), requires of her, however, to work as hard as the servants and exhibits
none of the exclusions that prohibited the mixing of classes and ethnicities
back in England. With a new moral force, which diverges from that prescribed by Victorian domestic ideology, she shows an expansive ethical
receptivity in the form of hospitality, especially when a despondent couple
with a child knock on her door. The scene parallels the earlier scene on the
train, where Elizabeth had helped an immigrant with milk for her baby.
Here, however, the nomadic immigrants do not avoid Elizabeth's gaze,
considering her receptive to and tolerant of their troubles, since she too
lives in Canada and shares with them 'the collective will [of the Canadian
inhabitants] to recognize themselves as a part of a common experience'
(Riendeau, xvi):

> And he looked under his eyebrows at Elizabeth, at the bright fire behind her,
> and all the comfort of the new farmhouse. Yet under his shuffling manner
> there was a certain note of confidence. He was appealing to that Homeric
> hospitality which prevails throughout the farms of the Northwest. (250)

And while hospitality can never be absolute and can never completely
mask economic inequalities[14] – the couple are impressed with the rela-

tive luxury of the farmhouse – Elizabeth's new, genuine empathy for the strangers reveals her willingness to be deeply transformed by their lives, so diverse yet intersecting with her own. In their wandering fate, they come to represent not only Canada, but also herself, and her wandering trajectory towards freedom from societal restrictions: 'No! – in Canada the human will has still room to work, and is not yet choked by a jungle growth of interests', she thinks (250), optimistically envisaging the future of the couple – a future which mirrors her own to a certain extent. The last lines of the novel confirm this fusion not only of ethnicities, but also of mentalities: 'in tending [the poor couple], she had been also feeding her own yearning, quickening her own hope' (254). and Elizabeth, pregnant with Anderson's child, imagines the freedom of a life in the making.

One question remains, however. I have been arguing that the train journey has been a means of feminist exploration of a woman's agency within the context of Victorian gender relations, on the one hand, and of empire, on the other. And yet the ending of the novel, at first glance, seems to deny the feminine empowerment reached by Elizabeth during her train ride. On deciding to marry Anderson, Elizabeth muses that 'She had made him master of herself, and her fate [. . .] he stood upon that dignity she herself had given him – her lover and the captain of her life' (238). It could be, thus, argued that despite the destabilisation of many binaries in the novel, colonial discourse prevails, this time as part of an internalised gender ideology, of a belief in woman's natural destiny to be conquered, mastered, body and mind, by man. Indeed, Ward has not fared well with feminist critics who have judged very negatively her fraught gender politics.[15] On the other hand, Beth Sutton-Ramspeck has comprehensively traced the 'contradictory attitudes [towards feminism] typical of Ward's work throughout her career' (205). I would like to argue that *Canadian Born*, like *Marcella* (1894) examined by Sutton-Ramspeck, 'illustrates Ward's balancing act' between forms of liberal feminism and social feminism of her period – 'liberal feminist self-development and social feminist self-surrender' (206).[16] It is obvious that *Canadian Born* promotes a version of womanhood that is in collaboration with – not submission to – masculine social positions, and Sutton-Ramspeck's reading of *Marcella*'s couple – 'Their mutual assistance in the private sphere will enhance their effectiveness in the public sphere' (206) – could very well apply to the later novel which closes with Elizabeth financially assisting the man who has helped her achieve liberation from paralysing social restrictions. Even though Anderson is dubbed 'master' and 'captain of her life', we understand that their intense attachment is reciprocal and that her money becomes a means not only of furthering her husband's career, but also of fulfilling her own responsibilities, equal to his own, towards her new country: she prepares to help develop a university,[17] found a training college, and build a cottage hospital (248).

Moreover, one cannot ignore the intense sexual desire that from the early pages of the novel dictates the decisions of Elizabeth Merton, leading her, towards the end, to propose marriage to Anderson and gladly leave her country and appurtenances. Elizabeth's gaze is clearly erotic as she peruses his body during their close encounters on the train, which has accelerated their acquaintance: 'Anderson's fair, uncovered head and broad shoulders were strongly thrown out against the glistening snows of the background' (87). In her exhilaration with speed, she sees him as a representative of the physical prowess and dynamic pace of the train, as well as of the natural beauty of the mountainous, and sexually suggestive, backdrop: 'The energy of the mountain sunshine and the mountain air seemed to throb and quiver through the persons talking – through Anderson's face, and his eyes fixed upon Elizabeth – through the sunlit water – the sparkling grasses – the shimmering spectacle of mountain and summer cloud that begirt them' (87). But one of the most intense scenes of sexual attraction blends sexual desire with the speed and danger of the train's movement along a perilous cliff. In this scene, which I discussed previously as an example of Elizabeth's mastering of her body, the heroine is intensely conscious of the magnetic effect of Anderson's body next to her as she takes the risk of leaning over the railing:

> And with the exhilaration, physical and mental, that stole upon her, there mingled secretly, the first thrill of passion she had ever known. Anderson sat beside her, once more silent after his burst of talk. She was vividly conscious of him – of his bare curly head – of certain lines of fatigue and suffering in the bronzed face. And it was conveyed to her that, although he was clearly preoccupied and sad, he was yet conscious of her in the same way. (168–9)

Such scenes demonstrate that Elizabeth's empowerment is as much sexual as it is social, and the deliberate precariousness of her body as she places it over the rail proves her willingness to embrace this intensely sexualised, albeit socially risky, subject position. During their second honeymoon in the untrodden parts of the Rockies, the narrative again insists on their mutually arousing eroticism, with Elizabeth constantly seeking his touch and Anderson 'with his arm about her, and the intoxication of her slender beauty mastering his senses' (245). Mastery and surrender seem to take on a particularly sexual overtone, with both lovers accepting their reciprocal power, while giving Elizabeth a clearly individualistic (feminist?) motive for having abandoned her country. Her desire for sexual pleasure and fulfilment has overcome national and social allegiance.

'In the Permanent Way of Civilization': Flora Annie Steel and the Railway in India

Despite her intimate engagement with themes of empire, for which one would expect her to be a favourite with postcolonial feminist critics, Flora Annie Steel (1847–1929) is one of the most understudied British authors of the colonies. A Scotswoman born in Middlesex (née Webster), Steel married a member of the Indian civil service and moved to India in 1867 where she lived for twenty-two years, actively engaged in administrative work at her husband's office as well as in educational initiatives, teaching and later on establishing schools for Indian girls. In her semi-official capacity as Inspectress of Schools she became a strong advocate of female education. On her departure from India it is reported that three hundred veiled women gathered at the railway station to see her off (Powell, 60).[18] Steel wrote many novels and short stories, most of them set in India, describing Anglo-Indian interaction, though, quite originally, some of her stories completely do away with the European presence, delving into the life of small Indian communities, rewriting folklore, or reconstructing Indian history. While one cannot deny the orientalist attitude inherent in Steel's mediation as narrator or historian, still her writing is endowed with an unusual imaginative insight and sympathy, spawned by her close affiliation with Indian women and men, her good knowledge of Punjabi, in which she could read, write, and speak, and her sincere attempt to discover and help perpetuate Indian folklore and traditions, such as traditional handicrafts and embroidery, which were threatened by the Western infiltration (Crane and Johnston, 73). Jenny Sharpe argues that in her conflicted attitude towards empire and her own role within in, Steel 'embodies the memsahib in all of her contradictions' (93). On the one hand, she did not absconc her role as British administrator of power in the colony, but, on the other, her stories convey an unusual insight into the lives of Indian men and women. Her intensive research into Indian culture resulted in some particularly Indocentric works. Jenny Sharpe writes that during her research for her most famous historical novel, *On the Face of the Waters* (1896), she 'immersed herself in her research, living on the rooftop like her heroine, roaming the streets of Delhi, and pouring [sic] over official records and histories' (87). Nevertheless, the same critic claims that this particular novel does not 'break with a colonial logic that explains the British retribution as a response to the massacre of innocents [. . .] hesitat[ing] to denounce the severity with which the rebellions were suppressed' (Sharpe, 101). Similarly, and more recently, Ralph Crane and Anna Johnston, while highlighting Steel's attempt to 'interpret the country and its culture using Indocentric rather than Eurocentric measures', conclude that 'Ultimately, though, it is difficult to escape the sense that in all her writing, her knowledge of India is used to control the natives, to support British rule of a subject race' (74). While this statement may be true for some of her writing, it does not do justice to Steel's work as a whole, which is not as straightforwardly imperialistic as most criticism contends.

In fact, early reviews of her writing repeatedly commented on the peculiar Indocentrism of her work, sometimes in order to praise her literary skills and at other times to complain that

> the stories are so taken up with the native that the settler is almost neglected. This seems hard since he alone will read them. The fact is, that the stories of the East without something Western in them are, like water without the whisky, a little insipid. (Anon., 'Book Reviews Reviewed', 163)[19]

'Her sterling and self-denying honesty' (Collins, 54), in other words, as she often excludes the West from the East, was seen as both a literary deficiency and a downplaying of empire. Many reviews compared her work to Kipling's, some finding her inferior, but others seeing in her work

> an even subtler appreciation of the Oriental standpoint – both ethical and religious – a more exhaustive acquaintance with native life in its domestic and indoor aspects, and a deeper sense of the moral responsibilities attaching to our rule in the East [than in Mr Kipling]. Indeed, if Mrs Steel shows any partiality, it is not towards Western modes of thought. (Anon., 'Book Reviews Reviewed', 163)[20]

A reviewer in *The Speaker* attributes Steel's superiority as a writer of Indian culture to her feminine sensibility which allows her to delve deeper than Kipling can into the everyday life of Indian communities. Steel reveals the 'hidden springs of native conduct' in a much more direct way than Kipling, according to this reviewer: 'The truth is that Mrs Steel and Mr Kipling paint different sides of the same picture, and that the normal (which is Mrs Steel's) side can never be looked on by Mr Kipling, whereas Mrs Steel can follow Mr Kipling a little further than he can follow her' (Anon., Rev. of *Voices in the Night*, 342). But is 'the normal side' admired by the reviewer also a normalising side? Is Steel's gaze, solely applied as it sometimes is at natives and the relationships between them, the appropriating gaze of the imperialist who applies her own regulating norms to Indian conduct and interaction? The reviews of the time, although steeped in imperial, orientalist discourse, seem to imply that Steel's gaze is more genuine and objective than Kipling's, to the extent that it challenges the hegemonic view of Britain's entitlement to transform the socio-political and cultural situation of India. What a reviewer such as J. P. Collins in *The Bookman* (1917) sees as 'the real essence of India' distilled in Steel's work (53), other, earlier, reviewers found threatening because it denied them a clear role and purpose as imperial administrators: 'India, Mrs Steel seems to say, can certainly not expect a solution of the problems which oppress her from the narrow creed of her alien masters, official even in their religion' (Anon., 'Book Reviews Reviewed', 163).

In a recent article in the *Feminist Review* (2010), Shampa Roy reappraises Steel's gender politics within the context of empire, arguing that in her writing about women in particular, Steel, unlike other memsahibs of that period, gestures 'at complex questioning of the bases of Imperial authority and its ostensibly benevolent intervention in the lives of Indian women' (55). In her view, Steel does not 'resort to the reductive Orientalist trope of feminine alterity as sexual threat or passive suffering, so popular among the Anglo-Indian fiction as well as non-fiction of reformist writers of her time' (Roy, 57). I would strongly agree with Roy that in many of her short stories, which have been largely neglected, her narration 'does not operate in a homogenous and non-complex manner in order to advance invariably a privileged Imperial perspective' (61). On the contrary, though certainly not free of the mediating authority of the Western narrator, her short fiction betrays a narrative instability resulting from what Ian Baucom has described as a 'slippage between what the colonial state wishes and what it achieves' (88); due to such fissures, the narrative surface of her writing often becomes roiled with ambiguities. In his book, *Out of Place*, Baucom explores the site of the gothic-style Victoria Terminus in Bombay as a 'disciplinary and reformative architecture of Englishness' (71), which, on the one hand, was meant to consolidate imperial power, but, on the other, may be construed as a conflicted space that 'produced not English but hybrid identities' (84). For in its intricate decoration of 'beasts and foliages of the subcontinent' the station 'is an England that has been tropicalized': 'Closely examined, the Victoria Terminus reveals that it has become what it was built to erase, that that imperial commitment to the production of the Same which it so massively symbolizes has been superinscribed by the "marks of difference"' (84). The tropical birds and plants that are embedded in the gothic architecture of the station, in Baucom's reading, on the one hand, demonstrate the colonial power to capture, tame, and exhibit alterity, but, on the other, they also disrupt colonial authority in a schizophrenic way: 'The same object produces all of these readings – not in sequence, but simultaneously' (85). Baucom argues in favour of this incoherence:

> The temptation to resist this derangement is strong. It seems better to assert mastery over this artifact, to identify it either as an apparatus of state discipline or as a hybridized and subverted architecture. But this temptation should be resisted. For it is, ultimately, the character of such overdetermined artifacts as the Victoria Terminus to produce not stable meanings but crises of reading. (85)

I believe that such an indefinitive reading, such a crisis, may be derived from Steel's work, which, equally if not more than Kipling's, which is Baucom's literary example, produces unstable meanings and lack of closures. Baucom's chapter focuses on the recurrent question found in Kipling's *Kim*, 'Who is Kim?', arguing that this 'ceaselessly repeated query invokes the barely hidden anxiety of that vast project of imperial adoption dramatized in Kipling's narrative' (88). Yet one of Steel's first stories, published in *Macmillan's Magazine* ten years before *Kim*, in 1891, is haunted by a similar question which commences her story, 'Lal': 'Who was Lal? What was he? This was a question I asked many times; and though it was duly answered Lal remained, and remains still, an unknown quantity – an abstraction, a name, and nothing more' (452). It is my contention that Steel's work, and especially, as we shall see, her writing involving the railway, constantly interrogates the Anglo-Indian interaction, even when the stories implicate no English characters whatsoever, exhibiting a reluctance to impose interpretations which tame or discipline the anarchic elements of Indian civilisation, those that by default exist outside the intellectual framework of the Westerner. The question, 'Who was Lal?', remains to the end and could be said to destabilise the whole of Steel's oeuvre. And though one could argue that in her collection of vignettes and characters of Indian life, Steel displays Empire's confidence in its ability to capture and exhibit its subjects (Baucom, 85), these subjects are never comfortably adopted and appropriated in the narrative, often eluding interpretation, with the narrator becoming self-ironising, respectfully withdrawing from further inquiry, and resorting to baffling indeterminacy.

Steel's volume, *In the Permanent Way, and Other Stories*, published as a collection in 1897 (though some stories had already appeared in periodicals since 1893), contains several stories which feature the railway. As has been argued throughout this chapter, trains and railway stations were significant contact zones which promoted interactive colonial encounters, not only in a literal sense but also in a wider socio-historical sense, since the railway in the colonies had been an important means of consolidating socio-political and cultural authority, as well as an instrument of technology and progress meant to civilise and advance the everyday life of the 'primitive' communities through which it passed. As Marian Aguiar maintains, 'Mobility is, after all, the primary function for a train; it was also the rationale for a colonial power that justified itself by the transferability of its ideals' (46). As a contact zone, the railway was a space in which the different trajectories not only of peoples but also civilisations intersected, and Steel seems especially sensitive to its ability to foster the co-presence of but also the unresolvable conflict between different perceptual and cultural frameworks. In my analysis I will focus on four of Steel's stories, 'In the Permanent Way', 'A Danger Signal', 'On the Second Story', and 'A Tourist Ticket', all of which are strongly suggestive of Steel's awareness of the aporias resulting from the railway's mission to discipline and homogenise the heterogeneous literal and conceptual space of colonial land and culture.

'In the Permanent Way' uses a narrative frame of a story within a story to relate the tale of a railway official, who during the construction of the 'Pind-Dadur' railway line through the desert, comes across an Indian man sitting on the sand at the exact spot on which the straight iron rails are supposed to be planted. The overseer of the construction, named Craddock, is very sensitive towards this apparently meditating man (later on nicknamed 'Meditations'), and keeps lifting him out of the 'permanent way' (the track on which the rails are laid), but to no avail as the man keeps returning to that same spot. Even when the line is completed and trains start using it, Craddock, as a driver, makes sure that the trains stop and move 'Meditations' out of harm's way before continuing the journey. One night when Craddock is drunk and the story's narrator needs to drive the train, due to lack of synchronisation between Craddock's and the narrator's watch, the train does not stop in time, killing both the Indian man on the track and Craddock who at the last minute jumps out of the train to save him. Both are buried in the permanent way, and the rail officials from then on, within the first narrative frame, feel obliged to stop, lift from, and reposition the running rail trolleys on the track, so as to avoid running over the altars of the two dead men.

In the only other, to my knowledge, critical reading of this story, Marian Aguiar argues that 'Steel uses the imagery of the train to present both conquest by means of technological development and Indian resistance' (45). The railway is the means of disciplining and conquering unruly land by means of charting space and imposing artificial lines and boundaries in the otherwise empty desert landscape. It is also a means of enforcing connectivity between not necessarily homogeneous regions, thus transforming relations between the parts of the nation and at the same time imposing the logic of Western politics upon these relations. But while both white narrators feel secure in their position as supervisors of the technology that confirms their political and cultural authority and superiority, throughout the story they are confounded by sudden disruptions and stops which are out of their control, resulting from the agency (or non-agency) of one Indian man. As Aguiar maintains, on the one hand, 'The British are charting space, entering it into an imperial, empirical order', but on the other, 'India's resistance is represented by the figure of the "Hindu saint"' (45). However, I believe that the function of the static, meditating man and of the barren space that he occupies in the desert is more nuanced, signifying not only India's resistance but also its potent historical continuity, since both man and desert space are shown to be firmly inscribed within a culture and a historical moment that are beyond the Westerner's understanding and which cannot be mobilised in the service of technology or any other Western modernising institutions. Rather than being an anachronistic space which exists in an anterior time, 'inherently out of place in the historical time of modernity' (McClintock, 40), the space is actually subject to a powerful human agency, whose historical situatedness is much more coherent than the incoherent, and, as it turns out, powerless modernity that the British are trying to impose with their technology. After all it is the Hindu man's participation within a firmly upheld religious tradition that manages to disrupt and undermine the agent of historical progress, of modernity, the railway. Nevertheless, the man's aim is only speculated and never confirmed; the British characters try 'to classify the creature' (29), to guess his sect, in accordance with their Western books on Hinduism, but their efforts, like their efforts to remove the man from the lines, are mocked by a pervasive ironic tone. Steel's narrative accepts its inability to incorporate Indian culture within its own intellectual and temporal zone, as up until the end of the story none of the characters manages to explain the purpose of the Indian sitting on the sand nor to calculate the time that he has been doing it: 'You see nobody really knew whether old Meditations was a *Saiva* or a *Vaishnava*' (42). Rather than coming into being through the representational strategies of Western literature, the Indian man is shown to already exist, to always already be, within a different time frame, beyond the understanding and the representational capacities of Western thought.

The first narrator acknowledges this indeterminacy at the end of the story, but without resolving the conflict between Western and Indian thought, without privileging the former. When he is told that two altars are raised for the 'hindu saint' (29), one for Shiva the Destroyer and one for Vishnu the Preserver, and that these symbols are appropriate for both Craddock and the Hindu man, the narrator closes the story with the thought, 'The jar of the points prevented me from replying' (42). He is silenced by the realisation that Craddock has been absorbed by the Indian culture, body and soul; his soul is dedicated to Hindu gods and his body, crushed in a tight embrace with the Indian, has become indistinguishable from that of the native. Aguiar asserts that Craddock and the guru have died 'locked in the intimate relation of opposites' and that there is 'a certain fatality in relations between Indians and Europeans when it comes to the grand imperial project – a relation as deadly to the English as to the Indians' (46). Nevertheless, the 'hybrid corpse' (Aguiar, 46) at the end is even more transgressive as a narrative and ideological tool because it suggests the blurring of the line between the British and the Indians in a way that threatens the hierarchies between superior colonisers and inferior colonised that imperialists such as Steel herself were meant to maintain. Steel's narrative on the contrary challenges the rationale of imperialism and questions the progress and enlightenment of the imperial civilising mission by suggesting that the traditions of the supposedly benighted peoples are planted firmly and permanently in the space that the railway officials see as barren and empty. According to this inverted view of imperialism's impact, the West's invasion of the East (by such means as the railway) can only be ephemeral and discontinuous, like the train that has to interrupt its journey and the rail trolley that needs to be disassembled and reassembled so as not to disrupt the peace of the man and later the corpses which lie in the very same space, the permanent path that the train unsuccessfully had claimed as its own permanent way.

The story also ironically undermines Western notions of time, by contrasting the time-tables and schedules that the train and the British characters are subject to and the incalculable time during which the guru has been sitting on the sand at the exact same spot. While the British have attempted to discipline the desert space by condensing and fixing the travelling time and distance between regions, the time-tables are constantly disrupted and overturned by the alternative fixity of the static man who imposes his own temporal and spatial reality on the train. However, the immobility of the Indian man sitting unperturbed on the sand does not emblematise static time, but the dynamic and meaningful passing of time, since it is this passing of many years that will ensure his immortality, according to the conjectures uttered in the story by both the British and the Indians. And by the end of the story the guru succeeds in being inscribed within time and memory, gaining permanence and immortality through the altars raised in his memory (and metaphysically, according to his own beliefs), while the train, for all its technological power and promise of temporal precision, will forever have to disrupt its schedules in order not to disturb this alien for the Westerner time frame. Steel's story thus suggests that clock time is unreliable and easily destabilised. After all Craddock and the guru die because of time failure: the former's watch stops working properly after a minor fall, and the narrator driving the train during Craddock's drunken stupor does not synchronise it with his own. As a result he does not stop the train in time, killing both the guru and Craddock who jumps out of the train to save him. The story traces the narrator's fear of impact and his agitation as he constantly looks at his watch calculating time and distance:

> the fear grew lest I should have been too late, lest I should have made some mistake. To appease my own folly I drew out my watch in confirmation of time. Great God! a difference of two minutes! – two whole minutes! – yet the watches had been the same at the distance signal? – the fall, of course! the fall!! (40–1)

His intense anxiety, resulting from the knowledge that time technology and locomotion are ultimately out of his control, is contrasted with the serene calmness of the guru who does not disrupt his own scheduled path towards immortality. The guru is able to control his body and its own temporality despite, or perhaps because of, death approaching, while the British men are confounded by that same technology – railways and railway time – they have constructed for the advancement and synchronisation of civilisation at a universal level.

Not only does the story mock the futile attempts of the British to impose Western timetables on India; it also challenges their belief in speed as a means of facilitating the imperial expansion project. The story starts with an evocative description of the narrator's perception of railway speed, produced, however, not by steam powered engines but by the will of the natives who are pushing the rail trolley on the tracks. As the narrator is pushed along the lines, he feels 'the propelling impulse of the unseen coolies behind, then the swift skimming as they set their feet on the trolly [sic] for the brief rest which merges at the first hint of lessened speed into the old racing measure' (27). Like on a proper train, on the trolley the source of power is unseen, yet on the latter vehicle, mobility is dependent not on technology but on the complicity or not of the natives. As the narrator gazes at the landscape in front of him, he imagines himself

Sitting on a stationary engine, engaged in winding up an endless red ribbon. A ribbon edged, as if with tinsel, by steel rails stretching away in ever narrowing lines to the level horizon. Stretching straight as a die across a sandy desert, rippled and waved by wrinkled sand hills into the semblance of a sandy sea. (27)

The interminable desert turns out to be forever beyond the conclusive grasp of the British, expanding and stretching to the extent that speed becomes irrelevant and the passenger feels as if he is going nowhere in a stationary vehicle. In other words, the landscape with its elusiveness and the 'coolies' whose will makes motion possible both mock the Westerner's assumptions of technological speed as a means of spatial discipline; it seems that what speed leads to is an aesthetic (and not political) annexation of territory: ribbons, ripples, and sandy waves suggest a merely imaginative, impressionistic, appropriation.

In 'A Danger Signal' Dhunnu, an aging Indian man and his grand-daughter Dhunni live in the middle of an unnamed desert area and their job is to lift the safety flag (red or green) to the trains traversing the crossing next to which they live. However, due to lack of traffic in the area, routinely only the green flag is lifted. Dhunni, who is described as a mischievous child longing for excitement, wants to lift the red flag, but dares not, until one day, after some years have passed, when she sees an unscheduled one-carriage engine approaching, she instinctively stops it. The handsome English boy on board decides to take her along with him in the carriage in order to see that she is punished for her insubordination by railway officials in a nearby town. But it turns out that her action has saved his life as it delayed his train and prevented it from crashing due to a broken line ahead. Half sorry, half glad that he has to part with her, the boy, who is smitten with her beauty, returns Dhunni to her home and the story once again ends with the silencing effect of an unanswered and unanswerable question: 'Dhunni stood gazing after the red and green lights with a dazed look on her face. The danger signal had come into her life – the train had stopped, and then – and?' (234).

In this story of colonial and gender encounters, the indefinite desert location – a 'sandy waste' according to the train driver – is once again contrasted to the fixity of the rail lines which are implanted in order to mark the otherwise unbounded space, and classify it within a rational system or network by which places are granted serial names – level crossing Number 57 – demarcating their position within recently charted ground. The disciplinary mission of the railway rendered through its punctuality and precision is challenged by the mischievousness of the young girl who constantly threatens to disrupt the logic of the crossing and the binary of danger and safety. In other words, while

Dhunnu and Dhunni are enlisted as crossing keepers to function within a system, an infrastructure, which dictates agency in accordance with its rational rules, the girl constantly undermines this function refusing to police and regulate the mobility of trains and bodies in the prescribed and predictable way within the wilderness of desert land. Instead, her agency disrupts the smooth running of the imperial machine. As Shampa Roy argues, contrary to other British women writers or reformers 'who reductively stereotyped Indian women as voiceless, helpless and ignorant and as invariably trapped in "pitiable states" and therefore requiring the benevolent gestures of their Western sisters' (60), Steel 'consciously disrupts the discourse of English feminine philanthropy' (64). Therefore, Dhunni's agency is not classified as pathetic and backward, as a sign of women's oppression in India, but is presented as self-liberating. In fact, while her grandfather warns her of the 'terrible consequences which followed on the unrighteous stopping of trains' (223), it turns out that her action, rebelliously raising the red flag, actually saves the train from collision. Technology is unreliable often leading to loss of life, while Dhunni's will and whim may grant salvation. The whole logic of danger and safety, supposedly ensured by the systematised routines of the railway – flags and signals – is overturned by Dhunni's spontaneous act; her arbitrary act of salvation is compared to the arbitrary breakdown of the line ahead: 'It was the veriest piece of luck! [. . .] If they had been five minutes earlier . . .' (232).

The story also juxtaposes Dhunni's attractive impulsiveness, as she lightheartedly and unrestrainedly, 'brimful of curiosity' (224), prances through the desert (despite the whacking that she sometimes unresent-fully accepts from her grandfather for her naughtiness), with the immobility of the passengers on the train, whom she describes as 'stuffed dolls' (223). Incarcerated within the carriage, deprived of independent mobility, the 'white dolls' are at the mercy of rigid schedules and mechanical efficiency, while Dhunni is able to escape the monotony of her position as a green flag signaller through her zest and wild imagination. When 'the pink and white child-dolls' fling a chunk of chocolate at her, she is enraged as she thinks that they have thrown stones (224). But the chocolate, which she eventually tastes and is enthralled by, inadvertently becomes the means of momentarily instilling submission and discipline to the colonised subject. And indeed, after tasting the chocolate, Dhunni 'smiled brilliantly at every train from that time forth, perhaps in hopes of more chocolate, perhaps from gratitude for past chocolate, perhaps because she really was beginning to be more sensible' (225). Yet, the tentative explanation rendered through the playful repetition of 'perhaps' points at the indefiniteness of Dhunni's adoption of Western habits. The chocolate is juxtaposed with the 'new suit of clothes and some jewels' that her future mother-in-law sends in preparation for her marriage; yet both are dismissively viewed by Dhunni who still longs for the excitement of the unknown: the danger signal – the red flag – initiating transgression which is more tempting than the ephemeral commodities that both cultures offer for superficial gratification.

When, finally, she gives in to her impulse and raises the red flag, the stopped train becomes the contact zone, a bewildered space, where the two different trajectories of West and East intersect, confounding not only the Indian but also the British subject. In his reading of Salman Rushdie, Baucom argues that in *The Satanic Verses*,

> The empire [. . .] is less a place where England exerts control than the place where England loses command of its own narrative of identity. It is the place onto which the island kingdom arrogantly displaces itself and from which a puzzled England returns as a stranger to itself. (3)

In Steel's story, it is the railway, the space of close encounters, that has this function of demonstrating the instabilities of imperialist narratives of identity. The English boy on board the train, who is at first annoyed by Dhunni's challenge to his authority, is eventually confounded not by her difference as an Indian girl, but by her sameness, as her beauty is not unlike his own, or unlike the beauty of English girls that he is likely to meet: '"By George! Craddock [. . .] I'd no notion they could look – er – like that. She is really quite a pretty girl". He could not help a smile somehow; whereat, to his surprise, she smiled back at him' (228). Moreover, while he incarcerates her in his carriage with the purpose of monitoring her actions ('I'll do *chowkidar* [watchman] till I can hand her over' [229]), it is he that comes under the surveillance of the girl who incessantly and fearlessly gazes at him. Feeling imprisoned within his own carriage by the captivating beauty of the girl and by her gaze to which he succumbs, he constantly envisages the end of this uncomfortable situation, looking outside the window, impatiently searching for his destination. In other words, his encounter with Dhunni causes him to lose command of his own self-definition and authority, while it is also described as a moment of racial panic, when due to mirroring – his smile is mirrored by her smile, his gaze by her gaze – the borders between self and other collapse. The unnamed English boy realises that *he* has become Dhunni's object of curiosity and that the dynamics of England's appropriation of the East as spectacle are overturned, with the strangeness of the West becoming the spectacle for its Eastern subjects. In an effort to reacquire control, the boy performs distancing tactics by relegating her to a regressive state of being – 'the little monkey' (230) – but he cannot

Figure 8. Rudolf Swoboda, *A Peep at the Train* (1892) Royal Collection Trust / © Her Majesty Queen Elizabeth II 2014.

ultimately dismiss her curious and defiant gaze which confounds him, to the point of his admitting, once again, his failure to apply alteritist stereotypes on her. The train and its occupant, rather than exhibiting their invulnerability to Eastern disorder, have been easily subjected to Dhunni's fecund imagination and unpredictable, though strong, will; the railway thus demonstrates the instability of boundaries between Western and Eastern will to power.[21]

The story also interrogates the effect that the imperial trappings, forcefully introduced in the desert space, have on Dhunni's consciousness. The interior of the carriage, described as a luxurious domestic drawing-room furnished with pictures on its walls, curtains, carpet, pink lamp shades, and comfortable arm-chairs, is contrasted to the starkness of Dhunni's crematorium-like home, just as the chocolate had been juxtaposed with the bridal presents. Yet the story does not privilege the Western commodities as a means of reforming the Indian girl. On the contrary, it is the English boy that experiences a reformation; he is transformed by Dhunni's presence to the extent that he finds himself wanting to entertain her by playing on his harmonium and singing for her better than he had ever sung before: 'And as he sang he felt with a certain anger that he had never sung it better – might never sing it so well again' (231). Moreover, her behaviour forces him to re-evaluate his imperialist belief in her otherworldly coarseness or her primitive inability to appreciate music when he admits that 'No one could have listened more eagerly' (231). With the English boy acknowledging the 'humour, the bitter irony' of his position as an entertainer of the 'wild' Indian girl, the narrative suggests the ineffectiveness of imperial command. As Baucom argues, from such encounters, 'a puzzled England returns as a stranger to itself' (3). In fact Steel from the beginning of the story, by imagining the Indian point of view, has subtly shown how English technology and culture are made strange in the eyes of the Indians, and how this strangeness is then experienced by the British themselves. The train, the symbol of imperial invasion, has from the start been viewed by Dhunni as a roaring monster, 'a great caterpillar with red and green eyes, and red and green lights in its tail' (221). Material reality – the railway – and its worshippers – the doll-like passengers – have become embedded within a foreign mythical context, and tropicalisation or exoticisation, if we can apply these terms to reverse Orientalism (Westernism?), has been initiated by Dhunni and her grandfather.

As Aguiar argues, 'the binary of inside and outside stands at the center of modernity's rhetoric of exclusion and is charted in the representational space of the train'. However, 'the boundaries between [inside and outside] are more fluid than they initially appear' (Aguiar, 94). In

Steel's story the imperial space inside the carriage, which initially seems to be impervious to the local space outside, becomes invaded by the will of the native girl, Dhunni, who not only does not put it in reverse mode towards regression and degeneration in accordance with the Westerners' fears, but actually saves it from collision and most probably death. In Steel's story, thus, the rhetoric of exclusion, exemplified by the seemingly insular train indifferently crossing the desert, becomes destabilised, as the upset power dynamics inside its carriage relentlessly question the hierarchy between rational European and threatening, or dangerous, native. Nevertheless, the ending of the story is not optimistic for Dhunni, just as it can't be so for the representative of England, the young boy, who is obliged to admit that even though he seems to have done the right thing by returning the girl to her home, 'it is a bit hard to know – to know what is fair and square – with – with some people' (234). In the conceptual framework of the young boy who needs to rationalise his experience, Dhunni has become 'some people', subjected to the generalising abstraction that the European ethnographic project deemed necessary. And as for Dhunni herself, Steel seems reluctant to reach a positive or negative closure which would secure her fate one way or another. The final open-ended sentence, 'The danger signal had come into her life – the train had stopped, and then – and?' (234), as the story resists closure, perhaps alludes to the unfinished business of empire and its undetermined effects on both English and Indian identity. Dhunni's exciting experience raising the red flag, being forced inside the bowels of the mystifying monster, and then incomprehensibly, but with seeming kindness, lifted out of it again, has demonstrated the permeability of boundaries between native and imperialist. But to what effect? Being 'in the permanent way of civilisation' (Steel, 'The King's Well', 150), Dhunni cannot help suffering a cultural hybridisation, like the guru, whose body literally melds with that of Craddock in the previous story.

Even though they do not illustrate physical contact between the natives and the British, the other two stories of the collection, for which the railway occupies an important role, 'On the Second Story' and 'A Tourist Ticket', also underscore this ambiguous hybridity. In the first of the two, the train becomes the aborted means of escape for a couple who according to Hindu tradition are not entitled to marry. Ramanund, an impious mathematician keen on Herbert Spencer and John Stuart Mill, falls in love with a devout and very sensible widow, Anunda, whom he meets at the shrine of the goddess Kali situated on the second floor of a building, one floor down from Ramanund's dwelling. When Anunda, who seems from the start unable to reconcile social and religious laws with desire, fails to keep her promise to elope with him via the train, Ramanund discovers her beheaded (perhaps sacrificed) in front of Kali's shrine and duly faints in horror. In her insightful reading of this story, Shampa Roy argues that in affirming Anunda's 'superior practical wisdom', 'the text actually reinforces the unchangeability of the Indian context and exposes the efforts of English-educated reformers like Ramanund as being hopelessly limited' (70). At the same time Roy affirms that Anunda's tragic death has been brought about by 'regressive practices' derived from the worship of the 'grotesque feminine power – the Goddess *Kali*. Terrifying and wrathful, the mother goddess seems to be symbolic of a kind of maternity and femininity that was completely opposed to the Victorian hegemonic ideal of womanhood' (70). In her otherwise very inspiring reading of Steel, Roy, by applying derogatory characterisations to the ancient religion, seems to attribute to Steel a blindness that, throughout her article, she attempted to absolve her from. I would like to propose that Steel's style and privileging of the Indian (albeit not unproblematically mediated) point of view, never actually deems the Hindu worship regressive. As a matter of fact, like in 'A Danger Signal' the Indian woman's enigmatic involvement in the narrative brings salvation.

In free indirect discourse, 'On the Second Story' ends with an ambiguous ironic tone; yet the worship of Kali does not seem to be the target of this irony:

> '*Jai Kali ma*! for She stayed the sickness' [said Ramanund's mother].
> Ramanund looked at her in dull dazed wonder. But it was true what she said. The cholera had slackened from that very time when he had been found lying at the Goddess' feet [next to Anunda's body]. (73)

Whereas for the Western reader it is difficult to accept that Anunda's sacrifice has brought about the abating of cholera, the narrative with its indeterminacy and ambiguous tone refuses to provide a more rational explanation. After all, the cholera pills that Ramanund circulated early in the story did not help relieve the ailing population. Moreover, the narrative remains undecided about whether an elopement by train would have been a preferable fate for Anunda, who has been conscious, from the first moment that she hears of the tickets to freely experienced passion that her lover has procured, of the gender and racial inequalities that the train in India perpetuated, despite its democratic promise that Ramanund believes in:

> 'Two railway tickets,' echoed Anunda in muffled tones from his shoulder; 'I came up in the railway from–'
> She paused, then added quickly: 'They put me in a cage, and I cried.'

'You will not be put in a cage this time,' replied Ramanund with a superior smile. (61)

As a means of gender and racial division, confinement, and subsequent psychological anxiety, the agent of modernity, the train, is thus more fearsome than the representative of 'the old ways', Kali, whose worship, despite its rigid, and for the Westerner regressive, practices, frees the spirit and may even save the body. At the end of the story, Ramanund becomes conscious of his own detrimental influence on Anunda, as, by requiring of her to embody the role of the liberated, modern woman, he inadvertently led her to death: 'Ah! why had he tried to interfere with the old ways? – why had he sought for more – why had he not let her be happy while she could, in her own way?' (72). The question of who is materially responsible for Anunda's death/sacrifice is complicated even further by Ramanund's mother who reveals to him that when he was 'found prostrate amid the blood of sacrifices' he was wearing one of Kali's garlands round his neck, as if Kali had favoured him with her trophy to thank him for fulfilling her wishes. Steel suggests that it was Ramanund's modernising impulses, thoughtlessly imposed on Anunda, as well as his hybrid Anglicised consciousness, that led to her death after all, with the Goddess recognising his confused agency as catalytic.

In my reading, Steel is not so much guilty of stereotyping the 'grotesque' old ways as of actually condoning them, and in doing so, she reveals perhaps her own conservativeness as a Victorian woman brought up within a system of gender ideology which dictated feminine self-denial and sacrifice. So, despite its otherworldliness, the image of femininity and maternity that Kali (and Ramanund's mother) propagates is, in its essence, not much different from its Victorian equivalent which found its expression in the 'angel in the house'. Both winged angel and eight-armed goddess functioned as symbols of women's self-sacrifice, whether they actually embodied the self-sacrifice, in the Western symbol, or ordered it in other women to ensure health and peace, in its Eastern manifestation. But perhaps Steel's conservatism also originates from her reluctance to apply Western, reformatory critiques on the Eastern traditions which, throughout her life and work in India, she tried to help preserve. Antoinette Burton has argued that 'there is little doubt that middle-class British feminists of the period viewed feminism itself as an agent of imperial progress, and their capacity to represent Indian women in turn as a signifier of imperial citizenship' (12). Yet Steel refuses to cast such a feminist, reforming, critique on Anunda's sacrificial death, perhaps out of respect for the unfathomable alterity of Kali worship or out of genuine bewilderment with its positive or negative effects on her believers. After all, Anunca's death is never confirmed, and the narrative applies its irony on Ramanund who from the start did not realise the liberating potentials of his lover's faith. With its inconclusiveness, the narrative challenges readers to decide for themselves whether sexual fulfilment via the cagelike train would have been a liberating option for Anunda or not.

In 'A Tourist Ticket' the failure of technology inadvertently grants salvation to Raheem, who had begun a pilgrimage via a train, but who gets crippled after a severe train accident which mostly affects the third-class passengers like himself. Raheem's intense desire for the pilgrimage and his naïveté in thinking that his money and the train may be employed as vehicles for gaining immortality are constantly juxtaposed with the devious actions of his brother and brother's girlfriend who are described as wasteful and selfish, to the extent that they steal his 'tourist ticket' in order to resell it and recklessly spend the money. Raheem discovers the loss of his ticket midway and is ordered to go back by the first train, but during his return as a despondent pilgrim, a horrible accident helps him recover his hopes of heaven. After the crash which shatters his legs, and which is described through Raheem's consciousness as an unidentified danger creeping up on him and suddenly striking, Raheem recognises his plight as an act of God, which exempts him from the duty of pilgrimage and therefore grants him salvation through other deeds which do not depend on Western technology and money. The theme of this story is again the permeability of cultural boundaries, a permeability expressed through Raheem's relationship with his modernised brother and the imperialist train. The narrative ironically contrasts the sincere faith in immortality that Raheem believes will be granted by his pilgrimage, with the 'tourist ticket' that is supposed to facilitate his journey. As a tourist on a vehicle of modernity, Raheem is subject to the contingencies and technical vulnerabilities of the train whose function is the fulfilment of transient pleasures or routine journeys, not the forging of the path to immortality. As Steel's previous stories have shown, the 'permanent way', the tracks, of the railway are always disrupted by the permanence of other fixed roots which tie the natives to their traditions and religious faith. The conflict remains unresolved as the narratives resist definitive closure.

In her effort to express this incompatibility of cultures and manners that complicate the plot of her stories, but also with her own inconclusive and ambiguous stance towards the imperial civilising mission, Steel invents a narrative style very unlike the realistic style of her era, one that is conscious of an alternative reality experienced in the colonies and one that cannot be embedded within the fixtures of the neatly organised realist plot. In other words, her style, which avoids explanations and closures and which resonates with an almost magical tone, materialises the incompatibility of different traditions, composing a hybrid realism that incorporates the extraordinary and the fantastic with the same sobriety as it does the mundane. Steel's narratives show, without prejudice or patronising attitude, that the extraordinary is no more surreal than the ordinary: the choices and decisions of the immoveable guru on the tracks are no more strange or absurd than those of the solitary young passenger in the luxurious drawing-room-like carriage traversing the expanse of the desert; the worship of Kali that leads to the death of Anunda is no more grotesque than the Western obsession with the monster or caterpillar train that in invading the desert confounds and irreparably alters Dhunni or kills the stationary guru in his tight embrace with the English railway operator; the mysterious subsiding of the cholera epidemic by an unknown divine force is no more extraordinary than the arbitrary, ordinary action of Dhunni, who by raising her hand prevents a train collision and saves the young English boy and his train driver. Steel's peculiar realism weaves a multi-lingual and multi-cultural text that fuses inexplicable and unexplained elements of India's traditions with those of her contemporary imperial culture. She thus creates an open-ended discourse which points at the limitations of the Westerner's rational, conceptual framework, when it comes to understanding the alien culture, and even at the detrimental effects of the hybridity effected within the colonial contact zones. Laura Bear has argued that 'the railway station from the end of the nineteenth century became the site of challenges to the legitimacy of British rule' (45). I believe that the railway, station and train, as the definitive contact zone, became for Steel the site of challenges not only to the legitimacy of British rule, but also to the legitimacy of their imperial narrative which relied for its stabilising realism on a rigid belief in progress and racial as well as ethical binaries. In this way, Steel's subversive narrative challenges the means of imperial self-definition.

Writing for *The Saturday Review* on the subject of 'An Indian Jubilee', on 7 November 1908, many years after her return from India, Steel writes still of the ineffectuality of the imperial mission in India:

> How idle it is to talk of a jubilee in connexion with any part of Indian life; above all, in connexion with that *curiously* complete, *curiously* incomplete civilization of its people which, until a short fifty years ago, seemed in its utter changelessness to mock at very Time.
>
> For, after all, what is a short fifty years in an unbroken history of three and four thousand? (571; emphasis added)

Steel acknowledges the little influence that the British have had during their fifty years of reign in India. Despite the railways, the telegraph post, and the signs of industrial progress, she writes, 'sooner or later you come upon the old order of things. Even the smoke of a factory chimney is lost at last in the unending levels of an Indian plain' (571). This ineffectuality is the result, in her view, of the inability of imperialists like herself to understand, penetrate, and influence the 'curious' progression of the Indian civilisation. She, thus, acknowledges the lack of synchronisation between the temporal framework imposed by the British (compactly represented by railway time) and the different conception of time by which the Indian people have experienced a long, complex, history, which cannot be infiltrated and transformed. It has been my contention that Steel's narratives have resisted the imperialist impulse to subsume and appropriate this history; and the railway settings have been especially conducive to illustrating the disharmony of opposites and the polarity of cultures and identities. Unlike other imperial narratives which deny the colonised races originary power of historical and cultural progress and development, Steel's narratives of the railway, through their imaginative insight, juxtaposition of others (natives *and* British), but also their indeterminacy and inconclusiveness when it comes to representing the intricacies of Indian culture, demonstrate the author's respect for the Indian alterity. Her stories also position Indian history within a parallel trajectory, within a temporal and spatial zone whose boundaries had, she admits, become permeable, but no more permeable than the walls of the rail carriages that were the vulnerable emblems of the 'universal' civilisation that the British were imposing on India.

Notes

1. See Hoganson, 200.
2. For a fuller analysis of this scene in relation to women's cosmopolitanism see my 'No Natural Place' article in *The Henry James Review*.
3. For a theoretical approach to the distinctions between settler colonialism and colonialism as well as an overview of the relevant criticism, see Lorenzo Veracini, *Settler Colonialism: a Theoretical Overview* (2010).
4. The British title, *Canadian Born*, also alludes (consciously or not) to a collection of poems of the same title published in 1903 by Emily Pauline Johnson, a prominent Canadian poet. We could speculate that Ward was perhaps advised to change her title when she was preparing to publish her novel in the States on account of its former use by Johnson in Canada. However, it is interesting that her title should echo a collection and poem by a female poet of mixed blood, whose literary preoccupations have been the dual heritage of Canadians, native and European. In fact, Johnson

herself was the daughter of a wealthy white woman from England and a Mohawk chief from Canada, and her poems attempt to resolve conflicts of ethnic ambiguity resulting from the fraught relations between natives, settlers, and the British. Her poem, 'Canadian Born', expresses a pride in this hybridity, for which, however, she was subsequently criticized for 'limited [. . .] effectiveness as a spokesman for Native people' (Francis, 120):

> No title and no coronet is half so proudly worn
> As that which we inherited as men Canadian born.
> We count no man so noble as the one who makes the brag
> That he was born in Canada beneath the British flag. (Johnson, p. 2,
> ll. 13–16)

5. See Guelke and Morin for a discussion of the way naturalist pursuits corroborated an imperialist agenda.
6. See (alphabetically) Elizabeth Bohls, *Women Travel Writers*, Antoinette Burton, *Burdens of History*, Nigel Leask, *Curiosity and the Aesthetics of Travel Writing*, Sara Mills, *Discourses of Difference*, Susan Morgan, *Place Matters*, Mary Louise Pratt, *Imperial Eyes*.
7. See Karen Morin's 'Peak Practices' for an analysis of women such as Isabella Bird and Rose Kingsley longing for risk and conquering their frailty.
8. See also Antoinette Burton, *Burdens of History*.
9. The novel exhibits little to no consciousness of the native Indians that formerly inhabited the lands now occupied by the settlers. In fact, despite its ambivalent take on imperialism by the heroine, the natives' rights to land are never considered and their territorial dispossession by the will of the white settlers never questioned or regretted. This interpretation is in line with recent theoretical approaches to settler colonialism which highlight the colonial settlers' annihilating drive as they conceptualised the new territory as vacant and available. In the words of Fiona Bateman and Lionel Pilkington, the presence of the natives 'was ignored, treated as a minor inconvenience [. . .] as dispensable' (1).
10. Even Anderson at times considers the burdens of time and the past, the debilitating force of origins and heredity (his own criminal father), which pull him back, while Elizabeth is only moving forward, ignoring the anchoring that history effects on her consciousness. The fear of degeneration seems to be deeply embedded in the male characters' colonial mentality.
11. All English characters in the novel see the immigrant settlers, who come from throughout Europe and America, as the new natives of the land. See Note 9.
12. In a discussion with Elizabeth, Anderson makes his nationalistic agenda clear: 'We have our own future. It is not yours [. . .] Canada will have her own history; and you must not try to make it for her' (158).
13. See Notes 9 and 11.
14. See Derrida, 83.
15. See Showalter's influential condemnation of Ward's outdatedness (227).
16. Sutton-Ramspeck compellingly argues that 'To ignore Ward and to deny her feminism are not only to distort and oversimplify the culture and gender

politics of her time but to silence one of its most prominent and interesting voices' (218).

17. Ward herself was one of the founders of Somerville College, Oxford.
18. All biographical information has been derived from Violet Powell's, *Flora Annie Steel: Novelist of India* (1981).
19. The review of Steel's *In the Permanent Way and Other Stories* quoted here was first published in the *Times* and subsequently collected under the title 'Book Reviews Reviewed' in *The Academy* (5 February 1898).
20. Originally published in *The Spectator*.
21. Rudolf Swoboda's 1892 painting, *A Peep at the Train*, similarly exemplifies the juxtaposition of two cultures and two kinds of gaze via the medium of the train. The painting, which focuses on Indian villagers peeping, according to the title, at an unrepresented train, whose tracks make but a small appearance at the left corner of the canvas, could, as Saloni Mathur has argued, very well have been titled 'A Peep *from* the Train', as 'the viewer is positioned as if he or she were on the train, looking out from a railway carriage at a passing scene' (101). Mathur rightly argues that it is impossible to determine Swoboda's aim in painting this cultural encounter between Western technology and picturesque India (102). However, by placing the viewer in the position of the travelling passenger, the painting hints at an unsettling exchange of gazes, during which the colonial subject remains unperturbed while train and passengers become entertaining spectacles, obliterated as subjects by the powerful gaze of the natives.

Chapter 4

Railway Space and Time

Industrial Traffic

The railway is at once the 'life's blood' and 'the triumphant monster, Death'. And in this dramatic enactment Dickens is responding to the real contradictions – the power for life or death; for disintegration, order and false order – of the new social and economic forces of his time.

Raymond Williams, *The Country and the City* (1973), 163

In his evocative description of urban alienation and indifference in the nineteenth century, Raymond Williams considers Dickens's railway in *Dombey and Son* to be a part of the impersonal institutional forces of modern society that physically and ideologically disrupt the established architectural and social order so as to impose new discipline and uniformity. Dickens's railway novel of the forties almost compulsively traces the impact of railway construction, journeys, and employment on character, perception, and urban planning, capturing both the vertiginous rhythms of technological progress and the alienating and dehumanising effects of mechanised mobility. Turning whole city areas into waste ground and houses into carcasses while preparing them for more efficient functioning within interconnected systems of technology and science, Dickens's monsters, dragons, and giants are the vehicles of socio-economic success at the expense of nature, of the physical manifestations of a historical past, and even of individuality. In Dickens's preoccupation with the railway we find a protomodernist vision of people as impersonal railway passengers, anonymous members of moving crowds which function as if automatically at the command of a timetable or a railway clock. Railways in *Dombey and Son* promise economic power but also bring tragedy and death. They embody speed but they also prompt meditations on fatality, on the 'swift course' of life mocked by the mechanical speed of the train, as Dombey realises during a dizzying railway journey after his son's death (280). They demand the efficiency of their workers but ultimately distort simple habits which define them as human: in order to sustain himself and function, Mr Toodle, the railway engineer, needs to '[shovel] in his bread and butter with a clasp knife, as if he were stoking himself' (514). Moreover, for Dickens the railway is not just a product and apparatus of industry and a metaphor for the speedy advance of science but also a reason for the construction of new spaces of transit as well as a means of remapping and reconceptualising space: 'There were railway hotels, coffee-houses, lodging-houses, boarding-houses; railway plans, maps, views, wrappers, bottles, sandwich-boxes, and time-tables [. . .] railway omnibuses, railway streets and buildings' (224). In his description, the new transitory spaces generated by the railway require a novel conception of experience as fleeting and contingent and thus dependent on equally ephemeral objects which facilitate or make comfortable this fast movement across and beyond cities; for the sandwich-box seems as indispensable as the map and the time-table. Railway spaces affected experience on many levels, practical as well as conceptual and visual.

A lot has been written about Dickens's treatment of the railway in this novel, as well as about his own involvement in a railway accident in 1865 which left him psychologically traumatised, and which curiously prefigured his death on the very same date of the accident five years later.[1] While I do not wish to add to the readings, I would like to examine the ways in which other writings of the period by and about women dealt with similar issues of the mechanisation of life and the concomitant alienation or estrangement from community that the railway brought about. In what ways and to what degree were women conscious of the social and psychological effects of the reconfiguration of familiar and public space by the railway? In this period of increasing industrialisation and urbanisation, the railway contributed to the construction of a new social and spatial experience for which mobility seemed to be a prerequisite as well as an outcome. In this chapter I would like to focus on the way Victorian texts deal with women's urban alienation and loss of individuality and community brought about by the expansion of the railway network which enabled and in some cases demanded radical uprooting and relocation. The issue of women's response to collective identities and spatial displacement – which is different from the displacement suffered by the heroines of the previous chapters – will initially be linked to industrialisation, class, and/or economic necessity. Next the chapter will connect railway traffic to the nervousness and fragmentation experienced by railway women as we move towards the fin de siècle and modernism, during which women start developing new narrative techniques that reflect changes in the perception of space and time that the railway stimulated.

In *The Country and the City* Raymond Williams argues that with the growth of cities, 'identity and community became more problematic, as a matter of perception and as a matter of valuation, as the scale and complexity of the characteristic social organization increased' (165). To Williams's list of complex institutions which made identity and communities more opaque, one may add the railway, whose technological and social organisation initiated profound changes in interpersonal interaction and perceptions of individuality and community. Frances Trollope's 1848 novel *Town and Country*, which begins with an apostrophe to 'Steam! steam! steam!' (1), goes back in time by fifty years in order to recapture a sense of individuality and discreteness that she believes the railway contributed in obscuring. If, as Williams believes, 'Most novels are in some sense knowable communities' (165), Mrs Trollope believes that the advent of the railway forfeited this knowability by undermining detail and accuracy to the extent that character and identity in novels, but also in life, suffered a levelling standardisation: 'our written details', she remarks, 'both of events and of character, bear about the same resemblance to those left to us by our fathers, as the glances of landscape afforded to the passengers of an express railroad train do to the meditative, lingering contemplation of the traveller' (2–3). She thus links the delimiting impact of speed on perception to the way individuality is or is not perceived and represented: 'this steam, which brings all the world together so easily, knocks off as many corners of character as of road, and thereby makes one people so very like another people, and one set so very like another set' (3). Railway speed, in her view, while shortening distances and lengthening lives, reduces individuals to 'jostling throngs' (4), for the fast receding of in-between space from one's consciousness has heralded the loss of distinctness and variety: 'for almost before 'tis seen 'tis gone' (4). In the way that it attributes to the railway changes in perception, space, time, and identity, Mrs Trollope's description evocatively introduces themes that preoccupied many women writers of the mid and later Victorian period. Railway speed, which served not only leisure travel but most importantly industry and urbanisation, is a persistent theme as it threatened to erase personal and collective histories and communities, with passengers increasingly treating the space rapidly traversed as a blank or static space, empty of signification, of lives, and of difference. As George Eliot famously wrote in the introductory chapter of *Felix Holt* (1866), 'The tube-journey can never lend much to picture and narrative; it is as barren as an exclamatory O!' (5). It is this tendency to view people and landscape indiscriminately and without imaginative investment, a tendency engendered by railway travel, that also affects narrative, as Mrs Trollope and Eliot believe, for which reason the former harks back to a time before the invention of the railway 'had caused them to be jumbled all together' (*Town and Country*, 5), fleetingly seen and swiftly forgotten.

Likewise, in *The Hidden Sin*, an 1866 novel, the Irish poet and novelist Frances Browne considers railway travel detrimental to community and individuality, as the passengers' new habits of hasty observation and meaningless interaction neutralise individuality and trivialise community. Browne compares the railway to the stagecoach or mail, emphasising through emphatic repetition that in the days of the latter 'there was life' on the roads, the highways, and the roadside inns, where there were acquaintances to be made, news to be heard, scenes to be witnessed, and landscape to be enjoyed (169); and thus 'life' consisted of individual and collective expression, communication, and knowability. Slow travel is seen as a means of safeguarding ties with community while creating the conditions for building new bonds with people and country or city. On the other hand, by the speedy railway journey communities are rendered unknowable and people turned into anonymous crowds: 'our haste reduces the multitude to one undistinguishable mass; their individualities and belongings utterly lost to the observer; people have no time to see or to talk in those flying trails of smoke and thunder, and life has become too great a scurry for either thought or enjoyment' (169). According to Wolfgang Schivelbusch, the motion of the train generated a novel perceptual ability in passengers, one that allowed them 'to perceive the discrete, as it rolls past the window, indiscriminately' (60–1). Yet, while in Schivelbusch's writing it is the scenery mainly which loses its differentiating marks as well as its dimension of depth due to the high velocity's new demands on vision, in Browne's description, speedy railway motion also affects the way human beings themselves are processed by travellers who, as hasty observers, reduce the foreground to an alienated and alienating background full of depthless faces and bodies – 'one undistinguishable mass'. Browne, like Frances Trollope before her, recognises the railway's negative effects on perception, communication, and community, suggesting that fleeting perception inevitably leads to the corrosion of human bonds and ultimately to a crisis of community and identity.

To a large extent the railway contributed to the dissolution of community in the industrial period, as it facilitated residential mobility which shook the stability of local social systems. Interconnected railway networks, which served industrial and commercial traffic as well as urbanisation and suburbanisation, increasingly disintegrated localised social networks which relied on the fixedness of roots and residence.[2] The role of the railway as such a vehicle of social fragmentation, personal displacement, and even identity revision or loss is explored in Elizabeth Gaskell's *North and South* (1855). In the novel, it is 'railroad time' that 'inexorably wrenche[s] [the Hales] away from lovely, beloved Helstone' (57), the familiar, knowable community whose distinguishing marks, such as the old church tower, ensure stability as well as human interconnectedness and dependence. Railroad time, which 'displac[ed] the sidereal rhythm of the natural world' (Ferguson, 'Introduction', 2) and thus stands for technological discipline, dissolves such community feeling by causing instantaneous and permanent displacement: 'They were gone', Margaret repeats twice at the very start of her trip to Milton (57), the repetition emphasising the immediate and traumatic radical uprooting she experiences, made possible by the speed and efficiency of technology.[3] The train approaching Milton forces Margaret to face her 'stern and iron' future (60), one that, like the rigid, iron railway line that carries her, implies the subordination of nature to technology: 'Nearer to the town, the air had a faint taste and smell of smoke; perhaps, after all, more a loss of the fragrance of grass and herbage than any positive taste or smell' (60). Margaret's baffled response to the fast approaching smoke viewed from the train window suggests perhaps the confusing effect of speed on the senses, which synaesthetically conflate the approaching visible darkness with the suspected but unconfirmed smell that must accompany it. The fact that the smell of smoke prevails in her consciousness prefigures the loss of natural surroundings that she will experience at her place of relocation. At the same time the train, which enables mass mobility, introduces Margaret to mass living conditions as, from the new urban viaducts which made industrial or slum areas visible to passengers from above, she catches a glimpse of the housing organisation of the industrial town: 'Quick they were whirled over long, straight, hopeless streets of regularly-built houses, all small and of brick' (60). Compared to Helstone, Milton for Margaret is an impersonal geography of uniformity and automation, one that confirms industrialisation's achievement of severing permanent relations to place. The action of the railway as it wrenched her away from home had already foretold this rupture from a qualitative to a quantitative experience of space and time.

At Milton Margaret feels and looks out of place, her precarious rambles in the city initially representing her reluctant trespassing of spatial and social boundaries. When she is freely accosted and at times indecently addressed by unknown working-class men, she realises the function of the street as a space of instability which threatens one's social, personal, and moral integrity. For example, though shocked by the men's words towards her, Margaret is also amused by them (72). By positioning her body where, according to the segregating rules of gender and class ideology, it is not supposed to be, she commits a transgression which challenges her sense of social and sexual self, while, at the same time, helping her turn the loss felt by her residential uprooting to a sense of personal gain and progress. And indeed as she acquires an urban identity and develops an empathic involvement in the scenes of industrial strife or poverty that she witnesses, the city becomes less estranging and her forays into its streets more determined. As Wendy Parkins has argued, by foregrounding Margaret's mobility, Gaskell makes her heroine 'a participant in, rather than an observer of, modernity' ('Women, Mobility', 507). Her mobility represents 'the agency of the modern female subject' ('Women, Mobility', 517).

However, the spaces of modernity are not always conducive to such agency, which may prove vulnerable when tested against a rigid social world of uncompromising prejudices. When one evening Margaret accompanies her brother to the train station – the setting that triggers the principal misunderstanding between herself and Thornton – she seems to be exercising an urban freedom earned by her previous spatial relocations and transgressions. However, at the station Margaret realises that social relations of power infuse space with ideological meaning which serves to maintain gender hierarchies and more particularly woman's rightful place. So although until that moment she had maintained a distinguished, honourable, and even haughty middle-class stance towards Thornton, her presence at a dubious location, the station, in the darkness, with a seemingly unknown man, immediately jeopardises her social and sexual identity, making her appear in the eyes of Thornton as a woman of loose morals. The space of literal mobility and traffic becomes, in the eyes of Thornton, a space of sexual traffic, with Margaret becoming the unlikely protagonist of such transactions. The train station, like other private and public spaces, is socially constructed, and though with her urban mobility Margaret has tried to challenge gender stereotypes which have tied her to the passive home life and the backward-seeming south, her adventure at the station reminds her of the rigidity of such restrictions. The incident is also indicative of the paradoxes of urban living, for though Margaret had hoped for anonymity at the impersonal station, she and her brother are recognised by three distinct townsmen who implicate her not only in the assumed sexual indiscretion but also in the death of a man. The train station thus emerges as a space of personal and social discipline, as Margaret is obliged to regulate her moves which at the start of this scene were characterised by fearlessness: 'Oh, I can manage. I am getting very brave and hard', she says, when she begins to ponder on the walk back from the station in the darkness (257). But later, after her unfortunate meeting with Thornton and the mishap with Frederick pushing Leonards off the platform, 'she felt she could not walk home along the road' (259), and hiding in the ladies' waiting room, she dares not raise her eyes to look at the porter who helps her into the carriage of the train that carries her home (260).

The train station also proves to be the epitome of state surveillance, as the various witnesses of the violent scene report on her presence there, making her the subject of cross-examination by a police inspector. But though Margaret manages to acquit herself temporarily through lying, her performance of 'regal composure' with which, during the questioning, she denies her presence at the station – 'I was not there' (269) – is not enough to save her from infamy. Instead it is Thornton who decides to save her from the public shame of feminine indecency and falsehood. So to the extent that in the north Margaret has tried to combine her new awareness of socio-economic and industrial relations with an idea of feminine strength and emancipation, the railway serves to dissolve this connection, fragmenting her identity and reminding her of the restrictions and prejudices that disable or discredit women's mobility. The railway thus becomes for Margaret the agent of a double severing, firstly from the closely-knit community which had defined her juvenile idea of herself and secondly from the identity she had gradually constructed as a gendered urban subject and an individual at Milton. Besides, the scene at the train station also proves to Margaret how fragile or insignificant her individuality may be taken for in such spaces of impersonal transit, since she is so easily depersonalised and misrepresented as a type, the type of a loose woman.

Forty years on, Sue Bridehead in Hardy's *Jude the Obscure* (1896) does not mind being misrepresented or maligned for boarding trains or spending time at a train station with a young man. She is not bothered when during her railway escapade with Jude they are taken for lovers and given an empty compartment all to themselves by a guard who acts in collusion with the new sexual mores that the railway had contributed in slackening (163). The geographic and sexual mobility of woman is taken for granted in this novel, whether it is forced by harsh economic conditions or by freely expressed erotic choices. And the railway epitomises this condition of ephemeral work and love, with woman having become a regular participant in its everyday routines. Furthermore, when Jude suggests that they go and sit in the cathedral at Melchester, Sue retorts that she'd 'rather sit in the railway station [. . .] That's the centre of the town life now. The Cathedral has had its day!' (160). With this comment, Sue acknowledges an oxymoron, that the spatial point of the town's decentralisation, the station, is precisely its centre; the locus that enables the dispersal of individuals and the dissolution of community is the focal point of urban life. Whether inward or outward, mobility defines town life, and Sue, more than Jude who admires the stability of static social structures such as those represented by Christminster or cathedrals, is attuned to its transient features. In a novel whose 'table of contents reads like a train schedule with its starkly enumerated list of points of arrival and departure' (Keep, 139), it is women who acknowledge this rupture of the continuity of locality and who experience most poignantly the precarious spatial and temporal co-ordinates that complicate their daily existence.[4] For the paths of Sue's and Arabella's lives are constantly subject to railway routes and timetables, their love affairs with Jude acquiring the arbitrariness of destinations chosen, abandoned, or switched.[5] Hardy's nomadic characters thus develop precarious relations not only to place but also to each other. They experience 'relationships as traffic' (Raymond Williams, 299).

Moreover, as Christopher Keep has argued, 'the speed and dynamism of the train seemed to many like Sue to represent a way of finally breaking free of the intense gravitational pull of history and convention' (139). In that sense mobility and restlessness are experienced by Sue as progressive means of challenging socio-cultural and gender hierarchies in the context of an unstable community network which, as has been shown above, is being constantly reconfigured and redefined in terms of its flexibility rather than its fixity. Nevertheless, this restlessness of continuous transit contributes to what Hardy and his critics have described as Sue's pervading nervousness, a nervousness that, as Nicholas Daly has argued, might have been caused by the 'modernization of the senses effected by the technological revolutions of the nineteenth century' such as the railway (*Literature*, 42). Modern nervousness thus seems to result from the subject's experience of time as transitory, space as discontinuous and fleeting, and action as fortuitous, an experience that makes Sue into an 'intellectualized, emancipated bundle of nerves that modern conditions were producing, mainly in cities as yet', according to a German reviewer's diagnosis reported by Hardy in his 1912 postscript to the novel (ix–x). It would not be an exaggeration to claim that Sue's infamous volatility matches the instability and fleetingness of location that the twists and turns of the railway plot precariously hinge upon. And yet it is this nervousness and her heightened intellectual life that saves Sue from the railway institutionalisation that has turned, conversely, Little Father Time into inert freight, a passenger without soul, without volition, and, in the words of Trish Ferguson, 'an automaton, the symbolic human embodiment of machine culture [. . .] Little Father Time is quite literally a deus ex machina, a god out of a machine, mechanized, like the railway' ('Hardy's Wessex', 71). In his dehumanisation, manifested in the rigid fixedness of his gaze and posture while in the carriage that brings him towards Jude and Sue for the first time (327), Little Father Time embodies what Sue with her heightened consciousness does not. For Sue, like Margaret Hale before her, resists the levelling deperson-alisation suffered by mass transit passengers. With her impenetrable obscurity, restlessness, and volatility she withstands, until the death of her children, her own assimilation within networks of institutional morality that the railway, as a battlefield of gender and class conflicts, paradoxically both challenged and strengthened.

Railway Time – Trains of Thought

> There was even railway time observed in clocks as if the sun itself had given in.
>
> Dickens, *Dombey and Son* (1848), 224

Trish Ferguson argues that Hardy's *Jude* dramatises 'the alienating dangers of time regulation, scheduling and the frantic pace of moder-nity' ('Hardy's Wessex', 73), a modernity embodied by the railway in the novel. With the expansion of the railway network in Britain in the 1840s it became obvious to the railway companies that the smooth running of the lines, the avoidance of deadly accidents, and the passengers' ability to catch their trains were contingent on time standardisation and preci-sion.[6] But as railway time progressively replaced local time in one region or city after the other, Victorian lives became 'subject to a temporal regimentation' (Zemka, 6) which instigated some resistance from those who aligned the time derived from the movement of the sun with leisure, the imagination, and a qualitative human experience. An article entitled 'Railway-Time Aggression' in *Chambers's Edinburgh Journal* (Anon., 1851) describes the imposition of standardised rail-time (the 'monster evil of the day') as arbitrary and its disruption and displacement of 'canonical' time (as guided by the sun) as aggressive (394, 393):

> [Old Time] is now obliged, in many of our British towns and villages, to bend before the will of a vapour, and to hasten on his pace in obedience to the laws of a railway company! Was ever tyranny more monstrous or more unbear-able that this? (392)

The article recounts several incidents during which the discrepancies between railway and sun time caused minor discomforts or misunder-standings between the fashionable members of a community, ending with a nostalgic call, urging men to 'rally around Old Time' (395). And yet the triviality of the incidents narrated and the leisurely conduct of all characters involved point to an important social and cultural crisis in Victorian Britain as the new time regime initiated by the railway could no longer accommodate leisurely activities which depended on approximate and not precise time. 'To become "as regular as clockwork" was the bourgeois ideal', according to Lewis Mumford in his seminal *Technics and Civilization* (16). Railway time, thus, regulated not only the mobility of travellers but also the social life of the middle and upper classes and the labour activities of the working classes. If, in the words of John Urry, time was newly conceived as 'a resource to be managed' rather than 'as activity or meaning' (99), daily leisure and routines had to be synchronised and disciplined. Ironically, this hostile to railway-time article ends by revealing its author's inevitable internalisation of the new time discipline: 'Englishmen! beware of delay in opposing this dangerous innovation! No time is to be lost' (395). While progressive innovation is shown to debilitate socio-cultural traditions, its concomitant dependence on punctuality and time economy already underlie the discourse of the writer. The phrase, 'No time is to be lost', acts in collusion with the mechanisation of time which ensured its measurable quantification. By the 1890s clocking-in machines were widespread, connecting definitive time with work and wages (Stevenson, 126).

Margaret Oliphant's short story 'A Railway Junction: or the Romance of Ladybank' (1873), which is set, as the title indicates, in a station, explores this tension between precise and approximate time. Waiting for his connection on the railway platform of a junction called Ladybank, Captain Cannon is reacquainted with a girl, Nelly, he had been smitten with some time before. Induced by love at first sight to abandon his friends and consequently miss his train, he eventually makes Nelly neglect her railway timetable by tempting her to a picnic during which he cultivates romance. For such a short plot line, the story is paradoxically long (twenty-three long *Blackwood's* pages), as Oliphant takes the opportunity to describe scrupulously and at length the sites – cities, monuments, and hills – encircling the station. After all, as Oliphant constantly suggests, it is the natural and historical surroundings that 'throw a more genial glow upon the weary roadside station' (421). The narrative therefore performs the expansion of the eye that the modern seclusion within insular spaces like the train compartment or the station has hindered. Moreover, it is as if with her story Oliphant was trying to fill the empty hours of those passengers stranded on the junction platform waiting for the train. Indeed the story seems to be about lost and gained time, explored both through the plot and the style. As Oliphant remarks, considering the hectic rhythm of life and work in the Victorian period, 'it is inconceivable how leisurely the people [who wait on platforms] are and how little it seems to matter to any one that they have an hour or two to wait at a junction' (421). The junction is described as a liminal space of modernity, a technologically constructed crossroad, occupying a site of no essential urban or historical significance in itself, paradoxically combining mobility with immobility, the speed of the trains rushing through it with the stationary posture of the awaiting passengers. Oliphant describes it as 'one of those purgatories of modern existence, those limbos of the weary and restless spirit' (419), suggesting the tortures of the modern consciousness, which, under the influence of timetables and routines, is obliged to endure spatial and temporal gaps in the otherwise fast process of living. The junction as limbo combines the worst of two worlds: 'the horrible sounds' of the perpetually moving trains, described as 'demoniac and excruciating', and 'the silence which intervenes', 'deep as death', 'the silence of useless and angry leisure, not knowing what to do with itself' (422). Thus railway spaces, and the junction especially, negotiate the otherwise incompatible concepts of mobility and immobility, work and leisure, sound and silence, time and timelessness, all of which are shown to be subject to technology and not to human agency.

The effect of the junction as limbo is also explored by Charles Dickens in 'Barbox Brothers', a story published in the 1866 Christmas issue of *All the Year Round*. Here Mugby Junction forces a stasis on the protagonist who jumps out of the train on arrival at this in-between space and who for several weeks is unable to decide which 'iron road' to take. Dickens's narrative explores this man's procrastination as the many possibilities of travel (the junction connects seven lines) confuse and immobilise him to the extent that he becomes known as 'the gentleman for Nowhere' (7). His static posture at the junction is contrasted with his lively imagination which he applies to the railway lines, pondering over the sharp, pulsating rhythm of the trains passing and the fleetingness of the vignette-like scenes of carriages and passengers rushing past: '*Then*, puppet-looking heads of men [. . .] *Then*, prodigious wooden razors [. . .] *Then* several locomotive engines [. . .] *Then*, along one avenue [. . .] *Then*, a struggling horse' (4; emphasis added). While engines, tracks, trucks of coal, and carriages have a non-ceasing, eternal, forward-moving life of their own, his own human life regresses, burdened by opportunities offered but not taken. As the railway lines become mirrored on his forehead, he starts looking more aged: 'Barbox Brothers stood puzzled on the bridge, passing his right hand across the lines on his forehead, which multiplied while he looked down, as if the railway

Lines were getting themselves photographed on that sensitive plate' (4). Railway time, thus, seems to take revenge on the man who is unable to partake in its mechanised routines. However, as in Oliphant's story, the expansion denied by the railway is offered by the surrounding countryside in which Barbox Brothers takes refuge and where he meets an invalid woman, whose lively imagination compensates for her inability to travel. Appreciating the power of the imagination in this physically immobile woman, which exceeds the power of railway lines and railway time, he learns to regard the junction as an inspiring social network that connects people rather than places. At the end of the story he decides to settle and live there forever, imposing the permanent qualities of nature on the otherwise ephemeral setting. Mechanical time is replaced with organic time and the dead time at the junction becomes productive time in terms of developing emotions and consciousness. Waiting for a train at a junction, therefore, offers Dickens as well as Oliphant the opportunity to criticise humanity's dependence on its own innovations that eventually cause the wasting away of meaningful experience.

And yet in both stories, this purgatory of modern existence, as Oliphant has called the junction, may have one redeeming quality in that it incites rebelliousness in the characters. They manage to escape the tyranny of purposeless waiting, Barbox Brothers, by turning his back on the railway lines, and Captain Cannon, by using the new etiquette of socialising to his advantage. In Oliphant's story the contingency of the encounter between man and woman and the emptiness of the hours of waiting lead them to defy the standardised social rules of interaction between the sexes, legitimising and rationalising the romantic opportunity offered by the railway station. Captain Cannon indulges in an extravagant exhibition of spontaneous emotion[7] when he abandons his friends and dangerously crosses the lines in order to reach Nelly, and Nelly daringly consents to a tête-à-tête picnic with him, a short walk from the station: 'Was it right, she wondered, thus to walk and talk alone with – a gentleman, that fiend in human shape, whom well-brought-up young ladies (of the old school) were taught to shun?' (431). Oliphant recognises that the spontaneous and unlikely intimacies flourishing in a station or on a train may spark romance. However, for the romance to develop it is necessary for the characters to reject the transitoriness that railway and junction signify. So Captain Cannon asks Nelly – who trusts him minimally, but apparently sufficiently because she has met him before at a friend's house – to walk with him away from the station and into a little forest, whose natural pleasures, together with the evolving romance, make Nelly miss her train. This romance gives Oliphant the opportunity to contrast the rigid time, indicated on the station clock to which the trains adhere, with the leisurely time passed by Nelly and Captain Cannon in the woods. Lewis Mumford argues that mechanical time is foreign to the human organism, which has its own regularities according to pulse, breathing, and mood shifts (15). By making the protagonists lose time and miss the train, the story demonstrates this incompatibility between mechanical and organic time as well as the narrator's reluctance to accept the fast pace and inevitability of mechanised mobility. The slow pace of the story and the meaningful experience with which Nelly's and the Captain's 'wasteful' time gaps are filled constitute a drastic reconceptualisation of the meaning of time and a means of withstanding the urban haste and confusion that the railway signifies. Ultimately, the junction is reinvented and feminised in accordance with its name, Ladybank, and loses its definition as a male industrial site, a bewildering labyrinth traversed by trains 'with a compound of all horrible sounds, jar, screech, creak, clang, and roar, demoniac and excruciating' (422). Instead it becomes a space for interaction and contemplation, one in which time can be condensed or stretched according to human will and whim. Similarly, its literal, physical presence as a neutral railway space is subjected to the characters' romantic imagination, so that finally the junction gets eclipsed by the adjacent beautiful landscape, which to Nelly, after her marriage to Cannon, seems 'a bit like Italy' (441).

Many women's texts of the late Victorian period offer a more internalised experience of the railway which seems to defy the rigid standardisation of time, precision, and punctuality that train travel required. But while in Oliphant we see a conservative impulse which privileges imagination over practicality and the permanence of nature over the transience of the railway, in other women writers we find more innovative and progressive approaches to railway time. Such texts, on the one hand, reject time-discipline but, on the other, explore and often manipulate in narrative terms the synchronicity and pulsating rhythm of the new experience of temporality. Thus in many cases, and quite paradoxically, train schedules, routes, and speedy passages through space evoke subjective and idiosyncratic experiences of time. I would like to argue, therefore, that in these late Victorian texts women are more attuned to time as duration, and that this original approach to time is derived from their experience of railway travel during which they subject external, mechanised ticking to internal processing.

As David Harvey has argued, modernity was affected, if not defined, by an experience of 'time-space compression', 'a speed-up in the pace of life, while so overcoming spatial barriers that the world sometimes seems to collapse inwards upon us' (240). Train travel was the medium *par excellence* that achieved this 'time-space compression', and though many male authors incorporated its physical or social consequences in their writing, women writers provide us, in terms of both plot and style, with an insight into the affected female consciousness. It could be argued that women's radical response to railway time is mostly derived from their responsiveness to the new demands the railway was making on vision. If, as Jonathan Crary contends, in the nineteenth century we have an 'uprooting of vision', in the sense that visual experience 'is given an unprecedented [sic] mobility and exchangeability, abstracted from any founding site or referent' (*Techniques*, 14), the train is one of the agents of this uprooting, rendering its passengers mobile observers of fleeting images, briefly or barely perceived, immediately forgotten, and swiftly exchanged. Women's multi-sensory and imaginative response to the ever-vanishing view from the carriage window testifies to what Schivelbusch has described as the transformation of landscape to panorama through train travel: 'The landscape [. . .] was no longer experienced intensively, discretely (as by Ruskin, the critic of rail travel), but evanescently, impressionistically – panoramically, in fact. More exactly, in panoramic perception the objects were attractive in their state of dispersal' (189). Women's highlighting of dispersed and disparate objects, merged by speed, results from this panoramic perception which tends to privilege unstable representation over literal reporting of view, impressionism over realism. Indeed while in the nineteenth century we see a cultural effort to stabilise, by means of realistic narrative techniques, a reality which increasingly defies control, women writers, from the early Victorian to the early modernist period, through their train narratives, which emphasise fragmentation, incoherence, and fleetingness, go against the rigid codification of perception and knowledge.

In an article in *The Englishwoman's Domestic Magazine* (Anon., 1855), the distortions to which perception is susceptible on the train are described as 'Railway Magic'. This author, addressing women and expressing a subjective appreciation of the journey often witnessed in writings by women, exalts the magical way in which distance, motion, and speed affect the visual perspective of the traveller, disfiguring the straight lines of the railway tracks or uprooting whole villages, churches, trees, and animals:

The trees are on the track; growing on the track! On the track indeed [. . .] And the worker of all this *diablerie*! You can see the fluttering of her blue robe just there in the horizon. She has gone on to conjure again. It is Distance!
   'Stop the train! Let us off! Conductor, driver, somebody, anybody!' There's a *village* on the track [. . .]
   Look behind you. Back goes the village that had been frightened away by

the whistle, and the stacks and the trees grow 'beautifully less' [. . .] There's a something on the track again. It's a fly – it's a frog – it's a child – it's a *man* – six feet high – a soldier – a magistrate. On we go. We have passed him. We have left him. Five feet high – four feet high – a child – a frog – a *nothing!* (373)

The last section of the passage quoted emphasises the flux and eva-nescence of perception which appears to be, perhaps partly, perhaps totally, affected by the new tensions vision was undergoing under such conditions as the high velocity of the train. In the nineteenth century fragmented vision and subjectivity were often attributed to the speed of train travel by socio-medical discourses, such as a *Lancet* pamphlet on *The Influence of Railway Travelling on Public Health* (1862), which examined its effects on visual observation: 'The pace, also, prevents the traveller from that observation of natural objects and sights of interest on the road, which made coach travelling a source of mental relaxation and a pastime. The passenger is forced into subjective sources of mental activity' (qtd in Schivelbusch, 118n). Woman's subjective response to the train, as articulated in the work of Elizabeth Barrett Browning, Rhoda Broughton, Margaret Oliphant, Mona Caird, Katherine Mansfield, and many others, may be said to express her affinity with the ephemeral, fugitive, and unstable aspects of modernity, as the emphasis in these writings is not on controlling the landscape but on presenting an inco-herence that parallels the incoherence of mental activity. So panoramic scanning of the scenery leads to simultaneous immersion and detach-ment, absorption and distraction. While male writers lament the train journey's obliteration of 'the space between points', 'the in-between, or travel space' (Schivelbusch, 37),[8] we see women savouring the spectacle deemed useless by geographers. Their simultaneously engaged and distracted glance offers an intense sensuous, emotional, and intellec-tual experience. Georg Simmel, in his analysis of 'The Metropolis and Mental Life' (1903), argued that the excessive stimuli characteristic of urban life ('the rapid crowding of changing images, the sharp dis-continuity in the grasp of a single glance, and the unexpectedness of onrushing impressions' [410]) forced (male) city dwellers to blunt their sensibilities by adopting a blasé attitude; but in women's texts about rail travel the alternating landscapes crowding mind and vision become vocal and physical – evocative – presences subject to the timelessness of consciousness, to inner time.

In *Aurora Leigh* (1856), Elizabeth Barrett Browning offers one of the earliest cases of finite rail journeys treated as infinite opportunities for introspection and observation. The mobile external scenery gives rise to a volatile imagination which energises the landscape, making it reflect the mobility that the body but also the mind are undergoing. Browning captures precisely the subjective experience of time and space while on the train, as Aurora subjects the journey and the powerful emblem of speed, the train, to a more powerful human faculty, the imagination, that blurs landscapes and suspends time:

> But presently the winding Rhone
> Washed out the moonlight large along his banks,
> Which strained their yielding curves out clear and clean
> To hold it, – shadow of town and castle just blurred
> Upon the hurrying river [. . .]
> So we passed
> The liberal open country and the close,
> And shot through tunnels, like a lightning-wedge
> By great Thor-hammers driven through the rock,
> Which, quivering through the intestine blackness,
>   splits,
> And let it in at once: The train swept in
> Athrob with effort, trembling with resolve,
> The fierce denouncing whistle wailing on
> And dying off smothered in the shuddering dark,
> While we, self-awed, drew troubled breath, oppressed
> as other Titans, underneath the pile
> And nightmare of the mountains. Out at last,
> To catch the dawn afloat upon the land! (262–3)

Aurora's consciousness is affected by speed and its demanding claims on the faculty of vision, transforming the fleeting images viewed from the moving train's window pane into fleeting sensations which transplant the actual scenery that goes past and are unaffected by the real time in which the journey takes place. So objects viewed from inside the carriage become unmoored and fractured, random impressions, reflecting the fragmentation of being that is characteristic of modern subjectivity. This constant dislocation of perception and the temporal discontinuity with which impressions are narrated express a fragmentation of consciousness which undermines Victorian notions of female identity as fixed and coherent.[9] In Aurora's mind, there were 'Hills, slung forth broadly and gauntly everywhere, / Not crampt in their foundations, pushing wide' (263). The unmooring of the natural or urban scenery, animated by the limitless flights of the imagination, ultimately represents the unmooring of woman, who, given up to the thrill of speed, indulges in the unlocatedness of a time-less and unfixed identity. Wolfgang Schivelbusch has written that one of the most popular metaphors for the train in the nineteenth century was the projectile or missile: 'The train was experienced as a projectile, and travelling on it, as being shot through the landscape

– thus losing control of one's senses' (54). Yet, while Aurora uses this image ('shot through tunnels'), she attributes the power of violent movement not to the train but to herself, as if it is her active imagination that splits the rocks through which she passes, while the train itself is passively 'swept in / Athrob with effort', its whistle 'wailing' and 'dying off'.

In the narratives of train journeys, thus, two conflicting gendered worlds are juxtaposed: the objective with the subjective; technology with imagination; organisation with confusion; punctuality with irregularity; the rational with the irrational. It could be argued that for women in transit the map of the imagination displaces the transportation map, by taking precedence over the geographical, scientific, or sociological details of location.[10] Similarly with their idiosyncratic experience of temporality they resist the automation and mechanisation of life that railway time enforced.[11] These impulses become clear in the train stories of Rhoda Broughton, which are rendered by means of an original style, a first person present and present continuous tense, in order to convey the immediacy of female bodily and emotional experience while on the train. In works like the overlooked novel *Nancy* (1874) and the short story 'Under the Cloak' (1873), which was discussed in Chapter 1, Broughton experiments with this technique tracing in real time the rapidly changing feelings of her heroines and prefiguring, I would like to suggest, a stream of consciousness that combines coherent thought with incoherent free association.[12] Both stories utilise to different degrees and with unequal emphasis the railway as the means by which the heroines travel. Yet in both stories the train journey with its technologically generated mobility becomes the external manifestation of the spontaneous inner flow of desires and fears, which race with equal speed through the mind and body of the heroines. In her work it is as if Broughton was attempting to represent the effects of modernity on the female consciousness, showing woman to be particularly attuned to its fleeting and transitory quality. In this way she challenges the normative, socially and culturally constructed view of woman as stable and unchanging.[13] Rather than providing men with the stability and comfort lacking in the dehumanised and alienating public sphere of socio-economic activity, Broughton's female protagonists, being no such homemakers, partake, sometimes with delight and at other times fearfully, of the discontinuity, fragmentation, transitoriness, and incoherence of modernity,[14] which they experience mainly through their senses. Broughton depicts her heroines as keenly prone to the effects of this new visual experience, their inner sensations paralleling the speedy passage of external visual stimuli. Lining the plot with the flow of emotions and sensual experience rather than events, Broughton follows inner time, depicting moments as uneven, short or long, overlapping, or even missing, as processed by the characters.

In 'Under the Cloak', a story of a woman robbed on the train, the heroine's emotions and sensations as she undergoes this trying experience, from before stepping onto the station platform, are rendered in a vivid present tense which follows inner time, reporting through free association the shifts of consciousness:

> [I] fix my eyes on the landscape racing by, and fall into a variety of thoughts. 'Will my husband really get up in time to come and meet me at the station to-morrow morning? He does so cordially hate getting up. My only chance is his not having gone to bed at all! How will he be looking? I have not seen him for four months [. . .] Shall we have a pleasant party at the house we are going to for shooting?' (101)

As Michel de Certeau says in his analysis of railway navigation, the view outside the window of the train compartment, despite its 'exterior silence', is what 'makes our memories speak or draws out of the shadows the dreams of our secrets [. . .] The cutting off [of the observer from the view by means of the glass pane] is necessary for the birth, outside of these things but not without them, of unknown landscapes and the strange fables of our private stories' (112). The glass pane is the only stable element dividing but also mirroring the slipping by of outer and inner, the silent objects receding outside and the mobile feelings progressing inside. In the story the mostly unreported external stimuli are overlaid by sensations, desires, fears, and memories, which pass with equal speed and are quickly exchanged for the next.

While describing the technique of free association, Freud wrote: 'So say whatever goes through your mind. Act as though, for instance, you were a traveler sitting next to the window of a railway carriage and describing to someone inside the carriage the changing views which you see outside' (qtd in Marcus, 'Psychoanalytic Training', 171). As Laura Marcus has argued, this passage 'relates in very significant ways to the question of the new forms of perception and mentation brought about by the experience of railway travel' ('Psychoanalytic Training' 171). The new means of transportation radically changed the way Victorians conceived of time and distance, and Broughton's heroine, despite her apparent adherence to traditional models of femininity, reproduces a dynamic model of mentation through her consciousness of simultaneity: 'Then I leave the future and go back into past enjoyments; excursions to Lausanne, trips down to the lake to Chillon [. . .] The time slips by: the afternoon is drawing towards evening; a beginning of dusk is coming over the landscape' (101). The simultaneity of past, present, and future, experienced on the moving train which obfuscates temporal and spatial distances through speed, triggers an accelerated rush of sensations, which, rendered in a fast-flowing style, resembles the processes of mentation described by William James in *The Principles of Psychology*: 'Consciousness does not appear to itself chopped up in bits [. . .] It is nothing jointed; it flows. A "river" or a "stream" are the metaphors by which it is most naturally described' (239). As Jonathan Crary notes, 'James uses the image of the stream to describe the fundamentally *transitive* nature of subjective experience – a perpetually changing but continuous flow of images, sensations, thought fragments, bodily awareness, memories, desires' (*Suspensions*, 60). Broughton's use of the present and present continuous tenses captures this sense of continuity that James conveys through his water metaphors. As James explains, 'The only breaches that can well be conceived to occur within the limits of a single mind would either be interruptions, time-gaps during which the consciousness went out altogether to come into existence again at a later moment; or they would be breaks in the quality, or content, of the thought' (237). Significantly, the heroine's stream of thought and sensation is interrupted only when she loses consciousness. The narrative gap coincides with the 'time-gap', in James's sense, that causes in her a total temporal and spatial disorientation: 'When I awake – awake with a bewildered mixed sense of having been a long time asleep – of not knowing where I am' ('Cloak', 107). By outlining this overstimulation of the senses and the consciousness by the speed of visual experience, Broughton daringly depicts the female character not as a stable, singular, and coherent entity, but as a consciousness in the making, a transient being, a life in the process.

Likewise in the novel *Nancy*, told in a similar first-person present, Broughton concentrates on the swiftly moving sensations and emotions of her eponymous heroine as she develops and reluctantly matures, moving out of her family home, first to go on her wedding tour and then to occupy her husband's home. The sensations of the body, acutely felt and reported, parallel Nancy's emotional development. And as in 'Under the Cloak', in this novel inner replaces outer, with the narrator following inner time, reporting thoughts and sensations that matter, however briefly, rather than events, which are often left out of the narrative. For example, the heroine's actual wedding is never described, as Nancy, during the ceremony, has a flashback that blocks out and transplants the external actions:

> Like lightning-flash there darts into my head the recollection of the *last time that I was married!* when, long ago we were little children, one wet Sunday

afternoon, for want of a job, I had espoused Bobby [her brother]; and Algy, standing on a chair, with his night-gown on for a surplice, had married us. It is over now. I am aware that several persons of different genders have kissed me. I have signed my name. I am walking down the church-yard path, the bells jangling gayly above my head. (*Nancy*, 74)

Broughton alternates between tenses (from present to past to present perfect and then to present continuous), treating time as 'durée', in Henri Bergson's sense, with no respect to the clock and to any linear sequence of events. The plot is propelled by movements of her consciousness rather than physical actions. This narrative style is explored to the full during Nancy's wedding tour by train, when she experiences anxiety caused by the 'incarceration', as de Certeau would say (111) – the 'oppressing' 'absolute tête-à-tête' with her husband that is enforced by the train's insulation (*Nancy*, 77). In this case, the view from the window provides escape from the stifling enclosure, a freedom, but also a unique experience of time, as the rapid alternation of the objects outside force time to race on, stop, or move slowly depending on the memory and desire that they trigger: 'All day I watch the endless, treeless, hedgeless German flats fly past [. . .] Oh, for a hill, were it no bigger than a molehill! [. . .] The day rolls past, dustily, samely, wearily . . .] The day falls, the night comes. On, on, on!' (79, 80). Certain sensations persist while others fade away quickly. The rapidly alternating external sameness, as one scenery fuses into the next, reflects the tediousness of the uneventful hours passed inside, the boredom Nancy feels in close companionship solely with one man, after a lifetime with many lively siblings in a noisy schoolroom. On her wedding tour Nancy experiences the paradoxes of train transport, as the freedom suggested by the idea of travel is contradicted by the reality of the confinement within the close quarters of the compartment and, by extension, of the marriage. As a semi-private/semi-public enclosure, the carriage foreshadows Nancy's role as a wife – her expected partial entry into her husband's public life and her equally partial entry into the private life of his home.[15] As a spouse, she is likely to suffer from the blurring of boundaries between private and public that characterised the Victorian married home, where women were often displayed as male acquisitions and their private lives were gradually thwarted. While her father's house ensured invisibility and hence a comforting privacy, as it was not her job to be hostess, in her husband's she will lose the freedom of not partaking in the theatricality of the drawing-room. In the insular train compartment Nancy finds herself already rehearsing this dreaded future role, her vivid spontaneity becoming the first casualty of the socio-cultural expectations she thinks she has to fulfil as a wife: 'Before I speak, I think whether what

I am going to say will be worth saying, and, as very few of my remarks come up to this standard, I become extremely silent' (77).

Moreover, both *Nancy* and 'Under the Cloak' use the train ride in order to undermine and reverse gender constructions which assigned mobility to men and immobility to women. Through her obsession with transience and flux rendered through her style of reporting female impressions, sensations, and emotions, Broughton presents woman as constantly in transit, responding to the fleetingness of life with an inner mobility that undermines male prerogative. Conversely, the men in her stories, whether they are criminals or husbands, are presented as immobile, static pillars, with little of the vivacity or ever-expanding interiority given to the heroines.[16] Broughton's men resemble characters depicted by male authors, who, as Nicholas Daly has argued, have adapted to the mechanical motion of the train (itself controlled by the rigid movement of the clock by means of timetables), and have 'become a little like automata' ('Railway Novels', 476). This is particularly well illustrated in 'Under the Cloak' where one of the thieves hardly moves because he is part man/part dummy, with false wax hands and an inexpressive mask for a face. Similarly, during the wedding tour in *Nancy*, Sir Roger, the heroine's husband, hardly speaks or moves, with Broughton concentrating instead on Nancy's constantly shifting states of consciousness. He exists in clock time – after all he holds the watch and tells the time (79) – reading the newspaper, which again helps to compartmentalise life, placing events within linear time slots. Nancy, on the other hand, partakes of the timelessness suggested by the speed of the train, the flux of the images, and the fragmentation of her own thoughts and sensations.

In both stories, thus, structured time and linear journeys are subordinated to the heroines' internal, chaotic mobility. Though women were expected by society to 'run on lines', as Diana Warwick in George Meredith's *Diana of the Crossways* believes (64), Broughton's heroines seem to prefer this figurative derailment, despite the dangers that it may incur. One of the most memorable scenes in *Nancy* is when we encounter her holding a precarious position on the top of a high wall that surrounds her father's garden with her legs dangling on one side (19), a posture that suggests her daring potential to challenge the physical and ideological boundaries that restrain her position and movement as woman. This hovering posture becomes, therefore, the visual equivalent of the 'state of transition' that Broughton envisaged for Kate in *Not Wisely, but Too Well* (138); it also stands for a proud stubbornness, characteristic of all the heroines examined here, with which they firmly embrace their liminal positions, refusing to adopt mainstream attitudes and mentally avoiding the pre-laid track on which they travel.[17]

Prefiguring the innovations and obsessions of literary modernism, Broughton explores the railway compartment or station as an interiorised space, transforming an inert place, subject to time constraints, into a discursive, multi-dimensional space, one that is subject to an idiosyncratic experience of time, structured by the randomness, incoherence, and mutability of the female consciousness processing it.

A novel that explores more emphatically woman's conscious attempt to escape the rigid constraints of temporal discipline is Mona Caird's *The Daughters of Danaus* (1894). Hadria, the talented composer and protagonist of the novel, who feels underestimated and trapped by her parents and later her husband, and who has allowed the most creative time of her life to be consumed by meaningless domestic duties, decides to flee from her socially prescribed roles and pursue a musical education in Paris. The description of her train ride to Paris has been rightfully celebrated for its unconventional, protomodernist, narrative treatment (Parkins, *Mobility*, 88), which captures the heroine's mental vagaries as she ponders on the incongruous sense data that bombard her consciousness: 'Disjointed, delicious impressions followed one another in swift succession, often superficially incoherent, but threaded deep, in the stirred consciousness, on a silver cord: – the unity of the creation was as obvious as its multiplicity' (295). Hadria, ahead of her time, and with philosophical insight that rehearses theories of consciousness, relates the succession of random external impressions to the flow of her 'superficially incoherent' thoughts and sensations. In doing so, however, she affirms the organising power of the consciousness, 'the silver cord', which subtly but firmly connects the fragments, providing unity to the subject. Thoughts and feelings are thus held together by an inner logic which defines experience as subjective and qualitative. Intriguingly the disjointedness of her railway impressions, which she views as forming a creation at once united and multiple, reflects her idiosyncratic way of conceiving musical notes in compositions that are deemed bizarre or too modern by her contemporaries. So her railway experience of time and space is intricately linked to creativity and the imagination.

Hadria views external time as an artificial construct which may be subordinated to the workings of consciousness and its inner time. In the following extract she provides a powerful reconceptualisation of time, relating it to her own feminine, and unorthodox or antilinear, aspirations.

> The speed was glorious. Back flashed field and hill and copse, and the dear 'companionable hedgeways'. Back flew iterative telegraph posts with Herculean swing, into the Past, looped together in rhythmic movement, marking the pulses of Old Time. On, with rack and roar, into the mysterious

Future. One could sit at the window and watch the machinery of Time's foundry at work; the hammers of his forge beating, beating, the wild sparks flying, the din and chaos whirling round one's bewildered brain; – Past becoming Present, Present melting into Future, before one's eyes. To sit and watch the whirring wheels; to think 'Now it is thus and thus; presently, another slice of earth and sky awaits me' – ye Gods, it is not to be realized! (294)

During her journey Hadria is sensitised to the fact that speed may challenge the structure and regularity of organised time as it causes a conceptual melting of past, present, and future which parallels the visual melting of one scene into another as the train pushes on. Although the railway depends on time discipline and the clock, speed in her view causes the rupture of such artificial temporal divisions. Thus Hadria on the train experiences time as subjective and fluid, characterised by the simultaneous layering of multiple time zones. As Patricia Murphy argues, 'Blending past, present, and future, the train ride unsettles conventional notions of time as an ordering principle to open up an alternative imaginative space' (168). Thus, not synchronised with the linearity that railway time (she calls it 'Old Time') supposedly enforces, Hadria appropriates the speed of the powerful train that promises to open up a new future for her:

What a speed the train was going at! One could scarcely stand in the jolting carriage. Old Time must not make too sure of his victory. One felt a wistful partisanship for his snorting rival, striving for ever to accomplish the impossible. The labouring visionary was not without significance to aspiring mortals. (296)

Murphy argues that for Hadria 'Old Time' represents masculine temporality which signifies discipline and death (167, 168). Hadria's journey thus becomes her means of challenging such masculine orderliness, which had in the past confined her within restrictive feminine roles and buried her artistic impulses. Significantly, Hadria's mother had similarly been stifled in her youth, having sacrificed her literary talent to the smooth running of the household. So during the journey to Paris Hadria does not 'run on lines' even though the train diligently follows its designated route. It is ironic, Murphy believes, that the symbol of masculine temporality, the train, is transformed 'from a sign of confining order to a vehicle of liberatory disorder' (169). Its roaring sounds come to represent the chaotic power of the imagination and the freedom of creative conception: 'The rattle and roar grew into a symphony – full, rich, magnificent, and then, with a rush, came a stirring musical conception: it seized the imagination' (295). And the empty, homogeneous, travelling time, which might in other contexts be considered a waste of time, becomes a series of unique and meaningful moments that challenge the imagination by proposing unforeseeable directions, unforeseeable futures: 'the interminable straight line of rails, leading – whither? [. . .] Wherefore? Was the inward tumult too evident in the face? Well, no matter. The world was beautiful and wide!' (295). The future has a realisable potential ('The Real!') while the restricting past becomes an unpleasant dream (294).

However, Hadria's potent embrace of velocity does not last long as she soon realises, while in Paris, that her 'past-fashioned self' holds her back, sending her 'spinning to hopeless distances' (307). Paris, where she is unable to fulfil her artistic aspirations, thus embodies not a potentially liberating future but the confirmation of futility. The unpredictable and limitless trajectories she had imagined while on board the train end abruptly with her understanding of her limited position as a woman who can never strip off the 'thick wrappings' with which society has covered her (306). The arrival at the Paris train station had already foreshadowed Hadria's disillusionment and the futility of her attempt to appropriate the speed of the train. Disembarking from the train of liberation she had been halted by the sternness and grimness of the Paris station as well as by the unavoidable practical routines which mocked her aspirations for mental and emotional freedom: 'The long delay in the examination of the luggage, the fatigue of the journey, tended to increase the disposition to regard the echoing edifice, with its cold hollow reverberations, as a Circle of the Doomed' (301). Her sense of time as a continuous process of becoming was thus contradicted by the repetitive and paralytic time structures represented by the circular, inescapable, doom the station stood for. And indeed Hadria is unable to exit this circle nor to rid herself of the societal gender expectations which command her return to England. Ironically, it is her mother's illness that forces her return, a narrative choice that suggests the futility of female aspirations if women themselves are unwilling to support each other. Mothering, as Ann Heilmann argues, 'is shaped by patriarchal power relations [. . .] [and] remains an instrument of oppression even when there is an explicit intention of feminist subversion' such as Hadria's abandonment of her own children (146).

On the train back to England Hadria is conscious of the delusions that the initial journey generated in her. She exists not in the timelessness of unrestricted potentials but in the rigid present of societal pressures which, having been internalised, punish the aspiring ego:

A thousand fears, regrets, self-accusations, revolts, swarmed insect-like in Hadria's brain, as the train thundered through the darkness, every tumultuous sound and motion exaggerated to the consciousness, by the fact that there was no distraction of the attention by outside objects. Nothing offered itself to the sight except the strange lights and shadows of the lamp thrown on the cushions of the carriage [. . .] Everything was contracted, narrow. (357)

The dark and shadowy carriage to which she limits her vision, as she is unable to extend her eye to the outer distances traversed, stands for the rigid railway time, 'Old Time', which disciplines her incoherent temporal and spatial fantasies. Old Time will always keep ticking no matter how much women want to change its rigid rules. Sobbing at the bedside of her adopted daughter, whom she is forced to surrender to the girl's biological father, Hadria can hear the inexorable 'tick-tack of the little clock telling off the seconds with business-like exactness' (446). The novel thus concludes that women's physical, temporal, and even mental mobility is futile, circular, with no outlets towards self-fulfilment: '[Women] were all spinning round and round, in a dizzy little circle, all whirling and toiling and troubling, to no purpose' (467). The clock's round shape and the repetitive movement of its hands stand for the quantification of experience and the inevitability of sameness which thwarts all attempts at escape: '[O]ld Time makes no comment, but moves quietly on; we fling the thing aside as tawdry, insufficient; the ideal is tarnished, experience of the world converts us – and still unmoved, he paces on' (480). The anxiety felt in the returning train carriage thus prefigures the temporal and spatial claustrophobia of Hadria's death in life experience back home. As Murphy writes, 'History is unmasked as a pretender to progress in *The Daughters of Danaus*, creating only the illusion of change while perpetuating static conceptions of womanhood across time' (177). Nevertheless, Hadria's mind-wandering by means of the train journey, even though it has not led to a spatial or social shift in her life, has managed to breach the rigid compartmentalisation of experience that railway time enforces. Her mobile, developing consciousness – Parkins calls it an 'enhanced subjectivity' (*Mobility*, 92) – which mocks the static passivity of the male characters, presents, by contrast, a warning about the dangers of restrictive time scheduling which threatens to extinguish progressive dreams of social and personal evolution.

Modernist Railway Anxieties

Women's protomodernist texts thus explore the image and idea of the train for the ways in which its speed and effects on vision mirror the flow of thoughts and trigger imaginative trajectories that undermine spatial and temporal boundaries. Moreover, for these texts, the capsule-like carriage is a 'chamber of consciousness'[18] in which subjectivity is given space to develop. As such, however, the carriage in railway stories of the fin de siècle by women may become a space of psychological anxiety and unease because it inevitably comes to represent patriarchal pressures, which find expression through railway speed, time, and incarceration. In Edith Wharton's 'The Journey' (1899), the train stands for inexorable life pushing on in defiance of the fragile consciousness of the heroine who, like Hadria, imagines the melting of past, present, and future within this spatial and temporal capsule. 'The Journey' tells the story of a woman who travels with her sick husband by train from Colorado to New York. On the train her husband's health increasingly deteriorates, and eventually he dies on the journey; the heroine tries to conceal his death as she is afraid that if found out she and the dead body will be left stranded on some remote railway platform.

Wharton uses the central reflector technique with the narrative following closely and in detail the progression of this woman's thoughts, memories, sensations, dreams, and feelings; short sentences and free indirect discourse reflect her anxieties and disillusionments. The man's imminent death generates in her feelings of resentment as it threatens to narrow the horizons of her future: 'she was never to be allowed to spread her wings' (28). The inescapability of the immediate setting of the carriage exacerbates this sense of restriction, and the journey, rather than representing the limitless trajectories of a multiplying life, becomes a slow passage of circular mobility. Twice in the story she describes her consciousness affected by the rush of the train, wandering not in a forward but in a circular motion reminiscent of the spinning movement that for Hadria represented the futility of women's aspirations in Caird's *The Daughters of Danaus*: 'deeper and deeper into circles of wakeful lucidity' and 'spinning like leaves, in wild uncoiling spirals' ('Journey', 27, 44). Slowed down by the protagonist's thoughts, fears, and meditations on sickness, the train thus exemplifies the defeat of her ambitions and her incarceration within a marriage that has thwarted her hopes and energies.

Additionally, the train makes her painfully conscious of her alienation from her husband whom she now considers a stranger. The unavoidable close proximity with the ailing man paradoxically reveals their apartness: 'Like two faces looking at one another through a sheet of glass they were close together, almost touching, but they could not hear or feel each other' (27). Though joined by the marriage, they are in reality divided by their diverging thoughts and their selfish egocentricity which makes them impenetrable to each other. The journey thus becomes an opportunity for self-exploration during which the heroine faces her own lonely estrangement not only from her husband but also from the unknown people that surround her in the carriage. The train epitomises this modern alienation especially felt in spaces of proximity and contact. However, it is marriage that is shown to be the most devastating alienating force of the story. The unity it presupposes is merely artificial, as the wife realises, and yet as a social force it forges for the partners a common future, in life and in death. For the husband's terminal illness seems to signal a deadly future for his young wife too, as she imagines the obliteration of the self after the loss of its legally bound half. For the heroine the vibrating train with its 'impetuous rush' comes to represent this doom: 'life itself [. . .] was sweeping her on with headlong inexorable force', but 'sweeping her into darkness and terror', into death (43). In this dreamlike state she imagines herself already dead, a lifeless body lying next to that of her husband's, spiralling downward in a 'black whirlwind' (44), which may represent the inevitability of death for the woman whose only outlet from a meaningless life as a daughter has been her entry into a similarly meaningless life as a wife. Women are condemned to repeat stagnant roles, and the train, despite its promise of routes and destinations, demonstrates the futility of their misguided quest for self-fulfilment. The female protagonist of this story, then, unable to imagine a life outside marriage or even widowhood, becomes a victim of railway time and speed. The train does indeed become an inexorable patriarchal force, and the journey leads to death. Just before its arrival in New York a sudden jolt makes her fall 'face downward, striking her head against the dead man's berth' (45). Though inconclusive, this abrupt ending to the story provides little hope that the black whirlwind dreamt of a few moments earlier has not been tragically prophetic.

The fin-de-siècle railway stories demonstrate little progress as far as women's fearless mobility is concerned. Representing the claustrophobia of marriage but also the inevitability of unwanted sexual proximity, trains continue to be geographies of fear, explored, nevertheless, by women writers, not for their potential for sensationalism but for the narrative possibilities offered for psychological penetration. George Egerton's (Mary Chavelita Dunne Bright) 'Virgin Soil' from the collection *Discords* (1894) is another case in point where an unnarrated train ride becomes the definitive moment in a young woman's life. Forced to have sex on the train with her new husband on their first trip together away from her maiden home after their wedding, the heroine returns to the same platform of her home town, five years later, in order to reproach her mother for never preparing her for the compulsory sexual intimacy that marriage entailed. The hermetically sealed train carriage, with its drawn curtains, served to imprison her within a marriage of repulsive sexual contact: 'I felt it vaguely as I stood on the platform waiting; I remember the mad impulse I had to jump down under the engine as it came in to escape from the dread that was chilling my soul' (158). Egerton's heroine, who strongly believes in female sexual autonomy and a woman's right to choose sexual partners, utters a poignant protest against the sexual coercion and incarceration that comes with marriage. She also realises that trains, with their privé carriages, act in collusion with marriage practices that physically subjugate woman. In the end she boldly and decisively leaves her loathed husband, and by forging for herself a different railway (and sexual) trajectory, away from the physical and psychological hell that marriage signified, she asserts her rights as a woman with independent desires: 'She hurries on, feeling that her autumn has come to her in her spring, and a little later she stands once more on the platform where she stood in the flush of her girlhood, and takes the train in the opposite direction' (161).

A modernist story that focuses at length on the overpowering psychological unease and apprehension that women were experiencing in the spaces of the railway well into the twentieth century is Katherine Mansfield's 'The Little Governess' (1915).[19] In a modernist style of free indirect discourse, the story explores the anxiety of a reticent and insecure girl travelling alone across foreign lands to take up a position as a governess. The focalised narrative shifts quickly from one charged psychological moment to the next as she progressively experiences the platform rush, the novel sounds and sights of a station, the strange, 'dreamy and vacant' expressions in the faces of those employed in these spaces of transit (53), the penetrability of the train compartments, the disrespect of male passengers and porters towards her, and the fleetingness of the landscape racing past the window. Though train compartments were marketed to combine the safety and intimacy of private space with the publicity of commercial life, the little governess cannot from the start indulge fearlessly in pleasures, such as sleeping and reading, usually reserved for intimate spaces. She experiences the compartment as a '*locus suspectus*', 'a space characteristic of modernity because it is structured by the most contingent of intimacies, because it is dependent on anonymous, accidental and strangely personal encounters in public' (Beaumont, 'Railway Mania', 129–30). As a matter of fact she feels constantly exposed to masculine abuse, first by the porter who demands a hefty fee after forcing his unwanted services on her and next by a group of young men who try to bully her. The text concentrates on her self-consciousness as she tries to adjust her appearance and manners in order to become inconspicuous and avoid the threats. When an old man, who appears kindly and grandfatherly, enters her carriage she feels thankful for his presence which helps fence off the younger masculine threat, at the same time making the compartment more cosy and domestic despite its constant penetrability by noise and other potential intruders. The presence of the old man fools the heroine into reconstructing the space as a safe haven in which she can read the illustrated papers that he offers and even sleep: 'I never could have dared to go to sleep if I had been alone', she thinks (54).

However, her limited native upbringing, her naïveté, and ultimately her miscalculation of the motives and freedoms that an elderly gentleman would feel inclined to take with a young woman in public make her misread and rationalise his persistent gaze during their tête-à-tête in the compartment. Self-conscious of her tangerine coloured hair which she considers a 'tragedy', she speculates that 'Perhaps that was what the old man was thinking as he gazed and gazed [. . .] Perhaps the flush that licked his cheeks and lips was a flush of rage that anyone so young and tender should have to travel alone and unprotected through the night' (55). The story contrasts her shy yet intense curiosity as well as her ill-founded confidence boost with the man's erotic fantasy and desire that aim at disciplining her imaginative and physical adventure. It gradually traces the succession of her feelings and sensations as the man manages to win her confidence and gratitude through patronage (he shields her from the vulgar young men on the train and buys her strawberries), only to eventually lure her to his apartment and sexually abuse her. Being made to feel at home on the train, the little governess has become more vulnerable to the predator who is almost welcomed into her private space.[20] The story also exposes the disadvantages for women of the democratisation of travel, as the train, on the one hand, allowed the classes and sexes to mix within such microspaces as the compartment, but, on the other, did not equalise the rights, responsibilities, and expectations of men and women. The girl assumes that the man must be honourable because he is a titled gentleman, and the man assumes that the girl must be promiscuous because she is a working girl travelling alone by public transport. And the fact that they are travelling in the same space does not help them go beyond their social preconceptions: 'He had a title! Well, it was bound to be all right!' (58). It is ironic that the little governess thinks she can appreciate without apprehension the potentials of mobility only when she accepts the man's patronage and protection and when the initiative of her safety and mobility is taken away from her.

The train ride, as in Broughton and Caird, gives Mansfield the opportunity to experiment with choppy, elliptical, and at times incoherent

narrative. While on the train, the girl's impressions are unruly and fragmented as she reports the fleeting view from the window in a series of
disjointed images randomly selected and imaginatively rendered:

> Taller houses, pink and yellow, glided by, fast asleep behind their green
> eyelids, and guarded by the poplar trees that quivered in the blue air as if on
> tiptoe, listening. In one house a woman opened the shutters, flung a red and
> white mattress across the window frame and stood staring at the train. A pale
> woman with black hair and a white woollen shawl over her shoulders. More
> women appeared at the doors and at the windows of the sleeping houses.
> There came a flock of sheep [. . .] Look! Look what flowers – and by the
> railway station too! [. . .] Slower and slower. A man with a watering-can was
> spraying the platform. 'A-a-a-ah!' (56–7)

With her imaginatively invested observations, the little governess seems
alert to the fact that she is 'travelling across trajectories', 'speeding
across on-going stories' (Massey, 119). Doreen Massey has argued that
although the scenes from the train window may seem immobilised,
'trapped in a timeless instant', yet a train transects ongoing histories
(119–20). On a trip, Massey maintains, it is important 'to retain at
least some sense of contemporaneous multiple becomings' (120). By
capturing the brief but continuing life of the objects and people viewed,
the little governess expresses her consciousness of this uninterrupted
flow of life which matches the development of her own consciousness,
her life in the making. Ana Parejo Vadillo argues that 'speed produced
two parallel effects, the adaptation of the human eye to the transient,
and the transformation of the observer into a transient figure' (34). The
little governess's perceptions exemplify her consciousness of this double
transience, which is the inevitable condition of urban life and mass
transport. However, when the elderly man turns into a self-appointed
tour guide, offering to show her the sights of Munich, he attempts to
freeze and standardise the girl's vision, to transform her impressions
from unruly and fragmented to regulated and coherent. Jonathan Crary
has argued that in the nineteenth century attention was frequently
regarded by physicians, psychologists, and social critics as a means by
which vision became disciplined and the sensory world orderly and
productive (*Suspensions*, 17). The little governess, apprehensive of her
own freedom, is at first thankful for his initiative to direct her attention
towards worthy objects:

> So after that the little governess gave herself up to the excitement of being
> really abroad, to looking out and reading the foreign advertisement signs, to
> being told about the places they came to – having her *attention* and enjoy-
> ment looked after by the charming old grandfather. (58; emphasis added)

Nevertheless, the narrative goes against her wish for patronage and continues to focus on her rebellious vision and her random, trivial yet enjoyably transient observations rather than the cultural monuments offered: 'Fat, fat coachmen driving fat cabs' and 'funny women with little round hats cleaning the tramway lines' seem much more interesting to the girl than the 'thousands and thousands of wonderful classical pictures [seen] in about a quarter of an hour'. 'I shall have to think them over when I am alone', she ruminates (59), preferring the freedom of contemplation to the prescribed explanations. The narrative focalisation dramatises the importance of unique moments of perception that rupture the regularity and monotony of time-tabled experience.

Sadly, the story does not allow the little governess to enjoy with impunity her liberating mental and physical adventure. Male patronage is after all part of regressive gender practices incompatible with her rebellious thoughts and perceptions. Visual fulfilment, gained through the train ride and the tour of Munich, comes with a price. The more she clings, literally and figuratively, to his arm for protection and support, the more she rouses erotic desire which peaks in his apartment where he forces an indecent embrace and a kiss on her lips. Close proximity in the public carriage and the streets thus becomes an invitation for a private sexual encounter in the mind of the lecherous man. In Mansfield's story, therefore, the railway carriage is a disorienting space whose blurry function as a semi-private and semi-public setting generates conflicting expectations and desires; on the one hand, it promises woman freedom of movement and perception, and on the other, it upholds domestic and class ideology by imposing on the working-class girl harsh limits to her aspirations. Moreover, accurate time wins over approximate time, for her little mental adventure makes her lose time and thus miss her important appointment with her future employer: '"I wonder what the time is," asked the little governess. "My watch has stopped. I forgot to wind it in the train last night. We've seen such a lot of things that I feel it must be quite late"' (60). Railway time as well as gender prejudices inexorably prove their inflexibility at the end of the story, which gives the last word to a spiteful waiter who vindictively destroys her reputation and job prospects by telling her potential employer that she had gone for a walk with an unknown man. For such modernist texts the railway becomes a space of internal conflict, with women passengers struggling to negotiate regressive with progressive gender practices, persistent strategies of power with rebellious feminine instincts.

Notes

1. See Jill Matus, *Shock*, 33–4.
2. According to Michael Freeman,

   > Railways were not just agents of spatial concentration, they were vital means in the transformation or re-ordering of urban space itself so as to service the requirements of the urbanization of capital in any one phase of its evolution. Suburbanization was one forcible manifestation of this process, with all its attendant social fragmentation. Another was the destruction and renewal of the pre-existing urban fabric. (*Railways*, 122)

3. Gaskell's *Mary Barton* similarly explores the role of the railway in the uprooting of woman from community when it describes Mary's trip to Liverpool during which, watching the beloved familiar sights of Manchester recede from her vision, she feels as if she is emigrating (273).
4. In *Far from the Madding Crowd* (1895), Hardy had already expressed this dissolution of local community:

   > The change at the root of this has been the recent supplanting of the class of stationary cottagers, who carried on the local traditions and humours, by a population of more or less migratory labourers, which has led to a break of continuity in local history, more fatal than any other thing to the preservation of legend, folk-lore, close inter-social relations, and eccentric individualities. For these the indispensable conditions of existence are attachment to the soil of one particular spot by generation after generation. (393)

5. For a detailed analysis of the function of the railway in *Jude* see Charles Lock.
6. 'Railway companies in the mid-nineteenth century sent officials with accurate chronometers up and down the country, resetting station clocks to eliminate local times in favour of a national standard, Railway Time, established more or less throughout the land by 1848' (Stevenson, 124). On the history of the standardisation of time in the nineteenth century see also Harrington, 'Trains, Technology', Ferguson (ed.), *Victorian Time*, Zemka, *Time and the Moment*, and Sussman, *Victorian Technology*, among others.
7. See Christopher Matthews (443) for an analysis of the ways in which the train encouraged such exhibitions of spontaneous emotion.
8. Schivelbusch quotes examples from Heinrich Heine, *Lutezia* (1854) and Charles Dunoyer, *Esprit et méthodes comparés de l'Angleterre et de la France dans les entreprises de travaux publics et en particulier des chemins de fer* (1840).
9. In her book, *The Gender of Modernity*, Rita Felski has meticulously shown how woman was consistently constructed by cultural discourses 'as an authentic point of origin, a mythic referent untouched by the strictures of social and symbolic mediation; she is a recurring symbol of the atemporal and asocial at the very heart of the modern itself' (38).
10. Schivelbusch argues that 'The diminution of transport distances seemed to

create a new, reduced geography [. . .] On the map of the imagination, all of these would finally be reproduced and reduced down to the infinitely small!' (35). However, my point is that in women's writing speed changes completely the mental map of the locations and distances travelled, detaching whole towns and mountains and setting them down randomly whenever and wherever the consciousness processes or recollects them.

11. See Nicholas Daly, who argues that male fictional characters in Victorian sensation fiction by men are animated by machine-like energy, clockwork punctuality, and automatic behaviour ('Railway Novels', 474–5).

12. See also my reading of Broughton's 'Under the Cloak' and *Nancy* in *Critical Survey*.

13. See Felski, 38.

14. Here I am borrowing words from David Frisby's description of modernity (4).

15. On the subject of the honeymoon trip, Amy Richter argues that 'In a railway car, under the watchful eyes of her fellow passengers, a young bride first tried on her role as wife. Confined with strangers for hours at a time, she attempted to balance new marital intimacy with appropriate public conduct' (*Home*, 35).

16. Similarly, in Broughton's *Second Thoughts* (1880), the protagonist, Gillian, is obliged to visit her estranged father and is escorted on the train by a man whom she finds detestable and who is so motionless that she fantasises he must be dead (43).

17. One of the most captivating features of Nancy, in my view, is her stubborn refusal to acknowledge men's erotic intentions towards her. Rather than revealing her naïveté and/or ignorance of the ways of the world, I think that her attitude betrays her brave adherence to her own self-definition and her unwillingness to be constructed as an erotic object.

18. See Henry James, 'The Art of Fiction': 'Experience is never limited, and it is never complete; it is an immense sensibility, a kind of huge spider-web of the finest silken threads suspended in the chamber of consciousness, and catching every air-borne particle in its tissue' (194).

19. See also my reading of Mansfield's story in Gómez Reus and Gifford's *Women in Transit*.

20. Amy Richter argues that 'the protective language of the domestic realm', used to promote the safety of train carriages, in reality misled women ('At Home Aboard', 78).

Coda: Mrs Bathurst and Mrs Brown

As the temporal and spatial journeys of this book have, I hope, illustrated, literary railway spaces emerge first and foremost as spaces of ambivalence, where the precarious dichotomies between private and public, inner and outer, stasis and mobility, fragmentation and continuity progressively affect feminine perception, subjectivity, and identity. The more the railway consolidates its role as an ideological and technological tool of progress, the more women resist its authority as an arbiter of time, discipline, and manners. If in the 1860s and 70s women's resistance is expressed through strategies of masquerade and deception, in later years the train offers opportunities for agency in terms of escape, emancipation, sexual mobility, or other transgressive impulses. By the fin de siècle the enclosed space of the carriage has become the material equivalent to the chamber of consciousness in which layers of the mind are unfolded and mental trajectories followed. With this turn inward, the subjectivity of woman explored during her occupancy of a carriage seat becomes more elusive as interior monologue and free indirect discourse provide partial access to a conflicted self. Realist narrative practices falter as she progressively defies the standardisation of time, rejecting temporal and spatial precision. The woman in the train carriage becomes increasingly an enigma to herself as well as to her fellow travellers with whom she often experiences a mutual estrangement. Yet this obscurity may ensure the privacy of the soul.[1] It may also save woman from the levelling depersonalisation and uniformity that the railway introduced, as the early texts of Frances Trollope and Frances Browne anticipated.

Perhaps it is for this that the woman in the carriage becomes for Virginia Woolf the ultimate symbol of the difficulty of representing character in fiction. In 'Mr Bennett and Mrs Brown' (1924) Woolf challenges her adversaries, the Edwardian writers, to try and figure out the lonely figure of an elderly woman railway passenger sitting quietly in a corner of a carriage. Yet, rather than submitting to the objectifying or materialistic impulses that Woolf attributes to her imaginary male co-passengers – Bennett, Galsworthy, and Wells – Mrs Brown defies complete knowingness via traditional representational techniques. The train as a space of liminality in which identity is bared of the solidity of social and material appurtenances is perhaps the best vehicle to carry these elusive and potentially unknowable subjectivities. For Mrs Brown in the impersonal carriage represents this inaccessible otherness of human beings who find themselves in close proximity to each other but who will always remain intangible and obscure. However, rather than being a depthless face and body – as Woolf's literary adversaries would regard her – Mrs Brown is all depth and individuality. The train is the epitome of the modernist world of mobilities, discontinuities, dispersals, dissonance, and anonymity. And the female passenger, unlike the male, in her resistance towards previous immobilising narrative strategies, scopic practices, and ideological imperatives, embodies best this ambivalent consciousness in flux. 'But do not expect just at present a complete and satisfactory presentment of her. Tolerate the spasmodic, the obscure, the fragmentary, the failure' (Woolf, 24). Woolf's elderly passenger can never – and perhaps should never – be fully represented as a coherent being; instead she is a composite of discontinuous, partial insights into her largely inaccessible consciousness.

Perhaps the most obscure female figure related to the railway is Rudyard Kipling's Mrs Bathurst. Deemed as one of his most baffling and at the same time intriguing stories by a series of critics, 'Mrs Bathurst' (1904) persistently defies interpretation largely due to the ghostly presence/absence of the title figure who haunts the narrative as well as the main character, Vickery, who obsesses about her to the extent that he deserts the army and is later found dead, a charred corpse, next to a railway track. The enigmatic Mrs Bathurst's connection with the railway is minimal yet crucial. While in Cape Town, Vickery with his friend Pyecroft visit a circus movie theatre and watch a reel composed of London scenes culminating in the arrival of the Plymouth express at Paddington:

Then the Western Mail came in to Paddin'ton on the big magic lantern sheet. First we saw the platform empty an' the porters standin' by. Then the engine come in, head on, an' the women in the front row jumped: she headed so straight. Then the doors opened and the passengers came out and the porters got the luggage – just like life. Only – only when any one came down too far towards us that was watchin', they walked right out o' the picture, so to speak. I was 'ighly interested, I can tell you. So were all of us. I watched an old man with a rug 'oo'd dropped a book an' was tryin' to pick it up, when

Figure 9. George Gibbs, illustration from 'Mrs Bathurst' in Kipling's *Traffics and Discoveries* (Scribner's, 1909).

quite slowly, from be'ind two porters – carryin' a little reticule an' lookin' from side to side – comes out Mrs Bathurst. There was no mistakin' the walk in a hundred thousand. She come forward – right forward – she looked out straight at us with that blindish look which Pritch alluded to. She walked on and on till she melted out of the picture [. . .] (397–8)

Plagued by guilt for he thinks that Mrs Bathurst is looking for him in vain on the Paddington platform, Vickery, who, though married, had had an affair with her in New Zealand, visits the movie theatre every night, with timetable precision, in anticipation of her life-like appearance on the screen, until the circus is taken up north and he is presumed to have followed it after deserting the army. The absent presence of Mrs Bathurst, who, like the train, seems to trespass the boundaries of the screen with her movements and her gaze, haunts not only Vickery but also the rest of the soldiers who discuss her appeal, unable, nevertheless, to pinpoint the reasons for her alluring effect on them all. According to Pyecroft, she's got 'just It' (393), an obscure erotic charm which makes her indelible in their memory.

The movie scene quoted above bears a strong resemblance to the 1895 film by the Lumière brothers, *The Arrival of a Train at La Ciotat Station*, that was reported to have had a similar effect on the spectators who were allegedly terrified by the moving image of the train seemingly rushing towards them, out of the screen and into the movie theatre itself.[2] As Laura Marcus argues, as in the Lumière film, 'Mrs Bathurst, or at least her screen image, heads as straight as the engine, and might indeed be said to take the place of the train' ('Literature and Cinema', 341). As such, Mrs Bathurst, who embodies the train and at the same time the elusive 'It', is both threatening and alluring, present and absent, real and unreal, transient and permanent (in the sense that the film has immortalised her). Destined to repeat the same movements, out of the train and into the station, every night, she may seem at first to be restricted by both mediums of mechanical mobility and cinematic projection that make her presence possible. However, her elusive character and her obscure motives, which are never ascertained by either the author or Vickery, constitute her the definitive Mrs Brown, a woman whose consciousness lies beyond the regularity and regimentation of traditional narrative forms. As an anonymous woman in a transient setting she is divested of any social markers that would define her as a stable representable subject. And yet she haunts the narrative just as Mrs Brown would haunt Woolf and her contemporaries with her 'unlimited capacity and infinite variety [. . .] for she is, of course, the spirit we live by, life itself' (Woolf, 24). As Harry Ricketts argues, 'Mrs Bathurst' 'was, in effect, the first modernist text in English. Deliberate obliqueness, formal fragmentation, absence of a privileged authorial point of view, intense literary self-consciousness, lack of closure – all the defining qualities of modernism were present and correct' (288).

By employing both the train and the cinema in his baffling, elliptical, representation of Mrs Bathurst, Kipling seems to be acknowledging the contribution of both vehicles to the othering of woman. However, like Mrs Brown, Mrs Bathurst remains inaccessible to the male pen and imagination. On the railway platform and the screen, she eludes interpretation and intimacy, even though she may become the object of the gaze. She presents Kipling with the challenge of how to represent the unknowable otherness of woman, especially of the woman whose independence has been achieved through increased mobility and exposure. Thus Mrs Bathurst's obscure presence in the liminal spaces of the railway and the cinema defies Victorian ideas about the fixity of woman's destinations. While her power over Vickery seems permanent, her own trajectory is transitory, always in the making, an on-going story. In other words, this doubly unstable stage on which Kipling positions his spectral heroine has fluid and unmarked spatial and temporal borders. For not only are the borders of train and screen permeable, as we see in the reaction of the spectators who see Mrs Bathurst penetrating their own space, but time as well becomes unfixed, producing the sensation of simultaneous temporal zones. As Lynne Kirby argues in her analysis of the railroad in early silent cinema, 'the editing of disparate images, places, and times [in newsreels] produced something of a leveling effect, a simultaneity by virtue of the condensed duration of projection of pictures taken far away' (54). So for Vickery both the train and the movie break down the temporal and spatial distances between the present and the past and between New Zealand, South Africa, and London, causing in him confusion, paranoia, and obsession. He is believed to have died next to a track while following her cinematic image across South Africa, using perhaps the train, the main medium of this temporal and spatial collapse, as a means of approximating her elusive being. Railway female identities can be none other than such fragmentary, contingent, transient, and precarious identities, but woman's identification with such a subject position, as I hope this book has shown, can be liberating and self-inventing despite the isolation or uprootedness that such an existence may also incur in social terms.

Notes

1. Here I am of course thinking of Mrs Dalloway's distancing tactics which ensure the privacy of her soul.
2. See Laura Marcus, 'Literature and Cinema', 340–1.

Bibliography

Primary (pre-1925) Sources

Allen, Grant. 'The Adventure of a Cantankerous Old Lady'. *The Penguin Book of Victorian Women in Crime: Forgotten Cops and Private Eyes from the Time of Sherlock Holmes*. Ed. Michael Sims. New York: Penguin, 2011. 213–34.

Andrew, W. P. *Indian Railways: as Connected with the Power, and Stability of the British Empire in the East, the Development of its Resources, and the Civilization of its People by 'An Old Indian Postmaster'*. London: Cautley Newby, 1846.

Anon. 'A Gentleman Fined for Kissing a Lady in a Railway Carriage'. *Reynold's Newspaper* 585 (27 Oct. 1861).

Anon. 'A Night in a First-Class Railway Carriage'. *Dublin University Magazine* 70.418 (1867): 419–23.

Anon. 'A Railway Adventure'. *Chambers's Journal* 628 (18 Dec. 1875): 810–13.

Anon. 'A Railway Adventure'. *The Englishwoman's Domestic Magazine* 88 (April 1872): 212–17.

Anon. 'A Railway Carriage Adventure'. [E.N.] *Every Week* (6 Nov. 1891): 349–51.

Anon. 'A Trip by Rail; or, the Third-Class Passenger'. *The London Journal* 40.1025 (Oct. 1864): 213.

Anon. 'An Expensive Journey'. *London Society* 11.61 (Jan. 1867): 35–40.

Anon. 'Aunt Tabitha's Railway Adventure'. *London Society* (Nov. 1864): 417–22.

Anon. 'Book Reviews Reviewed: "In the Permanent Way and Other Stories" by Flora Annie Steel'. *The Academy* (5 Feb. 1898): 162–3.

Anon. 'Charge of Assaulting a Lady in a Railway Carriage at Bitton'. *The Bristol Mercury and Daily Post* (26 Jan. 1878).

Anon. 'Dastardly Assault on a Lady in a Railway Carriage'. *Lloyd's Weekly Newspaper* 2621 (12 Feb. 1893).

Anon. 'Fast Girls'. *The London Journal* 56.1442 (Sept. 1872): 196.

Anon. 'New Books Received'. *London Society* 25.145 (1874): 93–6.

Anon. 'Of a Respectable Couple who Met with an Accident on the Underground Railway'. *Tinsley's Magazine* 5 (1870): 55–63.

Anon. 'Opening of the First Railway in India'. *The Illustrated London News* (4 June 1853): 436–8.

Anon. 'Other Dangers of the Rail'. *The Saturday Review of Politics, Literature, Science and Art* 18.456 (July 1864): 106–7.

Anon. 'Philosophy of Sensation'. *St. James Magazine* (1862): 340–6.

Anon. 'Railway Magic'. *The Englishwoman's Domestic Magazine* [issue unknown] (1855): 372–3.

Anon. 'Railway Romance'. *Chambers's Edinburgh Journal* 150 (1846): 314–16.

Anon. 'Railway-Time Aggression'. *Chambers's Edinburgh Journal* 390 (June 1851): 392–5.

Anon. *Raped on the Railway*. [London: Charles Carrington, 1894].

Anon. Rev. of 'Canadian Born' by Mrs Humphry Ward. *The Saturday Review* (30 April 1910): 565–6.

Anon. Rev. of *Footprints in the Snow* by Dora Russell. *The Saturday Review* 44. 1136 (4 Aug. 1877): 150–1.

Anon. Rev. of 'Lady Merton – Colonist'. *New York Times* (16 April 1910).

Anon. Rev. of *Voices in the Night* by Flora Annie Steel. *The Speaker* (23 June 1900): 341–2.

Anon. 'The Charge of Assaulting a Lady in a Railway Carriage'. *Daily News* 9101 (25 June 1875).

Anon. 'The Fast Young Lady'. *Bow Bells* 42.1086 (1885): 523.

Anon. 'The Hole in the Wall'. *All the Year Round* 16.390 (13 Oct. 1866): 325–9.

Anon. 'The Novels of Miss Broughton'. *Temple Bar* 41 (1874), 197–209.

Anon. 'The Railway Companion'. *Household Words* 12.298 (1855): 441–4.

Anon. *The Railway Traveller's Handy Book of Hints, Suggestions, and Advice, Before the Journey, On the Journey, and After the Journey*. London: Lockwood, 1862.

Anon. 'Young Ladies of the Period: No. 4 – The "Fashionably-Fast" Young Lady'. *Judy* (19 Aug. 1874): 180.

Aytoun, W. Edmondstoune. *Norman Sinclair*. 3 vols. Edinburgh: Blackwood, 1861.

Barrett Browning, Elizabeth. *Aurora Leigh*. New York: C. S. Francis, 1857.

Bodkin, Matthias McDonnell. 'How He Cut His Stick'. *The Penguin Book of Victorian Women in Crime: Forgotten Cops and Private Eyes from the Time of Sherlock Holmes*. Ed. Michael Sims. New York: Penguin, 2011. 235–46.

Braddon, Mary Elizabeth. *Aurora Floyd*. Ed. Richard Nemesvari and Lisa Surridge. Peterborough: Broadview, 1998.

Braddon, Mary Elizabeth. *Lady Audley's Secret*. London: Wordsworth, 1997.

Braddon, Mary Elizabeth. *Wyllard's Weird*. 3 vols. London: John and Robert Maxwell, [1885].

Broughton, Rhoda. *Nancy*. Michigan Historical Reprint Series. Michigan: Scholarly Publishing, University of Michigan Library, 2005.

Broughton, Rhoda. *Not Wisely, but Too Well*. New York: D. Appleton and Co, 1868.

Broughton, Rhoda. *Second Thoughts*. London: Bentley, 1880.

Broughton, Rhoda. 'Under the Cloak'. *Temple Bar* 37 (1873): 205–12.

Browne, Frances. *The Hidden Sin*. New York: Harper, 1866.

Caird, Mona. *The Daughters of Danaus*. London: Bliss, Sands, and Foster, 1894.

Collins, J. P. 'The Reader: Flora Annie Steel'. *The Bookman* 53 (Nov. 1917): 53–5.

Collins, Wilkie. *Armadale*. Ed. John Sutherland. London: Penguin, 1995.

Collins, Wilkie. *No Name*. Ed. Virginia Blain. Oxford: Oxford World's Classics, 1998.

Davidson, Lillias Campbell. *Hints to Lady Travellers at Home and Abroad*. London, 1889.

Dickens, Charles. 'Barbox Brothers'. *All the Year Round* 16:400 (Dec. 1866): 1–10.

Dickens, Charles. 'Barbox Brothers and Co.'. *All the Year Round* 16:400 (Dec. 1866): 10–16.

Dickens, Charles. *Dombey and Son*. London: Collins, 1969.

Dickens, Charles. 'The Signalman'. *All the Year Round* 16.400 (10 Dec. 1866): 20–5.

Egerton, George. 'Virgin Soil'. *Discords*. London: John Lane, 1894. 145–61.

Egg, Augustus. *Travelling Companions*. 1862. Oil on canvas. Birmingham Museum and Art Gallery.

Eliot, George. *Felix Holt, the Radical*. Ware: Wordsworth, 1997.

Gaskell, Elizabeth. *Mary Barton*. Oxford: Oxford University Press, 2006.

Gaskell, Elizabeth. *North and South*. London: Penguin, 2003.

Gissing, George. *The Odd Women*. Intro. Elaine Showalter. New York: New American Library, 1983.

Guiterman, Arthur. 'Rhymed Reviews: Lady Merton, Colonist'. *Life* (12 May 1910): 55.

Haight, Gordon S., ed. *The George Eliot Letters 1852–1858*. Vol. 2. New Haven: Yale University Press. 1954.

Haight, Gordon S., ed. *The George Eliot Letters 1862–1868*. Vol. 4. Oxford: Oxford University Press, 1986.

Hardy, Thomas. *Far from the Madding Crowd*. London: Penguin, 2003.

Hardy, Thomas. *Jude the Obscure*. London: Penguin, 1994.

Harrison, Agnes T. 'Two Girls of the Period'. *Macmillan's Magazine* 19.112 (Feb. 1869): 323–39.

Hawthorne, Hildegarde. 'Mrs. Humphry Ward's "Lady Merton, Colonist"'. *The Bookman* (May 1910): 308–9.

[Hayward, William Stephens]. *Revelations of a Lady Detective*. London: George Vickers, 1864.

James, Henry. 'A London Life'. *A London Life and The Reverberator*. Ed. Philip Horne. Oxford: Oxford World's Classics, 1989. 3–146.

James, Henry. 'Criticism'. *Essays in London and Elsewhere*. New York: Harper, 1893. 259–66.

James, Henry. 'Miss Braddon'. *The Nation* (Nov. 1865): 593–4.

James, Henry. *The American Scene*. New York: Penguin, 1994.

James, Henry. 'The Art of Fiction'. *The Critical Muse: Selected Literary Criticism*. Ed. Roger Gard. London: Penguin, 1987. 186–206.

James, Henry. *The Complete Letters 1855–72*. Vol 1. Ed. Pierre A. Walker and Greg W. Zacharias. Omaha: University of Nebraska Press, 2006.

James, Henry. *The Portrait of a Lady*. London: Penguin, 2003.

James, Henry. *The Wings of the Dove*. Harmondsworth: Penguin, 1971.

James, Henry. 'Travelling Companions I'. *The Atlantic Monthly* 26.157 (Nov. 1870): 600–14.

James, Henry. 'Travelling Companions II'. *The Atlantic Monthly* 26.158 (Dec. 1870): 684–97.

James, Henry. *What Maisie Knew*. Harmondsworth: Penguin, 1974.

Johnson, E. Pauline. *Canadian Born*. Toronto: Morang, 1903.

Kemble, Frances Ann. *Records of a Girlhood*. 2nd edn. New York: Henry Holt, 1884.

Kipling, Rudyard. 'Mrs Bathurst'. *Traffics and Discoveries*. New York: Scribner's, 1909. 379–408.

Leith, Mary Charlotte. *Mark Dennis; or, The Engine Driver. A Tale of the Railway*. London: Rivingtons, 1859.

[Mansel, H. L.]. 'Sensation Novels'. *The Quarterly Review* 113.226 (1863): 481–514.

Mansfield, Katherine. 'The Little Governess'. *Katherine Mansfield's Short Stories*. Ed. Vincent O' Sullivan. New York: Norton Critical Editions, 2006. 51–62.

Meredith, George. *Diana of the Crossways*. London: Constable, 1905.

Oliphant, Margaret. 'A Railway Junction: or, the Romance of Ladybank'. *Blackwood's Edinburgh Magazine* 114:696 (1873): 419–41.

Oliphant, Margaret. 'A Story of a Wedding Tour'. *Nineteenth-Century Short Stories by Women*. Ed. Harriet Devine Jump. London: Routledge, 1998. 425–40.

Oliphant, Margaret. 'Novels'. *Blackwood's Edinburgh Magazine* 102:623 (1867): 257–80.

Oliphant, Mrs [Margaret]. *Salem Chapel*. Edinburgh: Blackwood, 1865.

Payne, William Morton. 'Recent Fiction'. *The Dial* 48 (June 1910): 393–7.

Ruskin, John. 'Of Queens' Gardens'. *Sesame and Lilies*. Ed. G. E. Hollingworth. London: Clive, University Tutorial Press, 1932. 50–82.

Russell, Dora. *Footprints in the Snow*. London: John and Robert Maxwell, [1877].

Simcox, Edith. Rev. of *Nancy* by Rhoda Broughton. *Academy* 90 (1874): 85–7.

Steel, Flora Annie. 'A Danger Signal'. *In the Permanent Way and Other Stories*. London: Heinemann, 1898. 220–34.

Steel, Flora Annie. 'A Tourist Ticket'. *In the Permanent Way and Other Stories*. London: Heinemann, 1898. 129–49.

Steel, Flora Annie. 'An Indian Jubilee'. *The Saturday Review* 106 (Nov. 1908): 571.

Steel, Flora Annie. 'In the Permanent Way'. *In the Permanent Way and Other Stories*. London: Heinemann, 1898. 27–42.

Steel, Flora Annie. 'Lal'. *Macmillan's Magazine* 63 (April 1891): 452–5.

Steel, Flora Annie. 'On the Second Story'. *In the Permanent Way and Other Stories*. London: Heinemann, 1898. 43–73.

Steel, Flora Annie. 'The King's Well'. *In the Permanent Way and Other Stories*. London: Heinemann, 1898. 150–64.

Swoboda, Rudolf. *A Peep at the Train*. 1892. Oil on canvas. Royal Collection Trust.

Temple, Helena B. 'A Hurried Journey'. *The Women's Penny Paper* 99 (13 Sept. 1890): 555.

Trollope, Anthony. *He Knew He Was Right*. 2 vols. London: Strahan, 1869.

Trollope, Mrs [Frances]. *Town and Country*. 3 vols. London: Henry Colburn, 1848.

Ward, Mrs Humphry. *Canadian Born*. London: George Newnes, [1910].

Ward, Mrs Humphry. *Lady Rose's Daughter*. New York: Harper's, 1903.

Wharton, Edith. 'The Journey'. *The Greater Inclination*. New York: Scribner's, 1906. 27–45.

Whiteside, Marcia. 'Ruby Denzel's Travelling Companion'. *Bow Bells* 34:880 (June 1881): 553–6.
Wood, Ellen. *East Lynne*. Ed. Andrew Maunder. Ontario: Broadview, 2000.
Wood, Mrs Henry [Ellen]. 'Going through the Tunnel'. *Johnny Ludlow. First Series*. London: Bentley, 1895. 117–32.
Woolf, Virginia. *Mr Bennett and Mrs Brown*. London: The Hogarth Press, 1924.

Secondary Sources

Agathocleous, Tanya. 'London Mysteries and International Conspiracies: James, Doyle, and the Aesthetics of Cosmopolitanism'. *Nineteenth-Century Contexts* 26.2 (2004): 125–48.
Aguiar, Marian. *Tracking Modernity: India's Railway and the Culture of Mobility*. Minneapolis: University of Minnesota Press, 2011.
Allan, Janice M. 'Dora Russell'. *A Companion to Sensation Fiction*. Ed. Pamela K. Gilbert. Malden: Blackwell, 2011. 361–73.
Anderson, Amanda. *The Way We Argue Now*. Princeton: Princeton University Press, 2006.
Augé, Marc. *An Anthropology for Contemporaneous Worlds*. Trans. Amy Jacobs. Stanford: Stanford University Press, 1999.
Augé, Marc. *Non-Places: Introduction to an Anthropology of Supermodernity*. Trans. John Howe. London: Verso, 1995.
Bateman, Fiona, and Lionel Pilkington. Introduction. *Studies in Settler Colonialism: Politics, Identity and Culture*. Ed. Fiona Bateman and Lionel Pilkington. Houndmills: Palgrave Macmillan, 2011.
Baucom, Ian. *Out of Place: Englishness, Empire, and the Locations of Identity*. Princeton: Princeton University Press, 1999.
Bear, Laura. *Lines of the Nation*. New York: Columbia University Press, 2007.
Beaumont, Matthew. 'Railway Mania: the Train Compartment as the Scene of a Crime'. *The Railway and Modernity: Time, Space and the Machine Ensemble*. Ed. Matthew Beaumont and Michael Freeman. Bern: Peter Lang, 2007. 125–53.
Beaumont, Matthew, and Michael Freeman. 'Introduction: Tracks to Modernity'. *The Railway and Modernity: Time, Space and the Machine Ensemble*. Ed. Matthew Beaumont and Michael Freeman. Bern: Peter Lang, 2007. 13–43.
Berman, Marshall. *All that Is Solid Melts into Air: the Experience of Modernity*. New York: Penguin, 1988.
Bhabha, Homi K. *The Location of Culture*. London: Routledge, 1994.
Bieri, Sabin, and Natalia Gerodetti. '"Falling Women" – "Saving Angels": Spaces of Contested Mobility and the Production of Gender and Sexualities within Early Twentieth-Century Train Stations'. *Social & Cultural Geography* 8.2 (2007): 217–34.
Bohls, Elizabeth A. *Women Travel Writers and the Language of Aesthetics 1716–1718*. Cambridge: Cambridge University Press, 1995.
Bryden, Inga, and Janet Floyd. Introduction. *Domestic Space: Reading the Nineteenth-Century Interior*. Ed. Inga Bryden and Janet Floyd. Manchester: Manchester University Press, 1999. 1–17.
Burton, Antoinette. *Burdens of History: British Feminists, Indian Women, and*

Imperial Culture 1865–1915. Chapel Hill: University of North Carolina Press, 1994.

Buzard, James. *The Beaten Track: European Tourism, Literature, and the Ways to 'Culture': 1800–1918*. Oxford: Oxford University Press, 1993.

Buzard, James. 'The Grand Tour and After (1660–1840)'. *The Cambridge Companion to Travel Writing*. Ed. Peter Hulme and Tim Youngs. Cambridge: Cambridge University Press, 2002. 37–52.

Carter, Ian. *Railways and Culture in Britain: the Epitome of Modernity*. Manchester: Manchester University Press, 2001.

Casson, Mark. *The World's First Railway System: Enterprise, Competition, and Regulation on the Railway Network in Victorian Britain*. Oxford: Oxford University Press, 2009.

Chase, Karen, and Michael Levenson. *The Spectacle of Intimacy*. Princeton: Princeton University Press, 2000.

Cohen, Monica. *Professional Domesticity in the Victorian Novel: Women, Work and Home*. Cambridge: Cambridge University Press, 1998.

Crane, Ralph, and Anna Johnston. 'Flora Annie Steel in the Punjab'. *Writing, Travel, and Empire: in the Margins of Anthropology*. Ed. Peter Hulme and Russell McDougall. London: Tauris, 2007. 71–95.

Crary, Jonathan. *Suspensions of Perception: Attention, Spectacle, and Modern Culture*. Cambridge: MIT Press, 2001.

Crary, Jonathan. *Techniques of the Observer: on Vision and Modernity in the 19th Century*. Cambridge: MIT Press, 1992.

Cresswell, Tim. *In Place/Out of Place: Geography, Ideology, and Transgression*. Minneapolis: University of Minnesota Press, 1996.

Cresswell, Tim. *Place: a Short Introduction*. Malden: Blackwell, 2004.

Daly, Nicholas. *Literature, Technology, and Modernity, 1860–2000*. Cambridge: Cambridge University Press, 2004.

Daly, Nicholas. 'Railway Novels: Sensation Fiction and the Modernization of the Senses'. *ELH* 66 (1999): 461–87.

Davidoff, Lenore, and Catherine Hall. *Family Fortunes: Men and Women of the English Middle Class, 1780–1850*. Chicago: University of Chicago Press, 1987.

de Certeau, Michel. *The Practice of Everyday Life*. Trans. Steven Rendell. Berkeley: University of California Press, 1984.

Debenham, Helen. 'Rhoda Broughton's *Not Wisely but Too Well* and the Art of Sensation'. *Victorian Identities: Social and Cultural Formations in Nineteenth-Century Literature*. Ed. Ruth Robbins and Julian Wolfreys. Houndmills: Macmillan, 1996. 9–24.

Deleuze, Gilles, and Félix Guattari. *A Thousand Plateaus: Capitalism and Schizophrenia*. Trans. Brian Massumi. Minneapolis: University of Minnesota Press, 1987.

Derrida, Jacques, with Anne Dufourmantelle. *Of Hospitality*. Trans. Rachel Bowlby. Stanford: Stanford University Press, 2000.

Despotopoulou, Anna. '"No Natural Place Anywhere": Women's Precarious Mobility and Cosmopolitanism in James's Novels'. *Henry James Review* 35.2 (2014): 141–56.

Despotopoulou, Anna. '"Running on Lines": Women and the Railway in Victorian and Early Modernist Culture'. *Women in Transit through Literary Liminal Spaces*. Ed. Teresa Gómez Reus and Terry Gifford. Houndmills: Palgrave Macmillan, 2013. 47–60.

Despotopoulou, Anna. 'Trains of Thought: the Challenges of Mobility in the Work of Rhoda Broughton'. *Other Sensations*. Ed. Janice M. Allan. Spec. Issue of *Critical Survey* 23.1 (2011): 90–106.

Epstein Nord, Deborah. *Walking the Victorian Streets: Women, Representation, and the City*. Ithaca: Cornell University Press, 1995.

Fantina, Richard, and Kimberly Harrison. Introduction. *Victorian Sensations: Essays on a Scandalous Genre*. Ed. Kimberly Harrison and Richard Fantina. Columbus: Ohio State University Press, 2006. ix–xxiii.

Felski, Rita. *The Gender of Modernity*. Cambridge: Harvard University Press, 1995.

Ferguson, Trish. 'Hardy's Wessex and the Birth of Industrial Subjectivity'. *Victorian Time: Technologies, Standardizations, Catastrophes*. Ed Trish Ferguson. Houndmills: Palgrave, 2013. 57–73.

Ferguson, Trish. Introduction. *Victorian Time: Technologies, Standardizations, Catastrophes*. Ed. Trish Ferguson. Houndmills: Palgrave, 2013. 1–14.

Francis, Daniel. *The Imaginary Indian: the Image of the Indian in Canadian Culture*. Vancouver: Arsenal Pulp Press, 1992.

Freeman, Michael. *Railways and the Victorian Imagination*. New Haven: Yale University Press, 1999.

Freeman, Michael. 'The Railway Age: an Introduction'. *The Railway: Art in the Age of Steam*. Ed. Ian Kennedy and Julian Treuherz. New Haven: Yale University Press. [2008]. 21–33.

Freud, Sigmund. 'The "Uncanny"'. *The Norton Anthology of Theory and Criticism*. Ed. Vincent B. Leitch. New York: Norton, 2001. 929–52.

Friedman, Susan Stanford. 'Periodizing Modernism: Postcolonial Modernities and the Space/Time Borders of Modernist Studies'. *Modernism/Modernity* 13.3 (2006): 425–43.

Frisby, David. *Fragments of Modernity*. Cambridge: MIT Press, 1986.

Gilbert, Pamela K. *Disease, Desire, and the Body in Victorian Women's Popular Novels*. Cambridge: Cambridge University Press, 1997.

Gómez Reus, Teresa, and Aránzazu Usandizaga, eds. *Inside Out: Women Negotiating, Subverting, Appropriating Public and Private Space*. Amsterdam: Rodopi, 2008.

Gómez Reus, Teresa, and Terry Gifford. Introduction. *Women in Transit through Literary Liminal Spaces*. Ed. Teresa Gómez Reus and Terry Gifford. Houndmills: Palgrave Macmillan, 2013. 1–14.

Guelke, Jeanne K., and Karen M. Morin. 'Gender, Nature, Empire: Women Naturalists in Nineteenth-Century British Travel Literature'. *Transactions of the Institute of British Geographers, New Series* 26.3 (2001): 306–26.

Harrington, Ralph. 'The Railway Accident: Trains, Trauma, and Technological Crises in Nineteenth-Century Britain'. *Traumatic Pasts: History, Psychiatry, and Trauma in the Modern Age, 1870–1930*. Ed. Mark S. Micale and Paul Lerner. Cambridge: Cambridge University Press, 2001. 31–56.

Harrington, Ralph. 'Trains, Technology and Time-Travellers: How the Victorians Re-Invented Time'. University of York, 23 Jan. 2003. Lecture. http://www.artificialhorizon.org 27 March 2014.

Harvey, David. *The Condition of Postmodernity*. Malden: Blackwell, 1990.

Heilmann, Ann. *New Woman Fiction: Women Writing First-Wave Feminism* Houndmills: Palgrave Macmillan, 2000.

Heller, Tamar. '"That Muddy, Polluted Flood of Earthly Love": Ambivalence about the Body in Rhoda Broughton's *Not Wisely but Too Well*'. *Victorian*

Sensations: Essays on a Scandalous Genre. Ed. Kimberly Harrison and Richard Fantina. Columbus: Ohio State University Press, 2006. 87–101.

Henry, Nancy. '"Ladies do it?": Victorian Women Investors in Fact and Fiction'. *Victorian Literature and Finance*. Ed. Francis O' Gorman. Oxford: Oxford University Press, 2007. 111–31.

Hoganson, Kristin L. *Consumers' Imperium: the Global Production of American Domesticity: 1865–1920*. Chapel Hill: The University of North Carolina Press, 2007.

Horne, Philip. Introduction. *A London Life and The Reverberator*. By Henry James. Oxford: Oxford University Press, World's Classics, 1989. vii–xxxiv.

James, William. *The Principles of Psychology*, vol. 1. New York: Cosimo Classics, 2007.

Kaston Tange, Andrea. *Architectural Identities*. Toronto: University of Toronto Press, 2010.

Keep, Christopher. 'Technology and Information: Accelerating Developments'. *A Companion to the Victorian Novel*. Ed. Patrick Brantlinger and William B. Thesing. Malden: Blackwell, 2002. 137–54.

Kennedy, Ian, and Julian Treuherz. *The Railway: Art in the Age of Steam*. New Haven: Yale University Press, [2008].

Kirby, Lynne. *Parallel Tracks: the Railroad and Silent Cinema*. Exeter: University of Exeter Press, 1997.

Langland, Elizabeth. *Nobody's Angels: Middle-Class Women and Domestic Ideology in Victorian Culture*. Ithaca: Cornell University Press, 1995.

Leask, Nigel. *Curiosity and the Aesthetics of Travel Writing 1770–1840*. Oxford: Oxford University Press, 2002.

Lee, Louise. 'Lady Audley's Secret: How *Does* she Do it? Sensation Fiction's Technologically Minded Villainesses'. *A Companion to Sensation Fiction*. Ed. Pamela K. Gilbert. Malden: Blackwell, 2011. 134–46.

Lefebvre, Henri. *The Production of Space*. Trans. Donald Nicholson-Smith. Oxford: Blackwell, 1991.

Lock, Charles. 'Hardy and the Railway'. *Essays in Criticism* 50.1 (2000): 44–66.

MacDonald, Tara. '"Vulgar Publicity" and Problems of Privacy in Margaret Oliphant's *Salem Chapel*'. *Other Sensations*. Ed. Janice M. Allan. Spec. issue of *Critical Survey* 23.1 (2011): 25–41.

Marcus, Laura. 'Literature and Cinema'. *The Cambridge History of Twentieth-Century English Literature*. Ed. Laura Michaels and Peter Nichols. Cambridge: Cambridge University Press, 2004. 335–58.

Marcus, Laura. 'Psychoanalytic Training: Freud and the Railways'. *The Railway and Modernity*. Ed. Matthew Beaumont and Michael Freeman. Oxford: Peter Lang, 2007. 155–75.

Martin, Daniel. 'Railway Fatigue and the Coming-of-Age Narrative in *Lady Audley's Secret*'. *Victorian Review* 34 (2008): 131–53.

Martin, Daniel. 'Wilkie Collins and Risk'. *A Companion to Sensation Fiction*. Ed. Pamela K. Gilbert. Malden: Blackwell, 2011. 184–95.

Massey, Doreen. *For Space*. London: Sage, 2005.

Mathur, Saloni. *India by Design: Colonial History and Cultural Display*. Berkeley: University of California Press, 2007.

Matthews, Christopher. 'Love at First Sight: the Velocity of Victorian Heterosexuality'. *Victorian Studies* 46 (2004): 425–54.

Matus, Jill L. *Shock, Memory and the Unconscious in Victorian Fiction.* Cambridge: Cambridge University Press, 2009.

Maunder, Andrew. '"Stepchildren of Nature": *East Lynne* and the Spectre of Female Degeneracy, 1860–1861'. *Victorian Crime, Madness and Sensation.* Ed. Andrew Maunder and Grace Moore. Aldershot: Ashgate, 2004. 59–72.

McClintock, Anne. *Imperial Leather: Race, Gender and Sexuality in the Colonial Contest.* New York: Routledge, 1995.

Mills, Sara. *Discourses of Difference: an Analysis of Women's Travel Writing and Colonialism.* London: Routledge, 1991.

Morgan, Susan. *Place Matters: Gendered Geography in Victorian Women's Travel Books about Southeast Asia.* New Brunswick: Rutgers University Press, 1996.

Morin, Karen M. *Frontiers of Femininity: a New Historical Geography of the Nineteenth-Century American West.* Syracuse: Syracuse University Press, 2008.

Morin, Karen M. 'Peak Practices: Englishwomen's "Heroic" Adventures in the Nineteenth-Century American West'. *Annals of the Association of American Geographers* 89.3 (1999): 489–514.

Mumford, Lewis. *Technics and Civilization.* London: Routledge, 1955.

Murphy, Patricia. *Time is of the Essence: Temporality, Gender, and the New Woman.* Albany: SUNY Press, 2001.

Nead, Lynda. *Victorian Babylon: People, Streets and Images in Nineteenth-Century London.* New Haven: Yale University Press, 2005.

Nemesveri, Richard, and Lisa Surridge. Introduction. *Aurora Floyd.* By Mary Elizabeth Braddon. Peterborough: Broadview Press, 1998. 7–30.

Parkins, Wendy. *Mobility and Modernity in Women's Novels, 1850s-1930s: Women Moving Dangerously.* Houndmills: Palgrave Macmillan, 2009.

Parkins, Wendy. 'Women, Mobility and Modernity in Elizabeth Gaskell's *North and South*'. *Women's Studies International Forum* 27.5–6 (2004): 507–19.

Parsons, Deborah L. *Streetwalking the Metropolis: Women, the City and Modernity.* Oxford: Oxford University Press, 2000.

Peterson, Linda H. 'Reconstructing British Domesticity on the North American Frontier'. *Victorian Settler Narratives: Emigrants, Cosmopolitans and Returnees in Nineteenth-Century Literature.* Ed. Tamara S. Wagner. London: Pickering and Chatto, 2011. 55–69.

Pike, David. *Subterranean Cities: the World beneath Paris and London, 1800–1945.* Ithaca: Cornell University Press, 2005.

Pittard, Christopher. *Purity and Contamination in Late Victorian Detective Fiction.* Farnham: Ashgate, 2011.

Pope, Norris. 'Dickens's "The Signalman" and Information Problems in the Railway Age'. *Technology and Culture* 42.3 (2001): 436–61.

Poster, Mark. *Cultural History and Postmodernity.* New York: Columbia University Press, 1997.

Powell, Violet. *Flora Annie Steel: Novelist of India.* London: Heinemann, 1981.

Pratt, Mary Louise. *Imperial Eyes: Travel Writing and Transculturation.* 2nd edn. London: Routledge, 2008.

Pykett, Lyn. *The 'Improper Feminine': the Women's Sensation Novel and the New Women Writing.* London: Routledge, 1992.

Richter, Amy G. 'At Home Aboard: the American Railroad and the Changing Ideal of Public Domesticity'. *Gender and Landscape: Renegotiating the Moral Landscape.* Ed. Lorraine Dowler. New York: Routledge, 2005. 77–93.

Richter, Amy G. *Home on the Rails: Women, the Railroad, and the Rise of Public Domesticity*. Chapel Hill: The University of North Carolina Press, 2005.

Ricketts, Harry. *Rudyard Kipling: a Life*. New York: Carroll and Graf, 1999.

Riendeau, Roger. *A Brief History of Canada*. 2nd edn. New York: Facts of File, 2007.

Roy, Shampa. '"A Miserable Sham": Flora Annie Steel's Short Fiction and the Question of Indian Women's Reform'. *Feminist Review* 94 (2010): 55–74.

Scarry, Elaine. *The Body in Pain: the Making and Unmaking of the World*. Oxford: Oxford University Press, 1985.

Schivelbusch, Wolfgang. *The Railway Journey: the Industrialization of Time and Space in the 19th Century*. Berkeley: University of California Press, 1977.

Schoenbach, Lisi. *Pragmatic Modernism*. Oxford: Oxford University Press, 2012.

Sharpe, Jenny. *Allegories of Empire: the Figure of Woman in the Colonial Text*. Minneapolis: University of Minnesota Press, 1993.

Showalter, Elaine. *A Literature of their Own: British Women Novelists from Bronte to Lessing*. Princeton: Princeton University Press, 1977.

Simmel, Georg. 'The Metropolis and Mental Life'. *The Sociology of Georg Simmel*. Ed. and trans. Kurt Wolff. Glencoe: Free Press, 1950. 409–24.

Simmons, Jack. *The Victorian Railway*. London: Thames and Hudson, 1991.

Smith, Sidonie. *Moving Lives: Twentieth-Century Women's Travel Writing*. Minneapolis: University of Minnesota Press, 2001.

Smullen, Ivor. *Taken for a Ride: a Distressing Account of the Misfortunes and Misbehaviour of the Early British Railway Traveller*. London: Herbert Jenkins, 1968.

Stevenson, Randall. 'Greenwich Meanings: Clocks and Things in Modernist and Postmodernist Fiction'. *Time and Narrative*. Ed. Nicola Bradbury. Spec. issue of *The Yearbook of English Studies* 30 (2000): 124–36.

Sussman, Herbert. *Victorian Technology: Invention, Innovation, and the Rise of the Machine*. Santa Barbara: ABC Clio, 2009.

Sutherland, John. *Mrs Humphry Ward: Eminent Victorian, Pre-Eminent Edwardian*. Oxford: Oxford University Press, 1991.

Sutton-Ramspeck, Beth. 'Shot Out of the Canon: Mary Ward and the Claims of Conflicting Feminism'. *Victorian Women Writers and the Woman Question*. Ed. Nicola Diane Thomson. Cambridge: Cambridge University Press, 1999.

Talairach-Vielmas, Laurence. *Moulding the Female Body in Victorian Fairy Tales and Sensation Novels*. Hampshire: Ashgate, 2007.

Trachtenberg, Alan. Foreword. *The Railway Journey: The Industrialization of Time and Space in the 19th Century*. By Wolfgang Schivelbusch. Berkeley: University of California Press, 1977. xiii–xvi.

Tromp, Marlene. 'Mrs. Henry Wood, *East Lynne*'. *A Companion to Sensation Fiction*. Ed. Pamela K. Gilbert. Malden: Blackwell, 2011. 257–68.

Urry, John. *Mobilities*. Cambridge: Polity Press, 2007.

Vadillo, Ana Parejo. *Women Poets and Urban Aestheticism: Passengers of Modernity*. Houndmills: Palgrave Macmillan, 2005.

Veracini, Lorenzo. *Settler Colonialism: a Theoretical Overview*. Houndmills: Palgrave Macmillan, 2010.

Walkowitz, Judith R. 'Cosmopolitanism, Feminism, and the Moving Body'. *Victorian Literature and Culture* 38 (2010): 427–49.

Welsh, David. *Underground Writing: the London Tube from George Gissing to Virginia Woolf*. Liverpool: Liverpool University Press, 2010.

Williams, Merle A. 'Transforming Hospitality and Friendship in Henry James: from "A London Life" to *The Awkward Age*'. *Transforming Henry James*. Ed. Anna de Biasio, Anna Despotopoulou, and Donatella Izzo. Newcastle: Cambridge Scholars Publishing, 2013. 196–210.

Williams, Raymond. *The Country and the City*. New York: Oxford University Press, 1973.

Williams, Rosalind. *Notes on the Underground: an Essay on Technology, Society, and the Imagination*. New edn. Cambridge: MIT Press, 2008.

Wolff, Janet. 'The Invisible Flaneuse. Women and the Literature of Modernity'. *Theory, Culture and Society* 2.3 (1985): 37–47.

Wolmar, Christian. *Blood, Iron, and Gold: How the Railroads Transformed the World*. London: Atlantic Books, 2009.

Wolmar, Christian. *Fire and Steam: How the Railways Transformed Britain*. London: Atlantic Books, 2007.

Zemka, Sue. *Time and the Moment in Victorian Literature and Society*. Cambridge: Cambridge University Press, 2012.

Index